Katie Schwab Sample Book

Edited by Clare Molloy

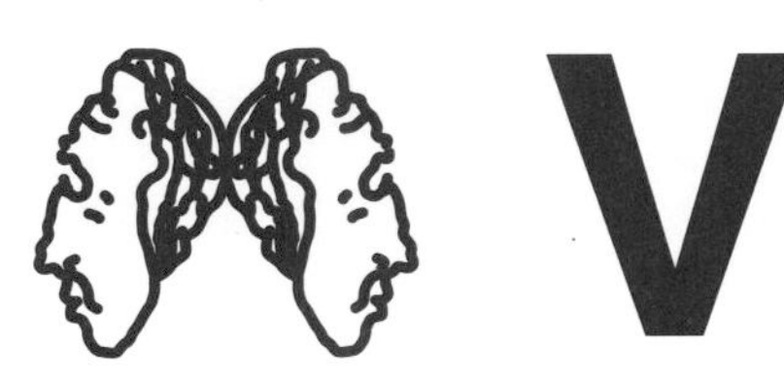

Dedicated to
the strength
of
Irene Schwab

Contents

Ending with a Yellow Ribbon

Roos Gortzak

It's winter. Vleeshal's heavy, black curtain is up again. Each year, when the temperature drops outside, it is installed to keep the cold out. It's hard to bring some warmth to this former meat market, a true refrigerator *avant la lettre*. The hanging of the curtain is a ritual of sorts, a marking of time, a way of moving with the seasons. It also acts as a gesture of care towards the hosts who are positioned at a close distance from the entrance door, ready to welcome whomever comes in.

When Clare Molloy and Katie Schwab stepped inside in September 2020, on their first site visit together, the curtain was packed away in storage, out of sight. It reappeared when Katie asked whether there was a textile in the space that could possibly benefit from an act of mending. Studying processes of repair in both textiles and civic architecture for her solo show in Middelburg, Katie was interested in caring for a material that was already there — as well as creating new works. On the bottom part of the curtain there were small holes, for which Katie made beautiful patches with colourful, zigzagging threads. After her exhibition, she generously gifted this work, *patches* (2021), to Vleeshal, for the curtain to stay strengthened and adorned (see the inside cover of this book and pages 84–85). Now when it's time to install the winter curtain, it not only brings warmth but also the joy of looking at the vibrant colours, the dance of the threads. It reminds me of the endless care and attention that Katie put into her exhibition, *small wares*.

And Katie was not alone. She worked with Clare Molloy, whom
I invited to curate an exhibition, solo or group, with whomever
she wanted. Clare and I met in 2014 when I was looking for
an assistant to collaborate on the *FdjT* festival I was curating,
for which forty students from art, theatre, music and dance
schools in and around Frankfurt developed new works. It was an
ambitious project, in which collaboration, experimentation and
play were main concerns. Clare embarked on this journey with
me, which proved to be a very intense six months. I could not
have done it without her brilliant insights, enduring enthusiasm
and sharp precision. It was also during this time that I applied for
the director's position at Vleeshal Center for Contemporary Art.
The image I started my job application with was of a painting by
Sanya Kantarovsky in which a hand moves a curtain. I compared
the situation of a new director stepping onto the stage with that
of a comedian who needs to win over her audience. A director
needs to fill the exhibition space with her programme, but it is not
a truly empty space. It has its own past, something I believe a
new director must consider. It's not a fully empty page, but a book
that doesn't yet have an ending. New chapters can be added.
Along the way, I realised that I wanted to give other curators the
opportunity to step onto the special stage that is Vleeshal.
I couldn't have been happier when Clare accepted my invitation.

I'm grateful for the dedicated work that Clare and Katie put into
their exhibition and this book you're holding now. The way our
winter curtain has been treated is just one example of the many
variations of care and repair they applied. This book has been
on their minds ever since they started working on the exhibition.
How could the book and the exhibition be related in terms of
materiality? How could their knowledge acquired from all the
research and conversations be shared with you, the reader?
I admire their "strength study", to refer to another work in the
exhibition (*strength study* from 2021 is pictured on the front and
back covers of this book as well as pages 86–91), to keep on
going, even when the funding for the book wasn't secured. I'm
thankful to graphic design collective Åbäke for being open to a
conversation about a book, when it was unclear what form it
could take – and with hardly a budget to speak of in the
beginning. Ironically, it is thanks to COVID-19 that we were able
to move money from our international nomadic programme
towards making books. I'm also grateful to the writers for
contributing such fascinating texts.

There are many things to learn from this book. How to work
together as a curator and an artist. How to repair a hole. How to
work site-specifically. How to be thankful. How to move mindfully
through this world. And how to weave a one-metre-long yellow
register ribbon through a book.

The People Who Made *Sample Book*

Clare Molloy

I was first truly bowled over by Katie Schwab's artwork in 2005. We were studying together on the art foundation course at Chelsea College of Art and Design in London, and Katie's work in the final exhibition was a playful sculpture. Frozen cubes of fizzy drinks melted in funnels that led to a collection of stilt-like plastic straws. The pop dripped slowly, creating patterns on the floor. It was a sculpture that celebrated colour, movement, process and gave a tongue-in-cheek nod to pop art. When Roos Gortzak, director and curator of Vleeshal Center for Contemporary Art, invited me to be the institution's 2021 guest curator, I knew that it was finally the moment to make an exhibition with Katie.

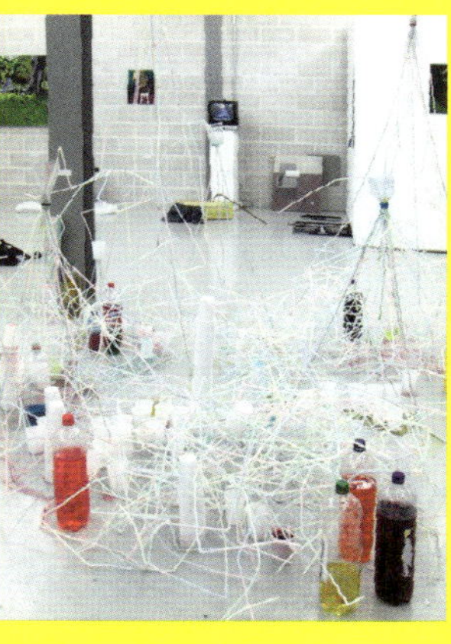

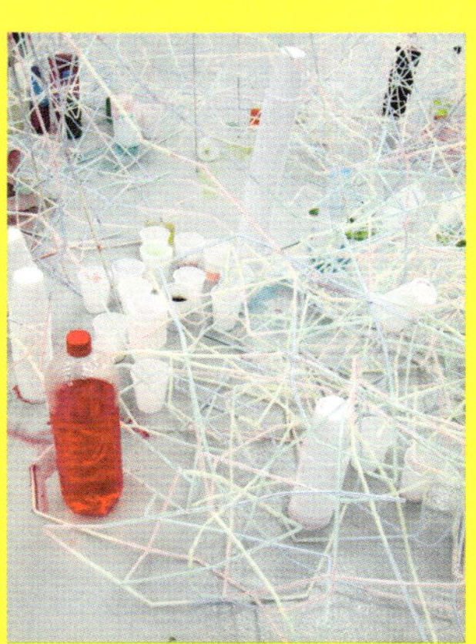

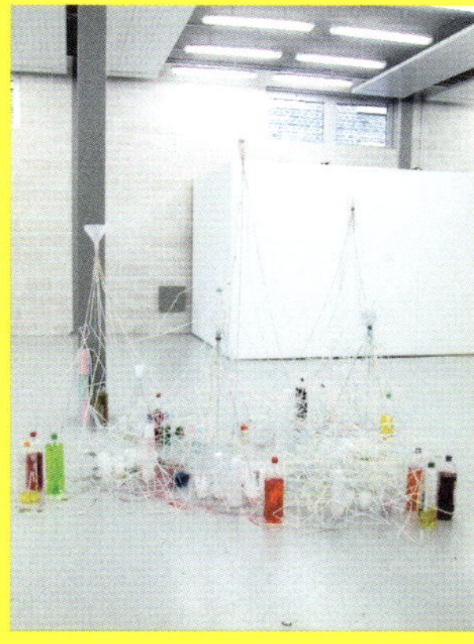

Katie's final exhibition piece (2005) at Chelsea College of Art and Design, London

Roos Gortzak and I met in 2014 when I assisted her on the festival *FdjT – What Happens in Offenbach Stays in Offenbach*, which, as the title suggests, I can't say anything more about. What I can say is that I wanted to work with Roos due to our shared interests in performance, scores and the living body in contemporary art, and because she was working with Cally Spooner, an artist whose examination of liveness ever intrigues me. In 2015 Roos started her Vleeshal programme with Cally. I travelled to Middelburg for the opening of *On False Tears and Outsourcing,* where performers created a seething and strenuous choreography of rugby-scrum huddles and corporate team-building embraces. Even then, after the performance, I had to wonder what Katie's colourful works might look like against the chequerboard floor. Without Roos' enormous trust and support that question would never have been answered and this book would not exist.

Since those early beginnings in the mid-2000s, **Katie Schwab**'s artistic practice has matured into a deep exploration of personal and social histories of craft and design. Her research focuses on twentieth-century domestic interiors and civic architecture. Katie's installations, textiles, furniture and moving-image works often have their roots in archival research and craft-based learning. This book documents an intensely productive period from 2020 to 2021 that led to her Vleeshal exhibition *small wares.* Our interview charts how this process unfolded on residency in Scotland, in her London studio, on production and research trips across the Netherlands, and over many a video call during the COVID-19 pandemic.

The first person Katie and I invited as an author was **Rebecca Lewin**, senior curator at the Design Museum in London. Rebecca has followed Katie's work since the earliest days, having also been on the Chelsea art foundation course. Her text unveils her unparalleled insight into how collaboration underpins Katie's practice. In 2013, Rebecca curated the exhibition *The Palace of Green Porcelain* with Katie Schwab and Dan Scott at Breese Little in London. Katie made a collection of glazed stoneware pieces, all titled after family, friends and peers with whom she had been in exchange during the process. This early example of consciously naming your influences found resonance in the fascination that Katie developed for the Middelburg darning samplers, which uniquely include not only the name of the darner but also the full name of their teacher.

One of the foremost experts on Dutch darning samplers is costume historian **Rosalie Sloof**, who is the curator of fashion and costume at the Nederlands Openluchtmuseum [Dutch Open Air Museum] in Arnhem. Texts that she wrote at the start of her career whilst working with the textile collection at the Victoria and Albert Museum in London were invaluable for Katie in gaining an understanding of how mending techniques were both learnt and preserved by darning samplers. Rosalie's essay here expands on how singular the Middelburg samplers are in textile history and what a resource they have become for researchers.

As well as darning samplers, looking into works created by textile and fibre artists was key to Katie's process. Having been both moved and influenced by the Anni Albers retrospective at Tate Modern, it seemed natural to invite one of the people behind that show to write about Katie's practice within the context of twentieth-century textile art. Enter the curator of international art at Tate **Ann Coxon**. Her writing, research and enthusiasm for textiles is evidenced in her essay that probes the notion of resilience as both a textile quality and a principle in how Katie's show was subtly guided by the idea of hidden strength.

The strength of Vleeshal's architecture relies, in its most elemental form, on a very specific type of stone, mined from a quarry located in the former Duchy of Brabant, or today's Belgium. You would be hard pressed to find an artist and writer in the Netherlands with more enthusiasm for both architecture and the humble brick than **Michiel Huijben**. Katie met Michiel at the opening of *small wares* and they spoke about weaving, brickwork and Gottfried Semper's writings on the origins of the wall. It was a serendipitous meeting between two people with a shared interest in design history. Invited to contribute a short story, Michiel draws on his meticulous research to construct a journey along the trade route of the River Scheldt, charting the spread of an eyebrow-raising architectural style known as Brabantine Gothic.

Intrigued by the material world and how it echoes through language, the artist and poet **m. patchwork monoceros** has a unique approach to text and textiles. Whether through weaving, writing or facilitation, their works reveal the somatics, or the internal bodily sensations, of grief. Katie and I first saw their work via *Stitch-Kin: an evening of poetry with melannie monoceros* broadcast by the University of Winnipeg during the COVID-19 lockdown of November 2020. It was mesmerising. Their poem for this book, *embossed vibrations*, is a channelled and sensuous imagining of visiting *small wares*. Originally written on a typewriter, here it is presented as a shape poem, conceived by m. patchwork monoceros with the book's designer Åbäke.

In the early development of *Sample Book*, Katie and I sat in a hotel room in Middelburg and shared all sorts of favourite books with each other from artists' catalogues to poetry volumes. The first thing to become clear was that the materiality of the book was just as important as its contents. The second thing to become clear was: the book had to have a register ribbon. One of the books Katie had with her was *The Knife* by Charlotte York, published by **Dent-De-Leone** and designed by **Åbäke**. The title on the front cover glinted with the murk of an oily puddle and the story was printed on silver-flecked pages made of pulped banknotes. These were our people. *Sample Book* is indebted to Åbäke's sensibility for material experimentation and the curiosity of the publishing hut Dent-De-Leone.

Holding the many strands of this book's making have been the steady hands of the managing editors. The start of the undertaking was helmed by curator, writer and occasional podcaster **Alix de Massiac**. Taking on the tasks of tracking down image rights, creating a plethora of captions and getting *Katie Schwab: Sample Book* over the finish line was the writer, editor and curator **Julia Steenhuisen**. It is an infinitely better book for Julia's care. I copyedited the texts, and the editor and translator **Jonathan Beaton** copyedited the conversation between Katie and myself. Commas, consistency and all things proofreading were also overseen by Jonathan with precision and poise.

Festooning and Sampling: Clare Molloy and Katie Schwab on the Process of *small wares*

Clare Molloy: As the texts by Ann Coxon, Rebecca Lewin and m. patchwork monoceros give such close readings of and insights into the exhibition *small wares*, what I'd like to talk about is everything that went on behind the scenes: your processes, your research and your experimentation.

Today you're in your colourful kitchen in London, I'm in my flat in Berlin and it feels very familiar to meet with you on a video call and speak about your work as this was our method of working together during the COVID-19 pandemic. Almost every Friday for over a year we spoke, you shared what you were working on at the studio and we shaped what would become the show. So, let's start at the top. How did your research begin for the exhibition at Vleeshal in Middelburg?

Katie Schwab: For me, the first step was looking at the Vleeshal's website and trying to get a sense of the space from the documentation of previous exhibitions. You had already been to Middelburg and knew the building, but I hadn't yet. It is a very visually striking interior and it was the chequered floor that I was immediately drawn to, but it was quite hard for me to get a sense of what the rest of the architecture was like and how the gallery space worked. It was clear that we'd have to go to visit the site, but we were in lockdown, so although that was the obvious starting point, this wasn't an option.

Something that I often do at the beginning of a project is to see if there is any specific textile history in the local area. I began with a simple online search into Middelburg textiles. I read that it was quite an agricultural area and it wasn't initially clear if there had been a textile industry in this region. However, one of the first things that stood out to me was an image of what's called a Middelburg darning sampler. It happened to be from the website of a textile historian and dealer called Meg Andrews, who I had previously met through her involvement with the Textile Society.

On her site Meg has an archive of pieces that she has sold. One such piece was the Middelburg darning sampler and it featured some text in Dutch. The listing has a description of the textile, which talked about how these samplers were made by young girls and women and how they were a record of practising darning stitches. As such, they often recorded the name of the student,

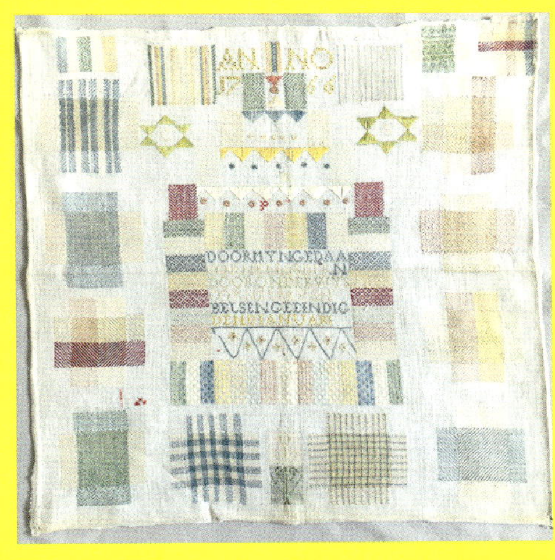

Darning sampler by Cornelia Smit (1766), Middelburg
Linen, 50 × 50 cm
Door myn gedaan Cornelia Smit door onderwys Cornelia van Belsen geeindig den 13 januari [Done by me Cornelia Smit under the instruction of Cornelia van Belsen finished the 13th of January]

13

the date, the location, but also the initials of the sewing teacher who was tutoring them. I was really interested in this acknowledgement of where skills and knowledge are inherited or passed on from, combined with the graphic and abstract forms on this embroidery sampler. The piece had been sold to a collection [it is now owned by the Historisch Museum De Bevelanden in Goes] and so I never saw it in person, but it was something I returned to a lot on the screen and was an important point of departure for the show's research. I wanted to know, was this kind of sampler part of a wider tradition of samplers?

C   M   : How did you go about pursuing that question?

K   S   : That question led me to the online archives of the Victoria and Albert Museum in London, the Cooper Hewitt in New York and the Nederlands Openluchtmuseum [Dutch Open Air Museum] in Arnhem. Browsing their archives, I found out that these textiles are called *stoplappen* in Dutch [*stoplap*, singular]. I was so intrigued by their formal properties: the grids, the overlapping points where two contrasting patterns or colours would meet. These were more interesting to me than the other type of Dutch darning samplers known as *merklappen*, which are more representational, with images of animals, plants, houses. I became curious about the more abstract forms: how had they come to have the shapes that they did? That's what led me to find out more about *stoplappen* as tools with which to practise stitches for darning, mending and repairing holes in fabrics.

C   M   : Being in London, one of your instincts was to try and see the *stoplappen* in the V&A's holdings. However, their storage was undergoing a move and so it wasn't possible to access this part of the collection. So, instead the focus became finding a way to get to Middelburg with the joint aims of viewing some darning samplers and of course seeing the Vleeshal exhibition space. We were incredibly lucky, travelling in the week just before the autumn lockdowns in Germany, the UK and the Netherlands, and arriving in Middelburg in late September 2020 for the first of what would be two site visits.

K   S   : Yes, during that first site visit we spent time walking around and getting a sense of the layout of Middelburg and also learning that the majority of the town had been rebuilt after WWII when bombing and fires destroyed large sections of the town.

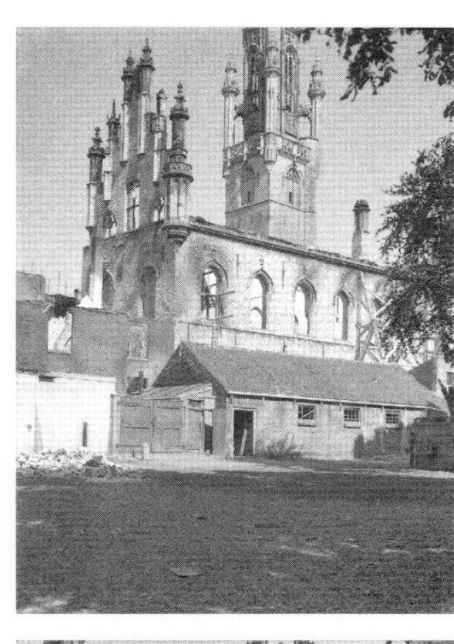

When we visited Vleeshal, Sandra Mujinga's exhibition *Midnight* was on display. The space was lit with very low lighting and she had created a temporary structure cloaking the whole space in blackout fabric, so it was actually really hard to see the Vleeshal space. I was climbing behind the temporary walls in order to have a look at the brick walls and I basically had to squeeze into the alcoves in order to inch along the sides of the space. In person, the black-and-white chequerboard flooring was still very striking and I could see the ceiling clearly.

This was when we began conversations with head technician Kees Wijker, who shared impressions and anecdotes of the building gathered during his work at Vleeshal since the 1990s. He said something that really stayed with me:

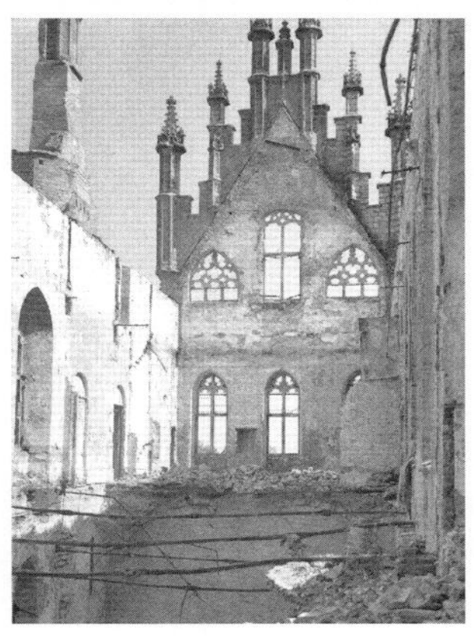

Middelburg Town Hall after enduring WWII bombing and fire on 17 May 1940 (photo: June 1940)

he described how the building was pitted with marks created by the act of exhibition making, what he called "The Scars of Vleeshal." He could look up at the ceiling and walls and identify which hole was made for what exhibition and even the particular year.

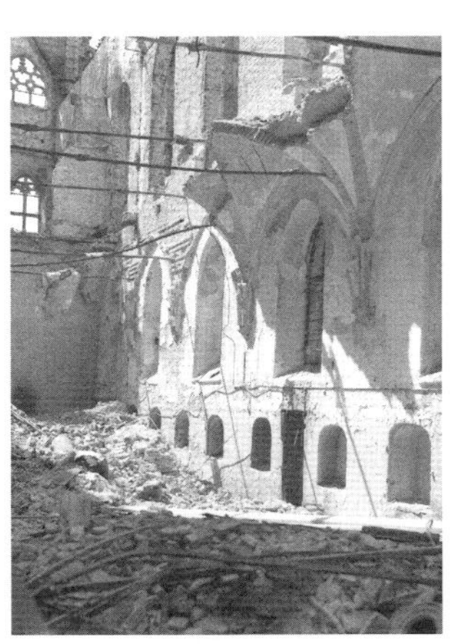

Vleeshal after WWII devastation of 17 May 1940 (photo: June 1940)

C   M   : Yes, it was almost like, should "The Scars of Vleeshal" be the title of a black metal album? Or the name of a tour in the public programme? Kees' tours through the building were fascinating.

K   S   : Kees also showed us around the basement and what we saw was quite unexpected: a giant concrete block. When the building had collapsed following a fire during WWII, all of the architectural rubble was gathered together, encased in wood, and concrete was poured over to create a new foundation. The Vleeshal stands on the ruins of its former self.

I had just completed a project in Plymouth, UK, where I'd been very interested in looking into its post-war architecture (see Rebecca Lewin's essay for further discussion, page 112). Plymouth had been badly bombed during WWII and a lot of the city had been rebuilt post-war. I already had an interest in what happens to the former footprints of a city and even what becomes of the former materials that these buildings were built or rebuilt from. The Vleeshal architecture itself is a combination of new and old – and new made to look old.

We also looked at the Vleeshal's archive of posters and exhibition documentation and one image that really stuck with me was from Christine and Irene Hohenbüch's 1994 show *To knit 2, purl 2*. They had created knitted structures across the whole width of the Vleeshal. There was something inspiring about this initial impression of a web or tangle of threads across the space that – due to the exhibition at the time – I still hadn't really been able to see yet.

C   M   : Even at this stage, there was a link emerging between architectural repair and textile repair techniques. We also visited the nearby Zeeuws Museum, intrigued about their textile displays, and it was there that we saw a book that inspired the title of this volume.

K   S   : Yes, in a gallery dedicated to regional costume there was an amazing sample book in a vitrine: it was from a company in Middelburg called Brouwenaar en Van de Kamer and contained many different types of gingham fabric. Customers could browse this book and select their cloth or, if it wasn't in stock, it would be ordered. This started me thinking about trade relationships in Middelburg, wondering where the cloth came from originally. There were cottons imported from India and silks from China. It was at this point that I found out about Middelburg being the second largest VOC [Dutch East India Company] office, and tangibly felt

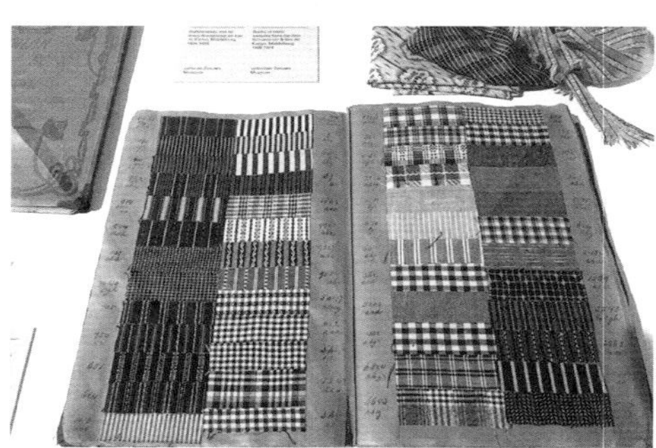

the weight of the colonial past informing both textile and architectural histories in the city. The darning samplers were often on linen and mended using cotton, linen or silk threads, so I knew at this point that I was going to interrogate these material histories.

A book of fabric samples from the Middelburg textile company Brouwenaar en Van de Kamer, 1906–1924

C   M   : What was also very unexpected was visiting the nearby town of Veere one evening and reading that it had links to the Scottish wool trade, which led you to look into the mediaeval wool trading routes between the UK and the Lowlands. British wool was exported to the Netherlands and Belgium to be dyed and processed into cloth. An intriguing map of material histories, regional expertise and trade routes was being formed.

Having seen Vleeshal and the Zeeuws Museum, the
next place that we travelled to was Tilburg, to visit
the TextielMuseum and to meet with its director,
Elles van Vegchel.

K   S   : The TextielMuseum is somewhere
that I'd wanted to visit for years. Elles took us on a
tour of the workshops in the TextielLab, which is a
research and development facility at the heart of
the museum. I was blown away by the production
facilities, seeing the looms and the sock knitting
machine, the testing stations and all the yarns –
there was so much possibility in that space. I think
from that point I knew that it would be really exciting
to produce an aspect of the show there.

C   M   : The TextileLab was so vibrant. Amid
the large machines there was actually only one
machine that was specifically demonstrated to us,
a wooden-framed band-weaving loom. One of the
museum guides asked us if we'd like to see the loom
in action, and when he turned it on, three wooden
boats at the front, which looked like the upturned
blades of ice skates, started to dance back and
forth. It was a loud, warm sound and a magical
moment. We subsequently found out that this was a
Brandenburg band-weaving loom dating from 1880
that had stood in the Haagse Passementfabriek
Brandenburg in The Hague.

With all these encounters still reverberating, you
returned to London. What were you working on
when you got back?

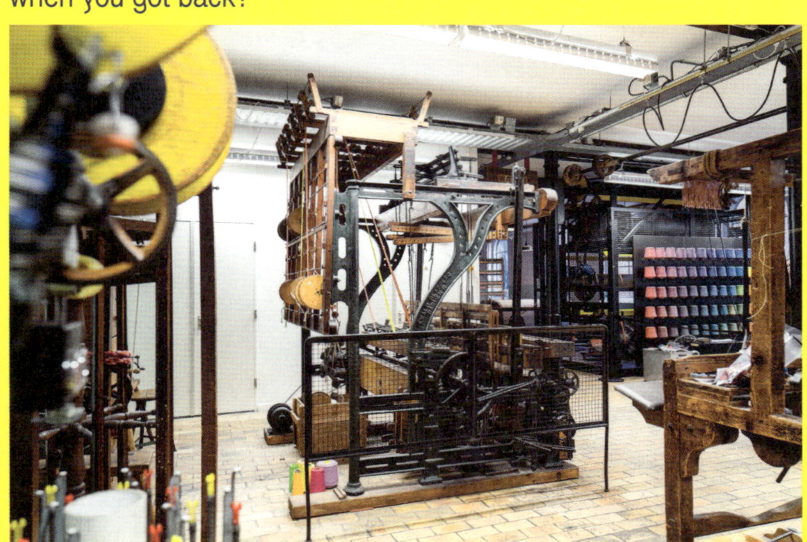

Band-weaving loom in the passementerie department at
TextielLab in Tilburg

K   S   : In the studio I was thinking a lot
about the dancing loom at the TextielLab, the
materials that were traded in the Zeeland area
and especially about the idea of sampling. I began
working on samplers and sampling. It's important
for me to say that I don't mean sampling in a
postmodern sense of taking lots of influences and
combining them with no sense of crediting where
they are from; I mean sampling in the sense of

17

learning about processes by patiently working with materials. Sampling with the intention of making a sampler.

One of the things that got me through the lockdown was working on a large improvised sampler. I worked on it a little bit every day. It's a new addition to a series that I've been working on for the last seven years, which is called *Work Hands*, a collection of small, improvised stitched works.

There are two ways of thinking about my samplers. There's the *Work Hands* series and there's the sampler that I made for my 2016 exhibition at Collective in Edinburgh. Titled simply *Sampler* (see pages 124–125), it is a four-metre-long work created by stitching on hessian with wool. The piece is a series of stitched visual quotes. I'd been looking at the printed, stitched and woven textiles of artists and designers from the 1920s to the 1950s and '60s, including Anni Albers, Phyllis Barron and Dorothy Larcher. *Sampler* became a way of thinking through their work, their processes and the abstract forms that appeared in their works. I made *Sampler* using wool that I had inherited from my grandmother after she passed away. She had always done a lot of embroidery, both decorative wall works and stitched cushions (see Rebecca Lewin's essay, page 112). I had these two modes of sampling already as part of my practice and then I started thinking again about the Middelburg samplers and I was really interested in this idea of acknowledging one's teachers. The Middelburg samplers were decorative pieces but they also had a real functional element to them; they were teaching you how to repair a hole. And so, in my studio, I was thinking about repair, holes and acknowledgement.

C   M   : Were you able to focus solely on this process or did you have other projects in the lockdown of autumn 2020?

K   S   : In October 2020 I was working in parallel on a new work for an exhibition that was looking critically at the history of the 1620 Mayflower crossing from the UK to what is now the USA. I was doing a lot of research into broadcloth production. This wool came from the UK, was dyed in Flanders and then transported across the Atlantic, where it was often used by colonisers as a good with which to trade with Indigenous peoples. Broadcloth is still produced in Yorkshire in the UK to this day; it's used for military uniforms, royal garments and even for snooker table baize. So, this fabric was hovering in my mind, too.

Prior to lockdown, I'd also been collecting woven ribbons from the 1940s, '50s and '60s. I started stitching some of these ribbons and rickrack to a black piece of woollen cloth, with the aim of tracing their movement across the fabric, but it was very difficult for the ribbons to hold these curves. There was a sample that had been up in the studio for a long time, but it had not really gone anywhere.

C M   : You showed me this sample on a video call and I loved the movement of the ribbons and the vivid green rickrack too.

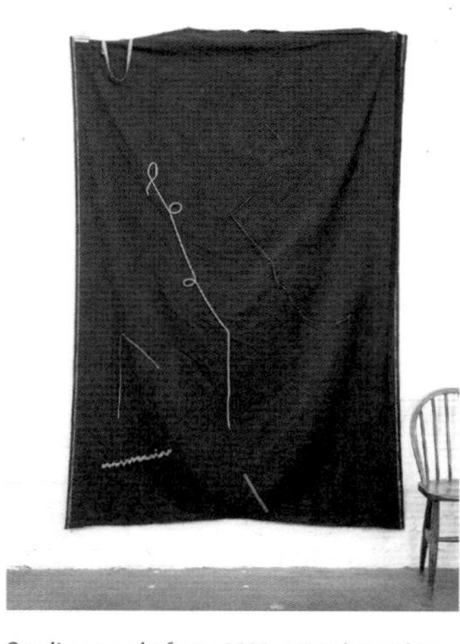

Studio sample from 2018, experimenting with ribbons and curves on superfine worsted wool and mohair

K S   : At that time I was thinking a lot about how to work with the curve as a form. As well as sewing the ribbons in curves, I was also doing lots of quilting, trying to work out how to stitch circles, or semicircles, or how to get wiggly lines. I was finding it very frustrating because generally when I work with patchwork it's an intuitive, improvised process. When you're working with curves, you have to plan a lot more and pin everything out and press everything with an iron, and it's much more precise.

I was looking at Barbara Brown's magnificent screen prints, which had these huge curves and waves and circles. And at the TextielMuseum I'd leafed through a book on Sheila Hicks in which there was a woven piece made with rickrack. I'd recently bought a big stock of rickrack – I was very intrigued by it as a material. And then I'd been thinking about Lenore Tawney's work (see Ann Coxon's essay for more discussion of Tawney, page 68), her loose woven structures which incorporate curves within the grid of the woven plane. I could really visualise setting up a loose warp on the loom and using your hand to weave these curves, going back and forth on yourself. I was intrigued by all of those processes and was wondering how to work with curves on an architectural scale as well as how to work with curvy materials. Working with curves to create curves.

This is also the moment when we were discussing Robert Morris' cut felt pieces together and I was also looking at Robert Rauschenberg's big fabric works with drapes in the middle and Lynda Benglis' "pour" works. What struck me about all of these works is that their forms feel organic, improvised, letting the material do its thing. It stood in such opposition to the frustration I was experiencing trying to sew a really precise curve!

C M   : You had already made a sampler on a large scale and now you were thinking of how to work with curves in a way that embraced architectural scale. Did this come from the ceilings you had seen in Middelburg? The Vleeshal's vaulted stone and brick ceiling and the concave wooden ceiling at the Zeeuws Museum?

K   S   : Yes, it did come from the ceilings. There was an important moment in the first site visit where Kees pointed out the point where the Vleeshal's ceiling transitioned from old stone to new stone, a subtle demarcation of the building's reconstruction. This, plus the dominance of the chequerboard floor, led me to thinking about potentially painting the ceiling. What soon became clear was that I didn't want to show any works on the floor; the curved ceiling and brick walls were to be the focus.

C   M   : The floor wasn't only something to negate though, it was also an inspiration for the initial palette of the show.

K   S   : Yes, and, as well as the chequered floor, it was also the influence of coming off the ferry from the UK and driving in the Netherlands for the first time. En route to Middelburg there were many black-and-white stripes to be seen: cycle lanes, zebra crossings, Belisha beacons. This, combined with the black-and-white gingham fabrics in the sample book at the Zeeuws Museum, led me to consider monochrome as being a strong palette to work with. As I generally use so much colour, this felt like an interesting challenge to embrace.

Thinking about this palette, I began to sketch drawings where I inverted the curves of the ceiling, making a series of black-and-white fabric loops that would hang from the ceiling – a graphic intervention in the Vleeshal. As I hadn't yet fully seen the space, I made the sketch on an installation view of a Jimmie Durham show at Vleeshal, in which his works were subtle and the architecture was really visible.

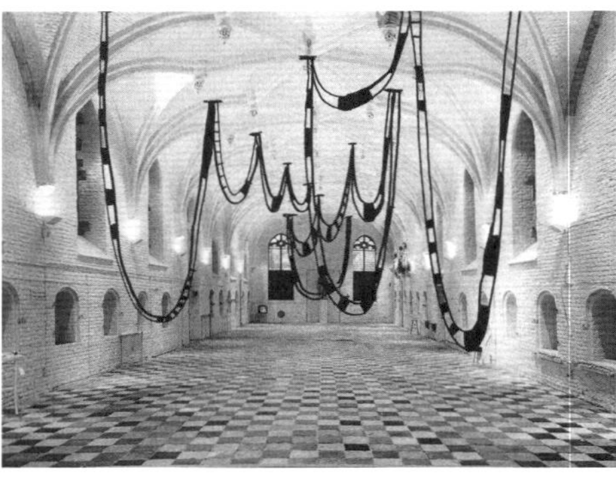

Katie's first sketches for the exhibition created in November 2020

C   M   : There was also an image that we came across just before you made those drawings. You were looking at the practice of William Morris and there was an image of Merton Abbey, the Morris wallpaper and textile works, where cotton fabric was being woodblock printed on long trestle tables and the caption described the fabric as being hung up to dry in "festoons." Suddenly the word festoon seemed the best word in the whole of the English language.

20

K   S   : Festoon! Yes! We were initially talking about William Morris because he had painted ceilings at the Red House in Bexleyheath.

C   M   : That's right, and the idea of trestle tables led us to think about vitrines running down the space as a way to demarcate the concrete block underneath the Vleeshal floor, to draw

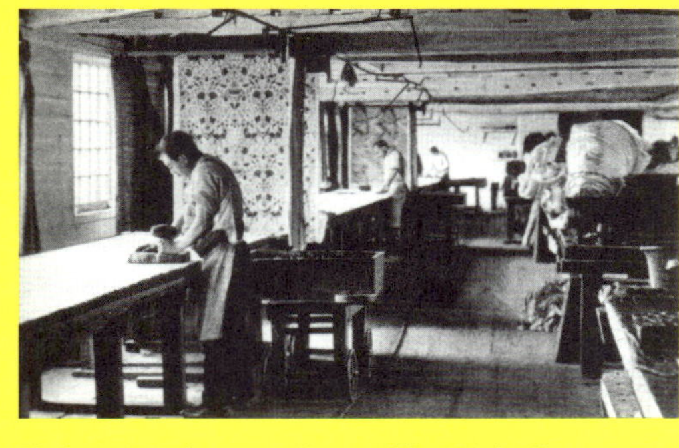

Block printing chintzes at Merton Abbey Works, Morris & Company, c. 1890

attention to this underappreciated structure that was giving the building its strength. But what seemed limiting about the vitrine as a display mechanism is that it only allows one side of what is displayed within it to be seen.

You had also shown me an image from a book that you'd ordered about Dutch samplers, *Door mijn gedaen* (literally "done by me," see Rosalie Sloof for more discussion of this sampler tradition, page 58). This book included a reproduction of *A Beautiful Reflection*, a painting by Nicolaas van der Waay that shows a darning sampler framed and displayed on the wall and this became, in a sense, an anti-guiding principle: not wanting to fall into the logic of framing textiles and only having one side viewable. It was essential that the form of display embraced the sculptural nature of textiles. And that it kept open the possibility of seeing the "back" of the piece.

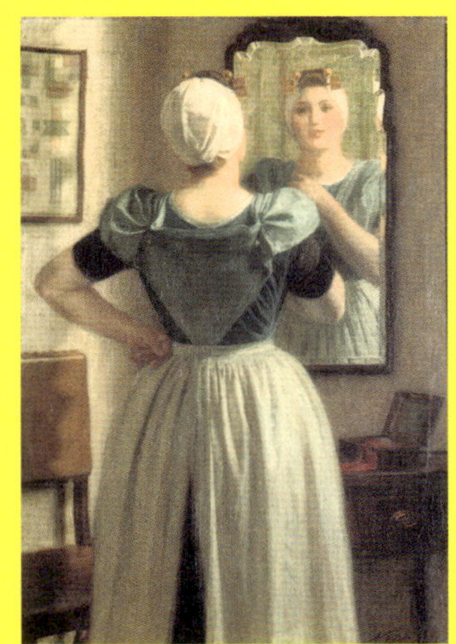

Nicolaas van der Waay, *A Beautiful Reflection* (n.d.)
Oil on canvas, 63 × 42 cm

K   S   : Right. By the start of 2021 I knew that I definitely wanted to work with the band-weaving loom that we'd seen and I reached out to TextielLab regarding production possibilities. They required an outline of a proposal of what the work would be, its size and materials plus a sketch of what the work would look like. So I had my early sketch of ribbons hanging from the ceiling in festoons and then I made a more detailed drawing of the stripes that these ribbons would have.

C   M   : I remember that the initial proposal for TextielLab stated the wish to produce one kilometre of striped ribbon on this loom.

K   S   : Exactly, and after submitting the proposal we had our first online meeting with Veva van der Wolf from the passementerie department,

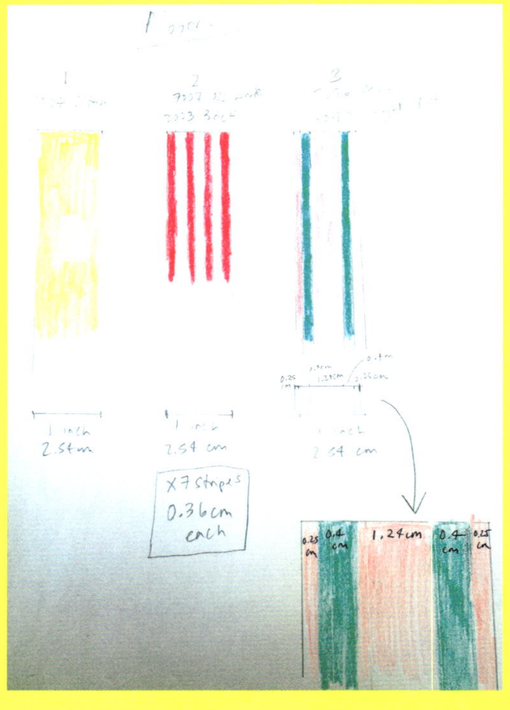

Sketch for dimensions of of the band-weave warp

where ribbons, tassels and cords are produced. Of all the amazing possibilities at the TextielLab, what struck me about this department is that the human body was still very much involved in the production process, rather than other departments where making was more digital or machine-led. I also loved the old timber of the machinery in the passementerie department.

It was fascinating talking to Veva, who was very into the idea of working with the wooden band-weaving loom as the TextielLab hadn't actually used it for a project before. So, it became a joint research venture. And there was a humbling moment when Veva explained that this type of loom might produce one kilometre of ribbon in its entire lifetime!

We agreed that woven samples would be produced and from that point we would enter into a kind of editing process based on the technical possibilities and how I wanted the piece to evolve. In March 2021 Veva posted the samples of black-and-white striped band weaves to the UK (see page 37). They were a combination of cotton and wool and one even included mohair. Materially they were very exciting but the colours made them feel flat. I had imagined them as striking, graphic elements, but where the black-and-white warp and weft met they became grey. Seeing this physical sample and understanding more about the production, it was clear to me that I wasn't going to be making a monochrome show – colour needed to enter. But the principle of the ribbon, how it was constructed and the changing of the yarns felt right.

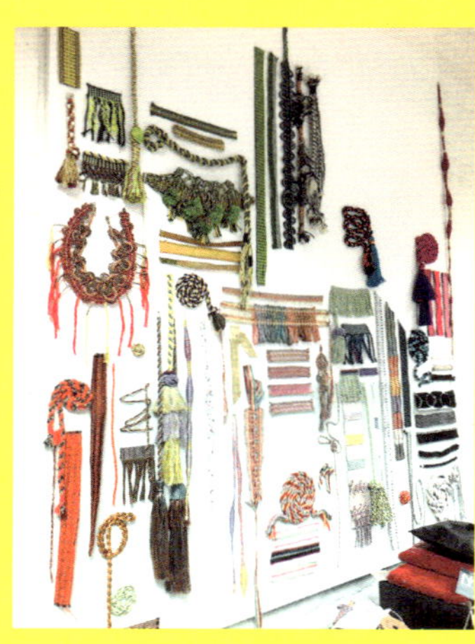

Ribbons, cords, fringing and tassels in the passementerie department at TextielLab, Tilburg in September 2020

C M : Once I had seen the sample, I also had to agree that colour must return! Especially with the black-and-white floor, it felt like a grey ribbon would simply disappear in the space. And with the knowledge that it wasn't going to be possible to create enough ribbon to festoon the ceiling, you returned to deeply engaging in the process of sampling in the studio, to see what other possibilities might emerge. You were preparing at this time to go on a residency in Scotland that had been very postponed due to the pandemic.

K   S   : I spent the month of May 2021 on a residency at Cove Park in Scotland. I travelled

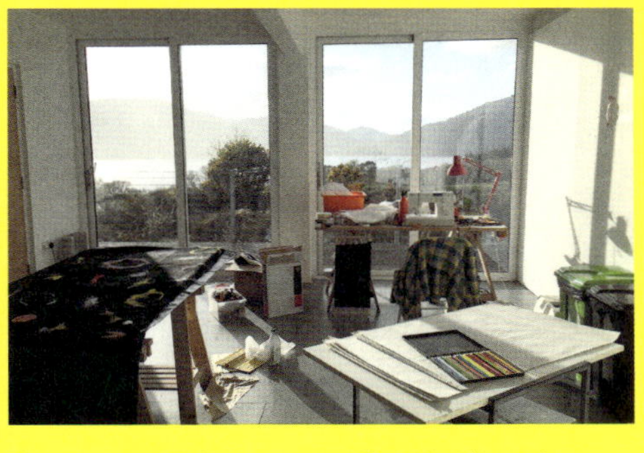
The view over Loch Long as seen from Katie's residency studio at Cove Park

just as we were coming out of lockdown here in the UK. Everything was still very cautious and it felt quite strange to be going anywhere. I loaded up the car with all the materials that I'd been thinking about with no clear plan of what was going to happen, but was open to spending a month making in the studio.

Cove Park overlooks Loch Long and is a very rural site. There are sheep wandering around the fields and you're surrounded by greenery. Every day I'd walk down to the studio and there was a huge gorse bush outside. The colours of the landscape were really vivid: the green of the hills, the yellow of the gorse, the blue of the sky and the loch.

C   M   : What was your starting point when you got into the studio at Cove Park?

K   S   : Before leaving, I visited my local haberdashers where I was drawn to materials that are used for darning and repairing – small wares used for strengthening and reinforcing. I ordered metres of rickrack and bias binding. Along with these purchases, I brought with me to Scotland my collection of ribbons, patchwork pieces I'd begun working on, samples of broadcloth and casein paint. At the beginning of the residency I began mixing up casein paints: chalky pigments made from milk protein. At this point I imagined that each of the Vleeshal's thirty-one alcoves might be painted with these natural colours.

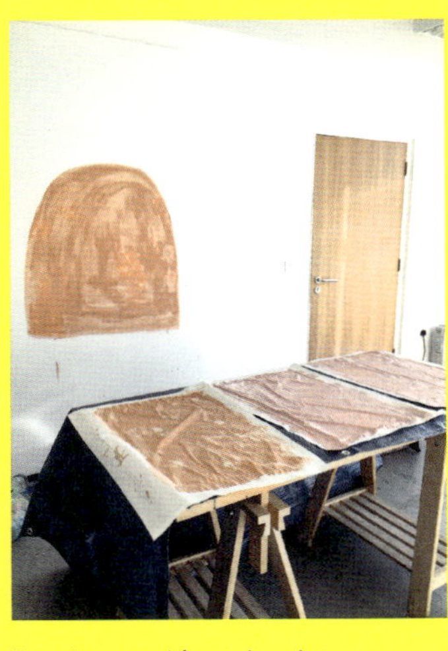
Experiments with casein paint

I was also thinking about natural pigments in a broader sense because in my research I'd come across the Zeeland tradition of dyeing fabric using madder plants. I had brought some madder to dye with and also gathered the deep yellow gorse petals from the bushes outside the studio. I began dyeing and trying out different recipes. I ended up with silks and cottons dyed in shades of red, orange, pink and yellow.

C   M   : Once you had begun making, were you freely moving between sampling processes?

K   S   : I was aiming to create thirty-one different samplers, or perhaps more accurately samples that might later become samplers, each incorporating a different material process related to the research. One sample was a patchwork piece of stitched silk, one was made up of lengths of bias

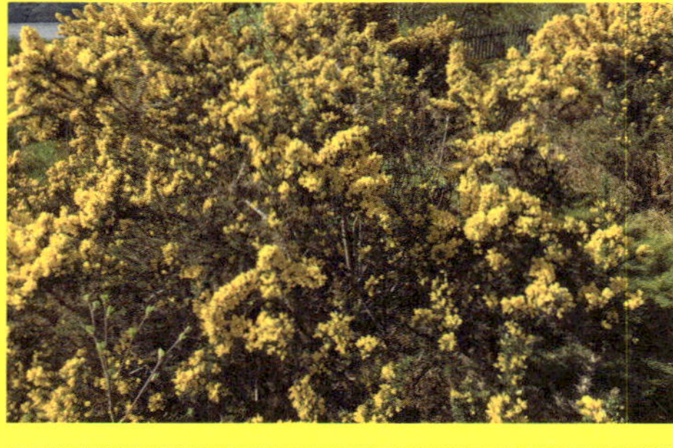

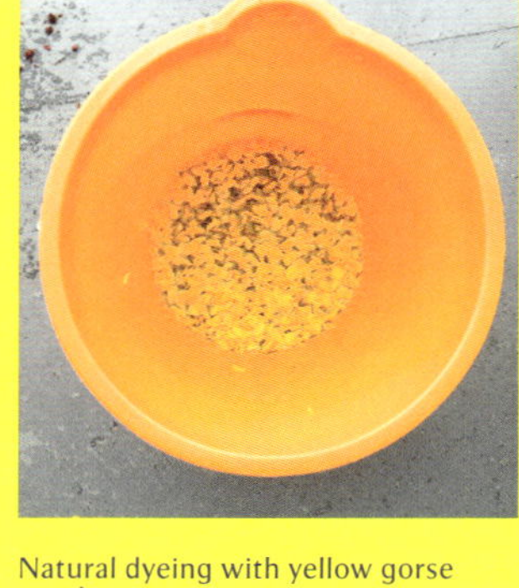

Natural dyeing with yellow gorse petals

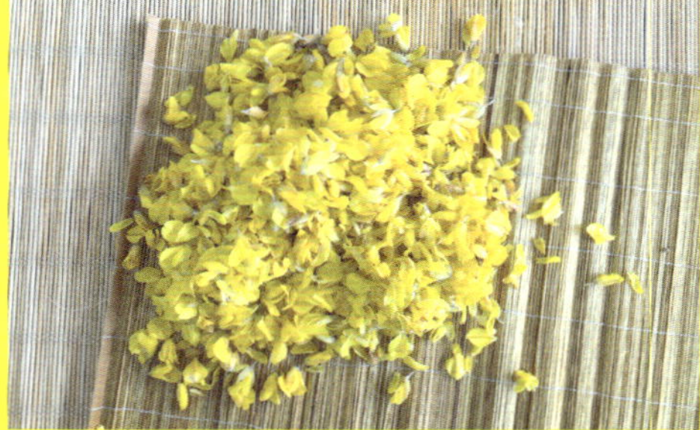

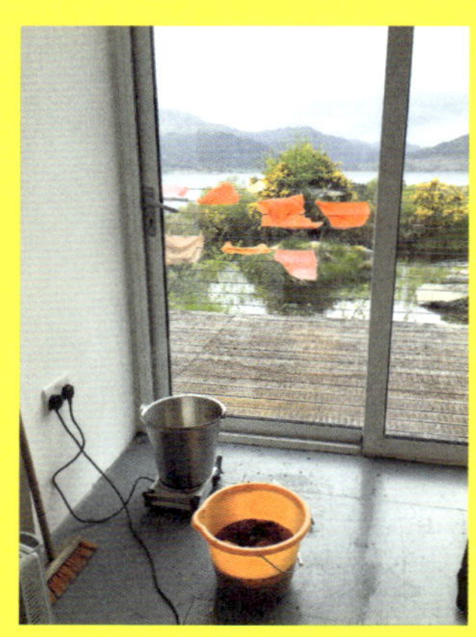

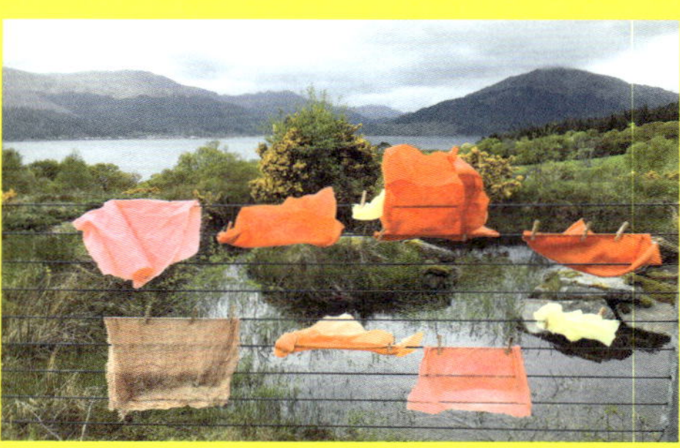

Dyed silk and cotton with madder and gorse

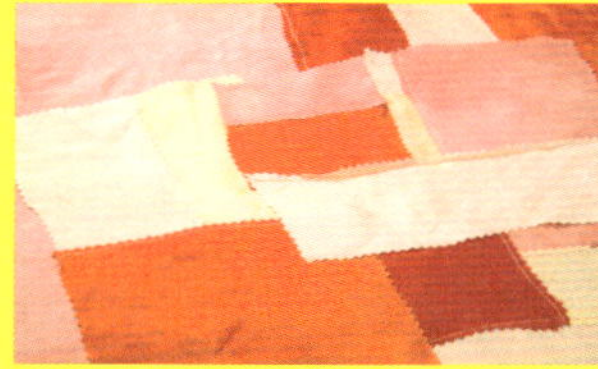

Patchwork dyed silk sample

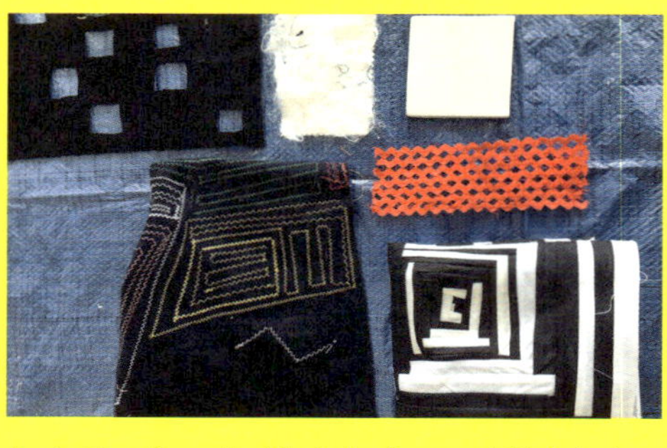

A selection of samples (clockwise from top left): holes in woollen cloth, felted wool, a ceramic tile, stitched rickrack, bias binding and zigzag stitching on woollen cloth

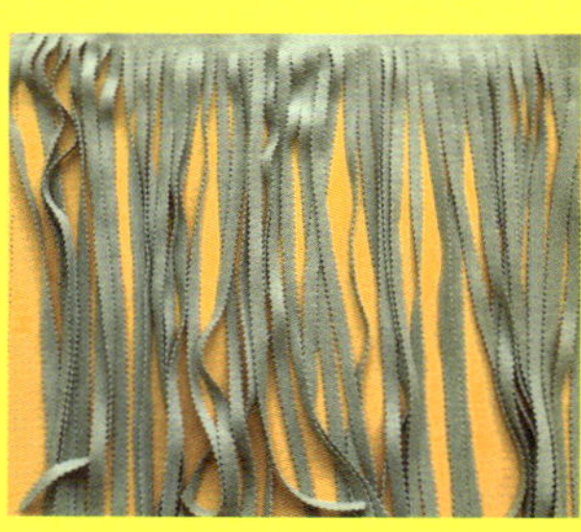

Broadcloth sample cut with pinking shears

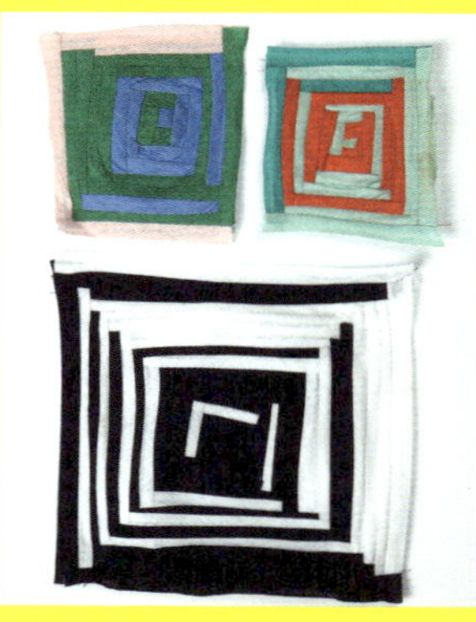

Early bias binding samples

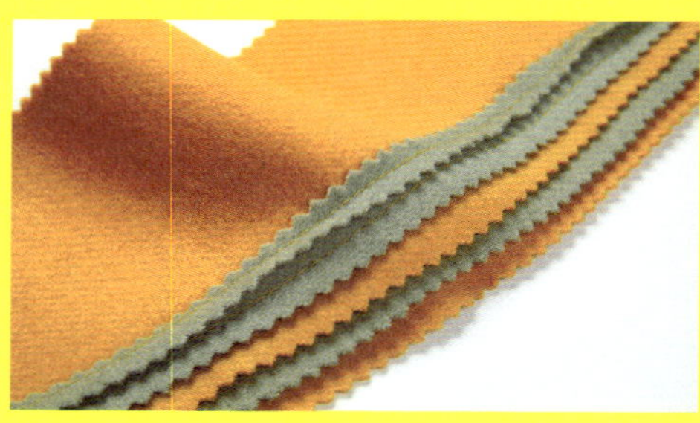

Broadcloth sample with a zigzag edge

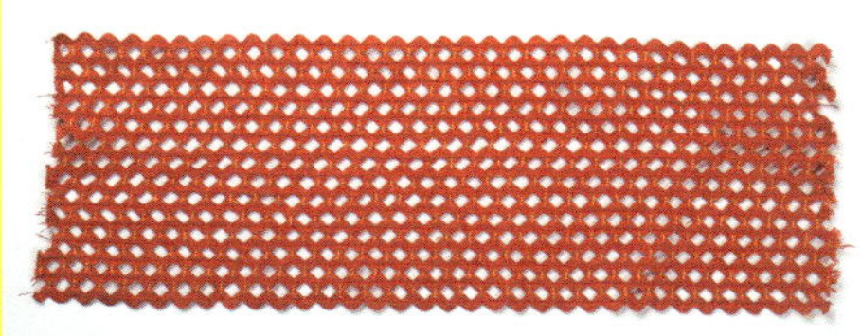

Rickrack sample

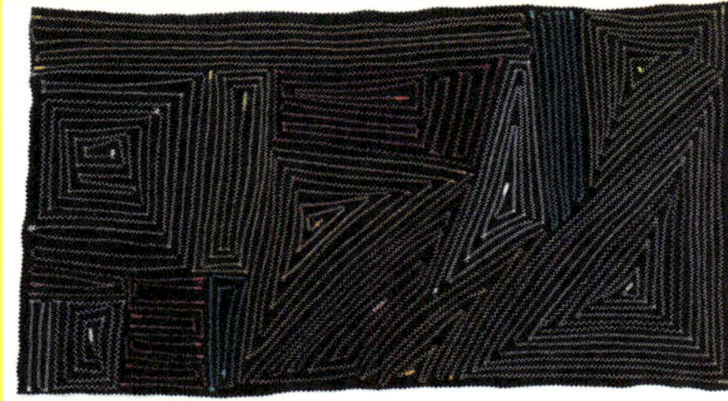

Zigzag machine stitching sample on woollen cloth, an early study for *patches* (2021)

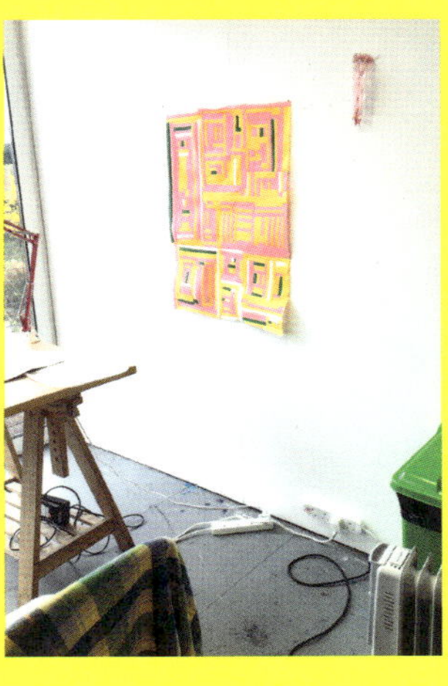

Pink, yellow and green bias binding sample that would later become the work *strength study* (2021)

binding, one was zigzag stitching on broadcloth. I was trying out as many different processes as possible. I was also collecting wool from the site that the sheep had left behind on branches and fences, and started felting and dyeing the wool. That was another kind of sampling that I thought might be incorporated into the show.

C   M   : We spoke twice while you were at Cove Park, so the online aspect of the exhibition preparations continued.

K   S   : Yes and it was also at Cove Park that we had our first online meeting with Åbäke, the graphic designer of this book, and so as I was experimenting with materials, the idea of shaping both an exhibition and a book was beginning; I was wondering how these related to each other in terms of shared material interests.

I returned to London in June with many different samples and material experiments, and we started speaking again about how to narrow this down or whether the idea of creating thirty-one samplers was still even the aim.

C   M   : You had created so many possibilities and we started thinking about: how to handle this breadth of samples? how to treat them? how to display them? One of your samples that we were both really excited by was an experiment of patchworked bias binding, which could be formed to hold its own shape. I was so intrigued by this idea of the bias binding revelling in its own strength, a fabric usually consigned to supporting hems and remaining hidden gaining some spotlight and supporting itself. We started talking about the work of Běla Kolářová at this point, too.

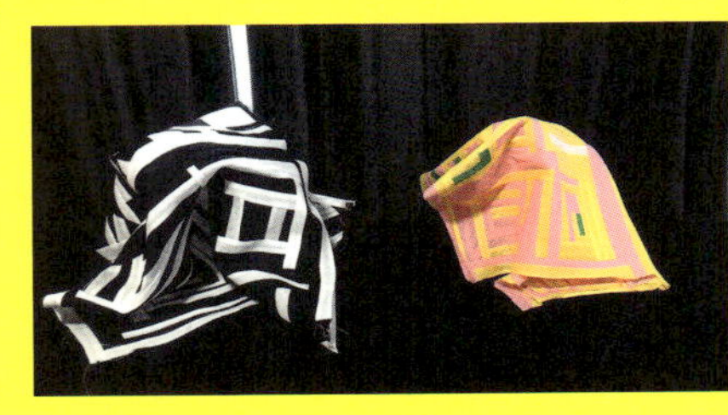

Bias binding samples

K   S   : Běla Kolářová's work was a wonderful reference because we had both seen her 2013 show at Raven Row in London, where there were many pieces made with press studs, hooks or pins. She also had a fascination for haberdashery and for hidden fastenings arranged in grids. There was a principle of very subtle, discreet objects that are not usually the main focus of attention coming together, and this approach of gathering objects en masse really carried through in her sculpture.

C   M   : We were also planning the second site visit to Vleeshal in July. There was an abundance of directions in which the show could go and I couldn't wait to see the samples in person.

K   S   : We had a few objectives for that trip. The first was for me to fully see the space! And the second was for you to see the samples, and for us to figure out if festooning could still play a role. Also how to deal with thirty-one samplers in the space. We also set up a series of museum and archive visits across the Netherlands as we hadn't yet seen any darning samplers in person.

The first thing we did when we arrived was to take all of the samples into the space – I had them stored in big chequered laundry bags – and to start thinking of them in terms of scale and colour and materials.

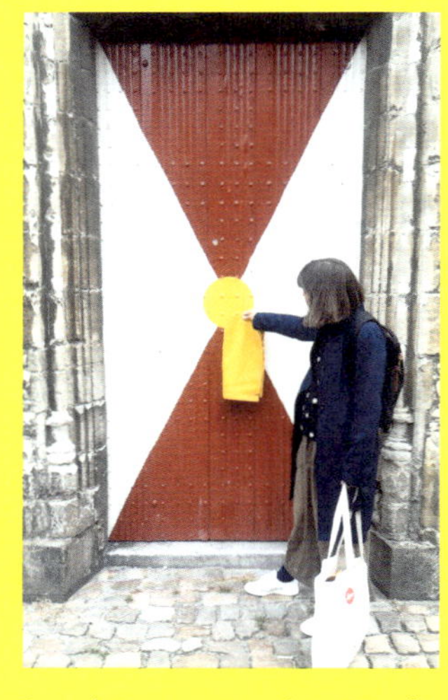

Serendipitous moment during Kees' tour: discovering that the broadcloth Katie has ordered has the exact same yellow as the Vleeshal's doors in July 2021

The second thing was to really see the building with Kees, he gave us a full-scale tour of the entire Vleeshal building: the exhibition space, the basement again, the parts that belong to the university, the town hall chamber, even right up into the attic. So, I went from not having seen much to seeing things that even Kees was encountering for the first time, like the roof. We saw what was behind the walls, above the ceiling, below the floor. I looked in particular at all the hardware in the spaces, the bolts and bannisters.

C   M   : It was a very illuminating tour. After this, we visited the archive of the Zeeuws Museum and met with the curator and head of collection, Karina Leijnse.

K   S   : I was finally seeing a Middelburg darning sampler in person! We went with the show's assistant curator, Luuk Vulkers and it was fascinating to be able to handle these textiles, to see the reverse of them and to look closely at the stitches.

26

C M : Karina shared this absolutely fascinating piece of knowledge about why the stitches were in colour: because if they had been white stitches on white cloth it would have been so much harder for the teachers to see their pupil's mistakes. It just felt like this complete confirmation that colour had to be in the show.

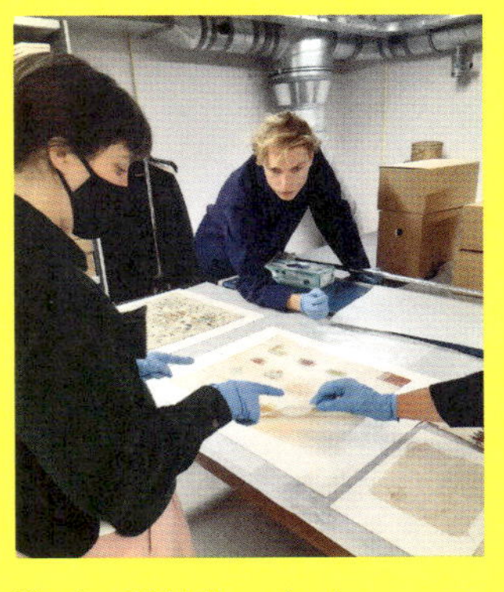

Viewing Middelburg darning samplers at the Zeeuws Museum depot in July 2021

K S : Yes, and the darning sampler colours became a guide for the show's palette. There were a few other formative moments in Middelburg. One of them was visiting a local charity shop after a long day in the gallery. We sat on their second-hand sofas and discussed how important it felt to have some kind of seating at Vleeshal, potentially upholstered or maybe even found materials. I began thinking about whether we could collect lots of sofas from the shop and bring them into the space. That got me thinking about reusing materials, which was a train of thought that came back later with the work *patches* for Vleeshal's winter curtain. This moment of rest in the charity shop was the earliest influence on what would become the work *alcove cushions*.

C M : We'd spent days in the Vleeshal space, sitting on the floor, looking at all the different individual samples and the flagstone floor was cold even in summer.

K S : Suddenly this practical element of textiles as being able to bring warmth to a space seemed essential for an exhibition that was going to be on display from autumn to winter.

C M : Returning the next day to the Vleeshal space and unpacking the individual sampler sculptures, we tried placing them in the alcoves and there was such an unexpected twist: due to the Gothic architecture, seeing the works in these recesses, they felt very shrine-like. And the idea of painting the alcoves seemed to underscore that atmosphere even more.

K S : It was not working. We took photos of each other standing next to the alcoves. And there was something about this relationship with the body, the scale of the body to the alcove that came across in these photos. As I sat in one of the alcoves I thought, "Oh, this is the perfect size." It felt like a very comfortable space for the body. This was a big shift: it suddenly wasn't important to delineate the concrete block or to necessarily have thirty-one samplers in the alcoves. It was about thinking of these alcoves as places from which the show could be viewed, to have the alcoves become seating.

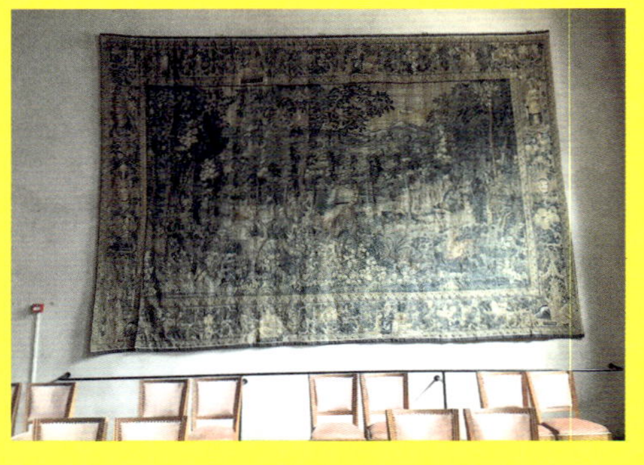

Protective barrier around a tapestry displayed in the former cloth hall that is located directly above Vleeshal in Middelburg Town Hall in July 2021

We also went to look at the former cloth hall, which is directly above Vleeshal, a former meat hall. And there were these two huge tapestries of hunting scenes hanging on the walls. They both had these bannister-like protection rails around the textile. I remember we talked about that display technique and the idea of the textile being at a remove, not being able to touch it. And being distanced from the materiality of it and not being able to see the back of the work either. We were also thinking about this as a former place of trade and exchange and purchase. It was then that idea of centralising the textile elements and liberating them from framing felt really important.

C   M   : On that day we also saw two further paintings of the wartime devastation wreaked on the town hall building.

K   S   : Seeing those paintings was really important, especially the Kimpe painting. Previously Luuk had sent us photos of the damaged building and one photograph in particular included a scaffolding structure holding up the roofless façade of the building. During our tour with Kees we'd seen these amazing red metal struts holding up the roof. Seeing these kinds of historical and contemporary support structures – scaffolds

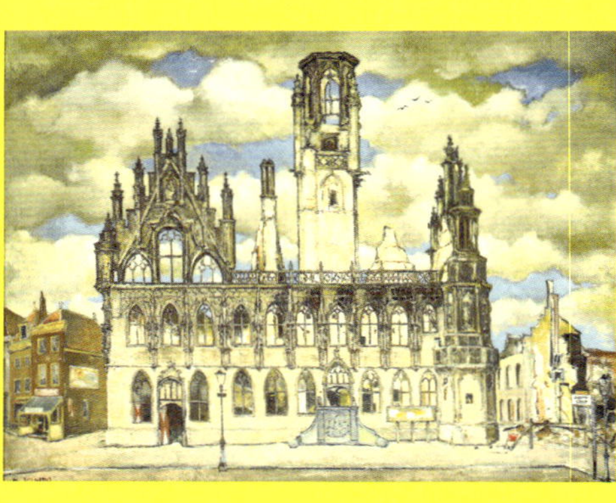

Reimond Kimpe, *Stadhuis van Middelburg na het bombardement* [Middelburg Town Hall after the bombing] (1940)
Oil on canvas, 100 × 130 cm, framed

and struts – that were there temporarily or permanently in the building and thinking back to the concrete block, the idea of strengthening, of holding up, really crystalised. We also saw a carpet winch in the cleaner's cupboard, which was this metal triangle suspended from the ceiling used for hoisting up the town hall's red carpet to clean it after events. We discussed the question of: will we have some kind of winch system for the textile works? How will the pieces be held up and

Vleeshal after WWII devastation of 17 May 1940 (photo: June 1940)

supported? So, we had
an idea of the direction
and the materials, but
we were still left with
some questions.

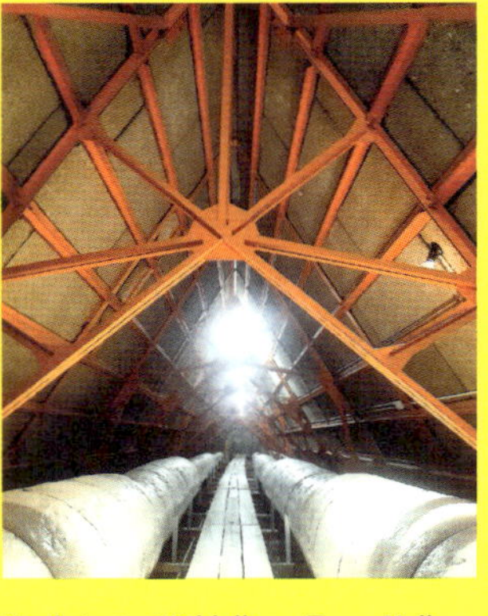

Roof struts, Middelburg Town Hall

C   M   : With all these questions
percolating, it was time to visit the
TextielLab for the second time, for you
to work with Veva on the weaving. And
I had ordered lots of books to view in
their library.

K   S   : Precisely. It was the point in the
production process where it was clear that three
colourful, striped band-weaves were going to be
produced of approximately twenty metres each,
and there was the task of choosing the yarns at the
TextielLab. We went to their yarn storeroom and
looked at all the options from the wools through
to the more synthetic or even paper yarns. But I
decided to pay homage to the darning samplers
themselves and work with a cotton warp, and then
the weft would be cotton, silk and linen. I spent
some time thinking about the principles of the band
weaves, how the stripes would occur and what
colours would overlap. Together with Veva I created
a plan for how the weavings would work.

C   M   : At this point you had to make more
precise drawings for the band weaves.

K   S   : I had done an approximate scale
drawing of how many centimetres of pink, followed
by how many centimetres of yellow and so on. The
palette of the band weaves was drawn from the
different shades from the madder and gorse dyeing
experiments I had done back at Cove Park, and
this palette was also a nod to the pink and yellow
stained glass windows at Vleeshal.

C   M   : In the afternoon you joined me in the
library.

K   S   : There were so many books on
passementerie that were interesting not only in
terms of their content but also their form. One in
particular was a very long, thin volume with different
examples of braids and trimmings.

C   M   : Oh yes, *Des dorelotiers aux
passementiers*, a catalogue from a 1973 show at the
Musée des Arts Décoratifs in Paris, which, along
with the proportions of your work *strength study*,
influenced the shape of this book.

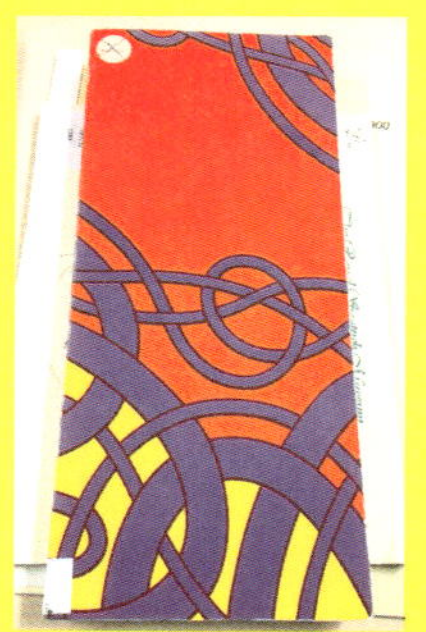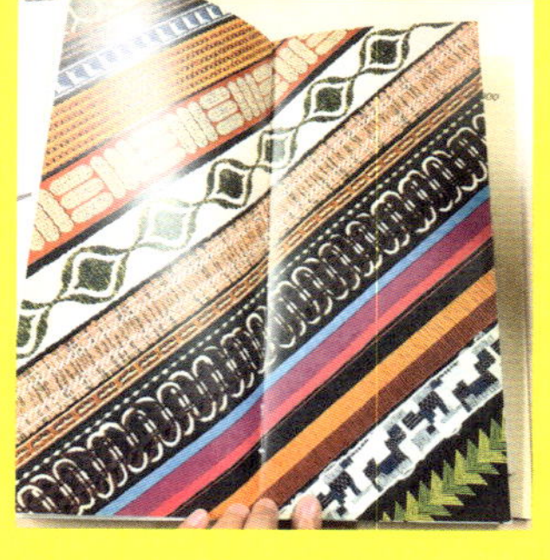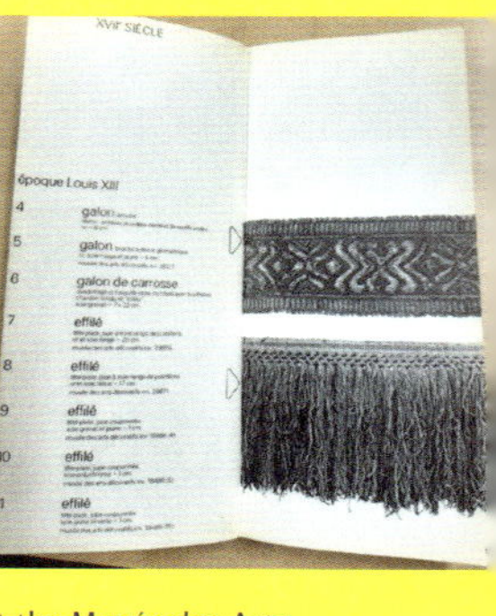

Des dorelotiers aux passementiers, catalogue from the 1973 exhibition at the Musée des Arts Décoratifs, Paris, at the TextielMuseum's library in July 2021

K   S   : Yes, the book had an amazing form. This was the day that I'd laid the material foundation for the band weaves and Veva then spent a week preparing the loom in my absence. This involved preparing the selected yarns, loading up the bobbins and "warping up" the loom. A week later, Veva and I spent some time together looking at the tension of the yarns and then introducing different colours at different points in the weaving.

C   M   : This was also a working process very influenced by the constraints of the pandemic. It was clear that Veva and yourself would be working remotely most of the time, so the drawings were a guide for those periods when you wouldn't be working together physically.

Before I would return to Berlin and you would set off across the country to see more Dutch darning samplers in the depots of the Musea Zutphen and the Fries Museum in Leeuwarden, we had one last destination to visit together with Luuk: Arnhem. Ironically it wasn't possible to see the darning samplers there at the Nederlands Openluchtmuseum where some of the oldest examples in the whole of the country are kept; instead we were going there to visit Werkplaats Typografie.

K   S   : Right, before my tour of archives and collections, we went to Arnhem to meet with Anniek Brattinga, who leads the two year MA course in graphic design along with Armand Mevis. Among her MA students was Marianne Noordzij, who was going to be designing the graphic identity of the exhibition. We spoke with Marianne about her work and the music she was making, previous projects that she had worked on, and then we shared all of the ideas and processes behind my forthcoming exhibition. I brought some of my samples and samplers with me, so there was also an exchange about materials.

C   M   : Even though so much was still undecided for the show, some things had already become clear: there would be band weaves, samplers and alcove seating in the show.

K   S   : Yes. You then returned to Berlin and I travelled to see darning samplers before heading back to TextielLab. In that interim week Veva had also added some different shades that weren't in the original yarn selection but were still based on colours found in the *stoplappen* – lilac for instance – in order to create more contrast. And this was when the production truly began.

When I returned to the UK in July, that correspondence with Veva continued online and she would send me photographs and say, "What do you think of this?" There was one really nice moment where she sent a picture of a repair where the thread had snapped. She had introduced a strengthening yarn, a different colour so that you could see a visible mend in the weave (see page 41).

C   M   : A repair to the weaving, how gratifying. Were there other surprises in the production process?

K   S   : Yes, other than the repair for which Veva had tied the yarn by hand, she'd also been trying out different ways of making holes in the band weave. So this was something we talked about a lot – how to make visible holes (see page 100). It was interesting because when the machine was running and then stopped, it took a little while to shut itself down. So, the yarn would trail out and form these unpredictable curves in the weave (see fourth image page 41). Veva was working on three of these band weaves simultaneously and changing the yarns in and out, based on the drawing that I had made. But she was also working with the personality of the loom itself and what it allowed for, and with yarns snapping or being added in, it was almost like dancing with the machine. There's so much movement in the loom and the body really interacts with it. It wasn't like you press a button and it goes and does its thing; it's still a very manual process and the hands are very involved. Gunnar Meier, Vleeshal's photographer, took photos documenting the weaving process and they capture so well Veva's interaction with and handling of the machine – it was amazing for me to see these images as Veva and I were working remotely at this point and it deepened my understanding of the process (see pages 36–43).

C   M   : By July 2021 another sampling process was happening. Having seen all of the hardware in the Vleeshal building, suddenly there was another principle that came in. It became clear that it wasn't just about the small wares – ribbons, bias binding, rickrack – it was also about how they were going to be displayed: they were going to have to be attached somehow to something. Whether that meant creating a metal bannister or loops or bolts, it became clear that creating a custom piece of hardware to perform this function was important, and you already had someone in mind who you wanted to work with.

K   S   : Yes, the person who I had in mind was someone we studied with in London from 2004 to 2005: Sam Fish, an amazing designer and fabricator who co-founded a hardware business called Swarf.

During the second site visit, I'd looked very closely at the bolts on the alcoves, which are used to close the individual oak doors that can be attached to them. Kees shared that these alcoves would have been used to store sharp knives and lock away valuables when the space was a meat hall. The bolts are on the doors and protruding from the walls are beautiful wrought iron bolt holes (see page 44).

We emailed Sam with an open query, with pictures of the blacksmithed bolt holes. We asked if it would be possible to produce a piece of custom hardware based on this form for the exhibition. What followed was an interesting conversation about how a piece of hardware like this could be made using a CNC (Computer Numerical Control) machine, then placing the pieces into a tumbling machine to soften the metal edges before being powder-coated. Again, influenced by stitches on the samplers, the colour I wanted was a very specific blue. Sam produced 100 of these hardware loops, which then became the fixtures and fittings that were used to hang the works in the show (see pages 44–47).

C   M   : And in the studio you were also in full production mode.

K   S   : Right, in my studio in Hackney, I was scaling up the production and initially focusing on three different elements for the show. There was a large textile to be suspended from the ceiling on custom Swarf hardware, a patchworked, improvised work made of bias binding, and a collection of broadcloth cushions with patchwork tops for each alcove.

I was also continuing production discussions with Veva about the patterns of the band weaves.

I also had a conversation with Kees where I asked him if there were ever any textiles used in the space, and he recalled a curtain hung across the inside entrance that kept the wind out

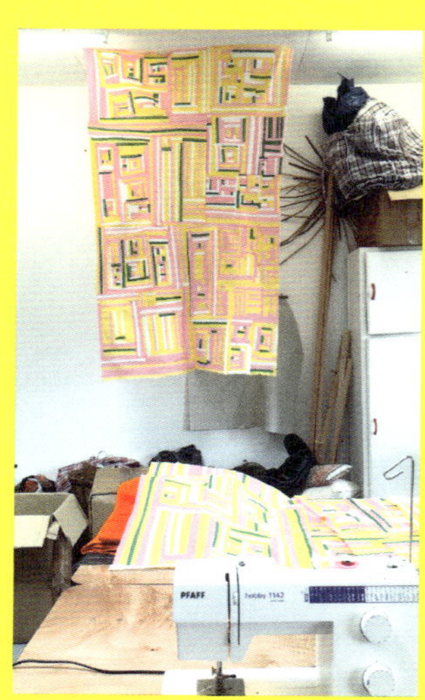

strength study in progress at the studio in July 2021

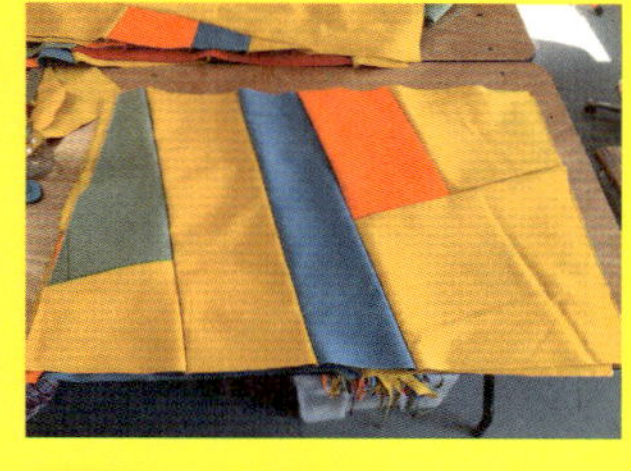

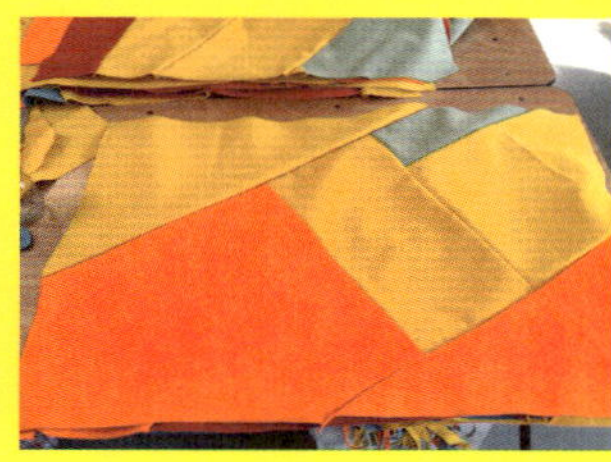

The tops of *alcove cushions* (2021) being made from "fents" – offcuts of broadcloth – in July 2021

of the space in the winter. He said he'd have to see if it was still there. This sounded promising and I asked him to keep an eye out for any holes, too. I got a very excited email from him about this curtain with a sketch attached, saying that he'd not only found the curtain but that it had two holes in it. It felt like a great opportunity to make a piece that instead of symbolically considering holes or scars or repairs, would instead actually serve a function. I could create a work to darn the curtain's two holes. I started sampling based on a sample that I'd made with zigzag stitching at Cove Park. I was already thinking about the principle of a visible strengthening-stitch and a zigzag is often used to reinforce a loose edge. I was looking at a book by Ann Ladbury on repair stitching and practising these sewing machine stitches on broadcloth offcuts.

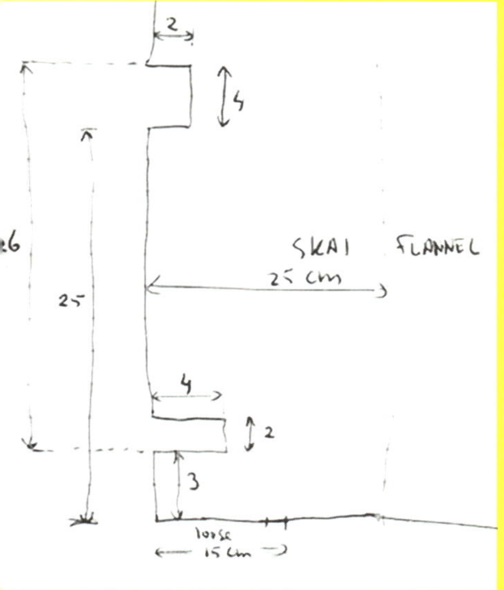

Kees Wijker's sketch of the holes in Vleeshal's winter curtains from July 2021

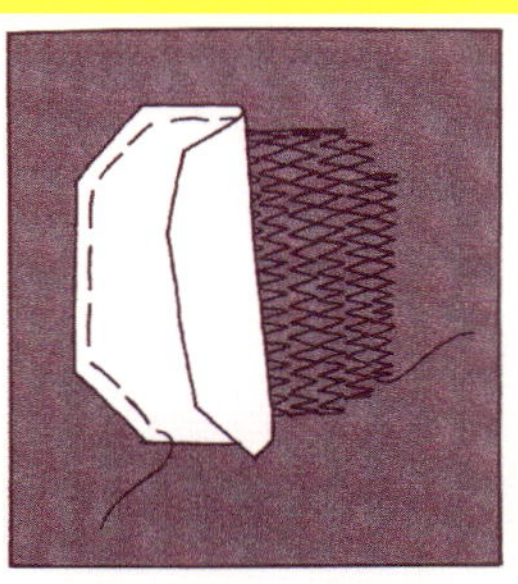

Reinforcing knees Apply decorative patches to RS of new clothes. Use shaped motifs, quilted fabric or make patch pockets. If a hole has formed, patch on WS before patching RS. If area is worn, reinforce with rows of zigzag machining parallel with straight grain of fabric before adding decorative patch to RS.

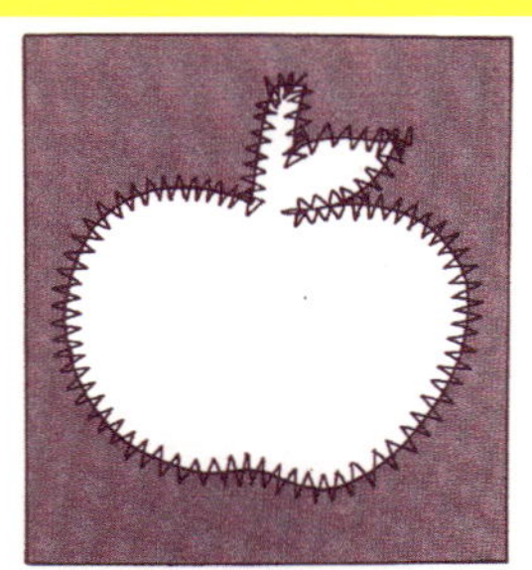

Quick hard-wearing patch Apply purchased patches of adhesive-backed denim or motifs. Press patch or motif RS up into position on RS of fabric and work loop stitch or machine zigzag round the edge. Trim away surplus fabric on WS and loop stitch, overcast or zigzag raw edges to neaten.

Illustrations from Ann Ladbury, *Sewing* (1978)

C M : By this point in August the show had resolved into four works. We were deep in conversation with Marianne about the graphic identity for the show and also speaking with Åbäke about how the form of the book could echo the forms in the exhibition. However, there was a long period where we didn't have any funding for the book, but it still seemed so important to make a publication. And as it was clear that it would be called *Sample Book*, we were then thinking about the idea of it maybe actually being a sample of a book – a one-off object, the fifth work in the show. We considered books that we loved that were made against all odds, like Irma Boom's tome *SHV Think*

Book 1996–1896, which is over 2,000 pages, or
even her tiniest books. We were also thinking of Etel
Adnan's drawings in concertinaed leporellos. There
was an early point where we thought that maybe
thirty-one samplers were going to be made not
for display in the alcoves but to be photographed
and live in the show as a thirty-one-page leporello.
You also shared with me books made by Ella
Steigelman, who I wasn't previously aware of.

K   S   : Ella Steigelman produced these
kindergarten exercises, stitches on folded papers.
They recorded stitching exercises that were in a
zigzag form. Funnily enough, have a project at
Collective in Edinburgh that's on display until March
2023 where I'm showing a zigzag screen in the
middle of the space. I hadn't thought about that
connection to this process of looking at leporellos
and concertina books!

C   M   : We shared this enthusiasm for
concertina folds and leporello books with Marianne
and she was able to incorporate the leporello into
her design for the exhibition booklet (see insert).
Even in August we didn't think this book would
receive funding, so there was this moment that, as
a joke, we said that we could always just print an
essay about your work on a tea towel instead. And
very suddenly we were both very passionate about
making a tea towel for the show in some capacity.
So, central to all of our conversations during the
process of making the show was when thinking
about supposedly flat forms like paper or fabric,
considering how this two-dimensional surface or
object becomes sculptural and how the sculptural
becomes architectural at a certain scale. So even
the printed booklet needed to avoid flatness.

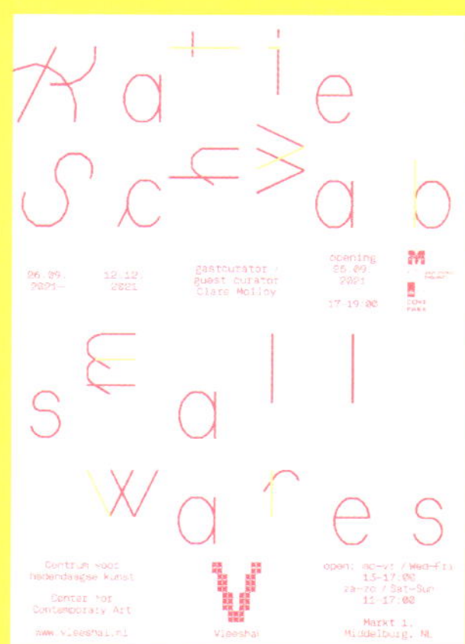

small wares exhibition poster
designed by Marianne Noordzij

K   S   : That was something
that I really enjoyed about the process,
always thinking about textiles in the
sense of sculpture. There was always
the conversation about not robbing
them of their three-dimensional
nature. Even in Marianne's choice of
typeface for the poster and booklet,
each curve is made up of lots of
straight lines – she found such an
amazing font. Luckily funding did come
through for this book, but the tea towel
idea persisted.

C   M   : And it became part of an edition
for the show. You've made stoneware plates and
ponchos as editions before – why did you want the
tea towel to become part of an edition?

34

K   S   : The tea towels served a practical purpose in the space. Some were screen-printed with the exhibition poster, others with ticketing information, and they were pinned onto the wall in a tiled pattern: they were the first thing that viewers saw when they entered Vleeshal (see pages 82–83). And I was already thinking so much about how artworks can serve a function outside of the exhibition space because of the domestic origins of the darning samplers. And so the idea of something from this show going back into people's homes felt completely appropriate.

Having worked with Sam to create this custom piece of hardware in such a small run, I also wanted to share this beautiful and practical design and not just have it as hardware for the art context. It just so happened that when installed on the wall you could perfectly pull a tea towel into the hardware hook and it stayed in place, so I wanted to give people a way to have these two prototypes in their homes. The boxed edition even comes with the correct wall plug, so you can order the edition, drill a hole, screw in the hardware and have your tea towel in position in no time. It is a small edition of just thirty, but I'd be very interested in making much larger runs of multiples for domestic use in the future.

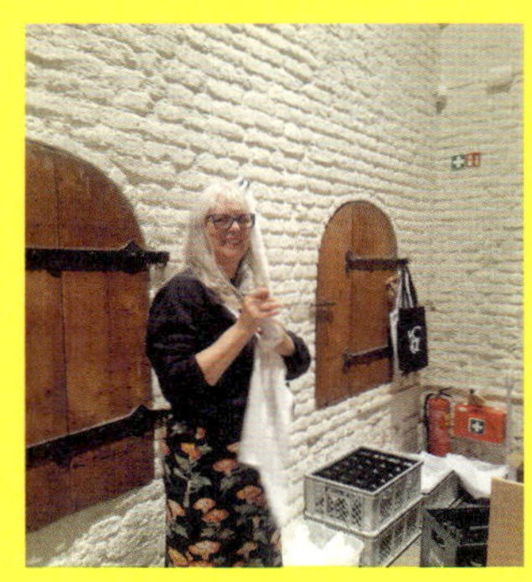

C   M   : An edition was displayed near the bar as part of the show and one of my favourite parts of the opening was seeing Suzan Van de Ven, one of the Vleeshal hosts, intuitively using the tea towel from the edition to dry glasses that she'd washed up. So brilliant.

Suzan Van de Ven putting the tea towel to good use at the opening of *small wares*

K   S   : Amazing! I definitely want the edition to be used. Some editions have been acquired by libraries or collections, where I'm not sure that they will be used, but my ideal scenario is that the exhibition, *small wares*, has an afterlife in domestic spaces, just as the darning samplers were displayed as well as serving as a useful tool in people's houses.

C   M   : I am intrigued as to what objects you will create for distribution in the future. For now, this book seems like a significant step in the direction of equitable distribution.

Band Weave Production at TextielLab, Tilburg with Veva van der Wolf
February to July 2021

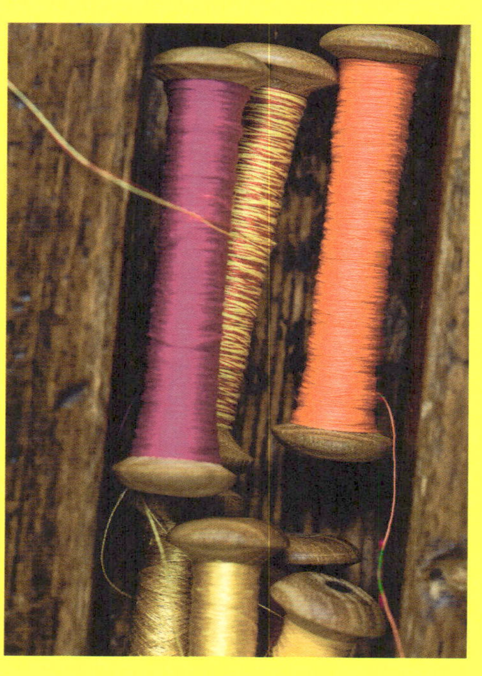

Yarns on bobbins

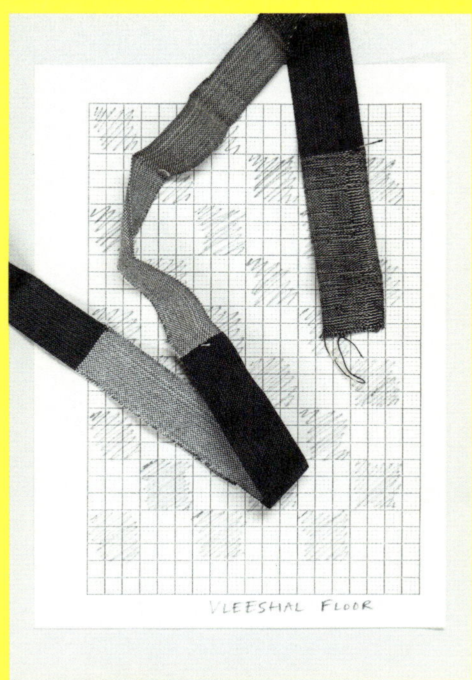

Black-and-white band-weave sample

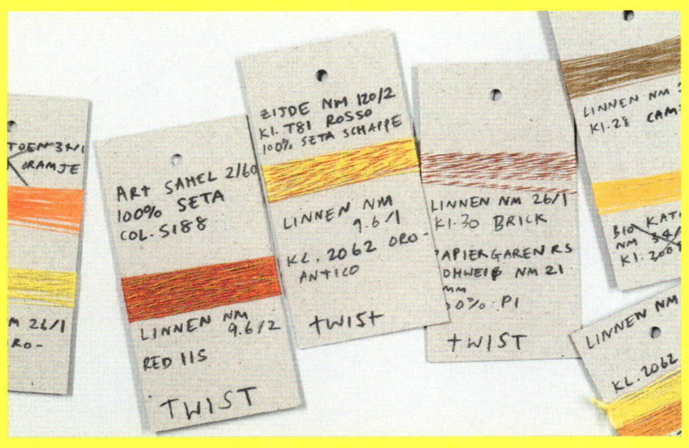

Yarn wraps made up by Katie to indicate the thread colour combinations in the band weave

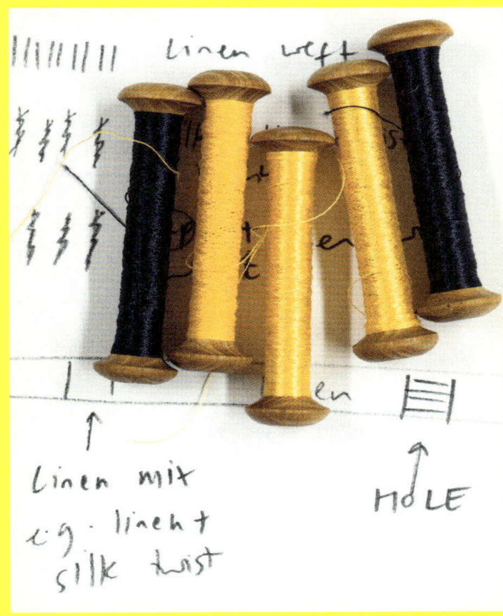

Sketches and design notes for the band weave

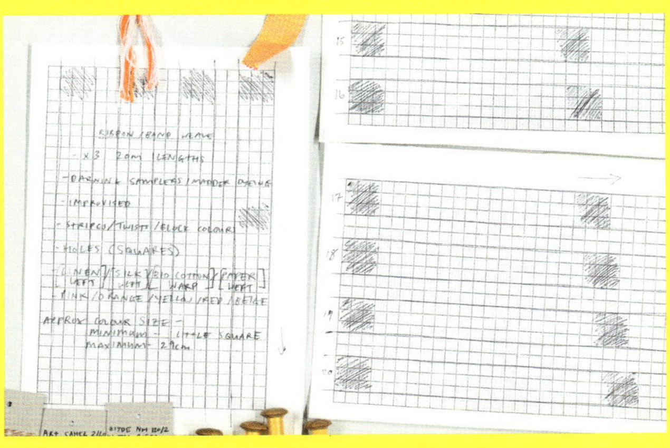

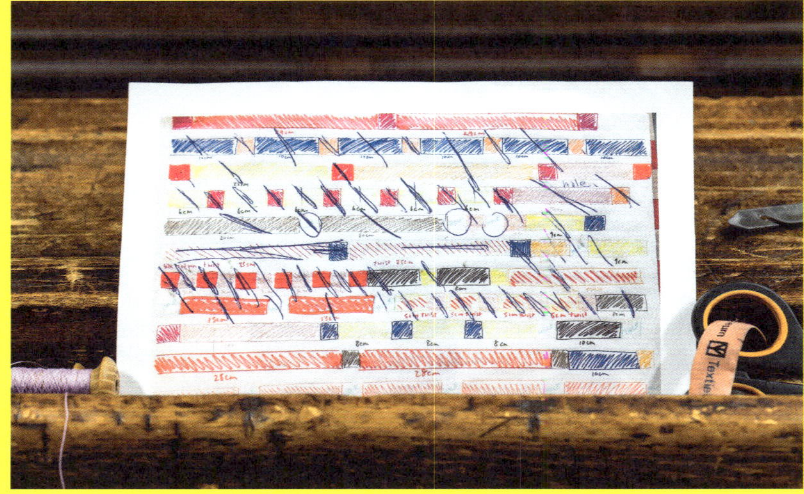

Katie's final sketch for the band weave

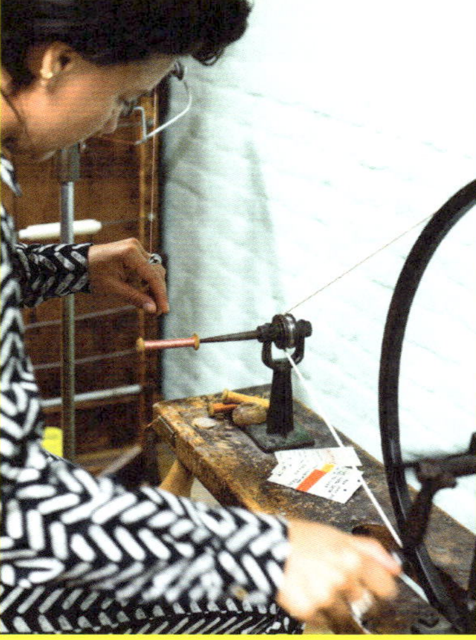

Veva spooling up bobbins for the band-weaving

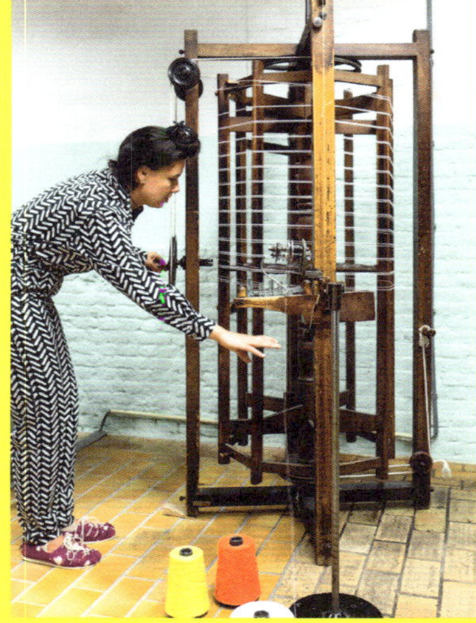

Veva working on the wool winder [*kettingscheermolen*] to measure out the lengths of cotton warp

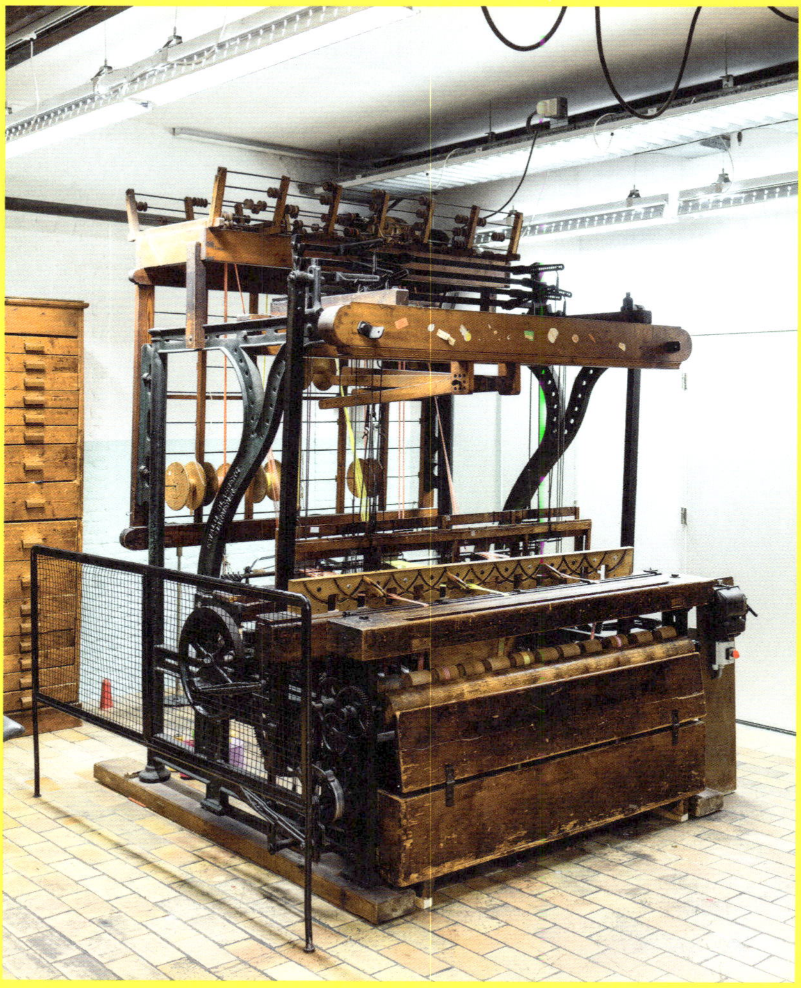

The band-weaving loom from 1880

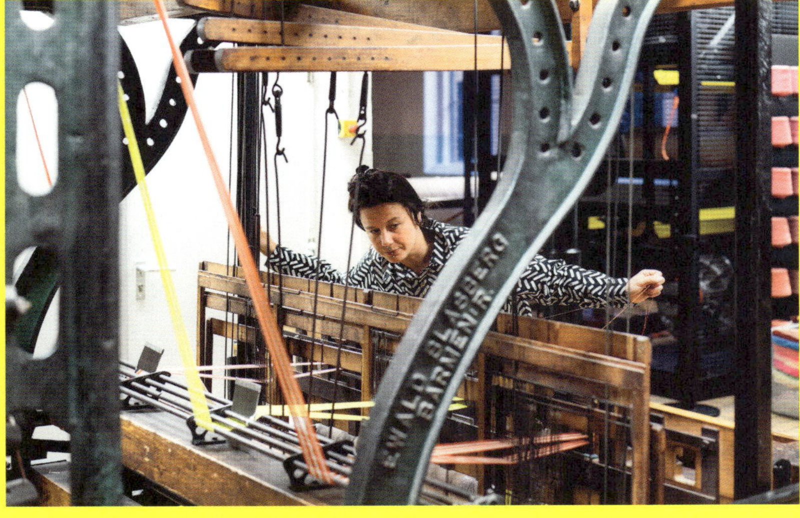

Warping up the loom

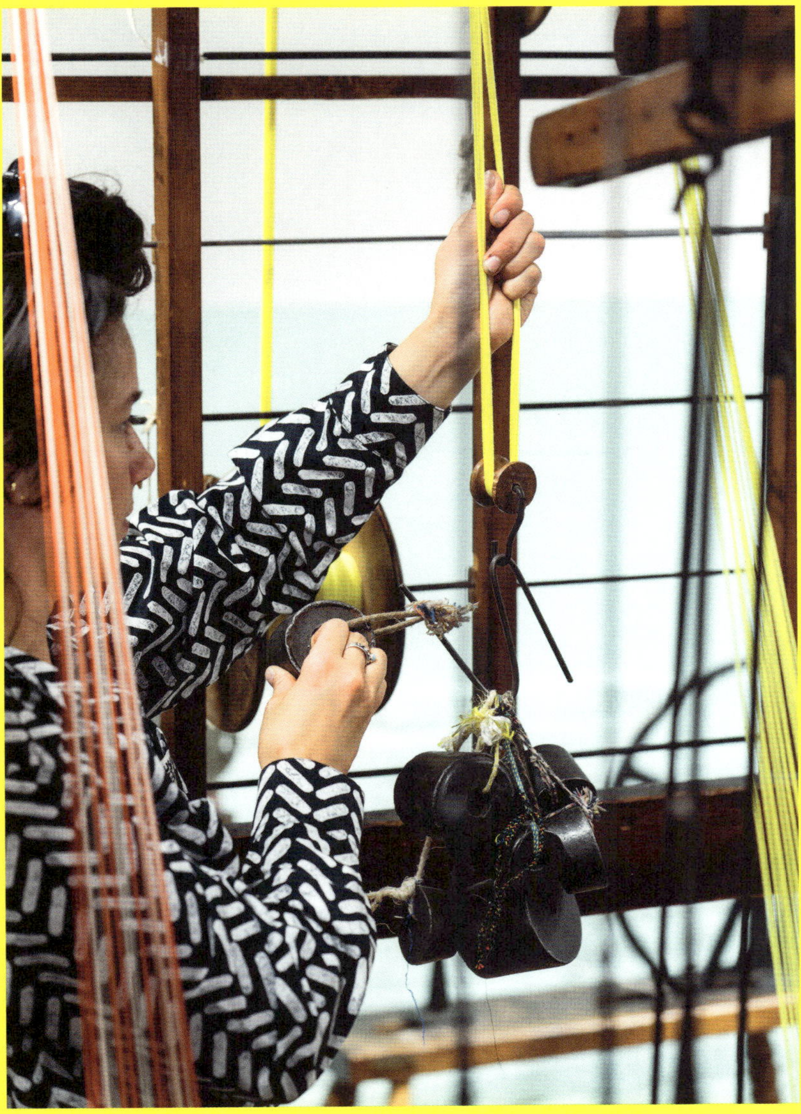

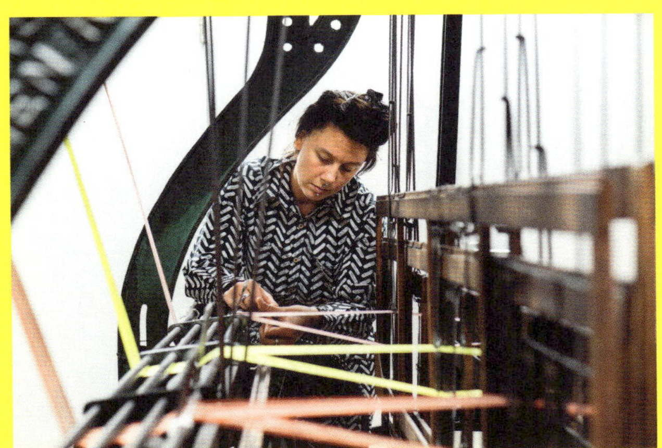

Hanging weights on the loom to adjust the tension of the warp

Adjusting the warp

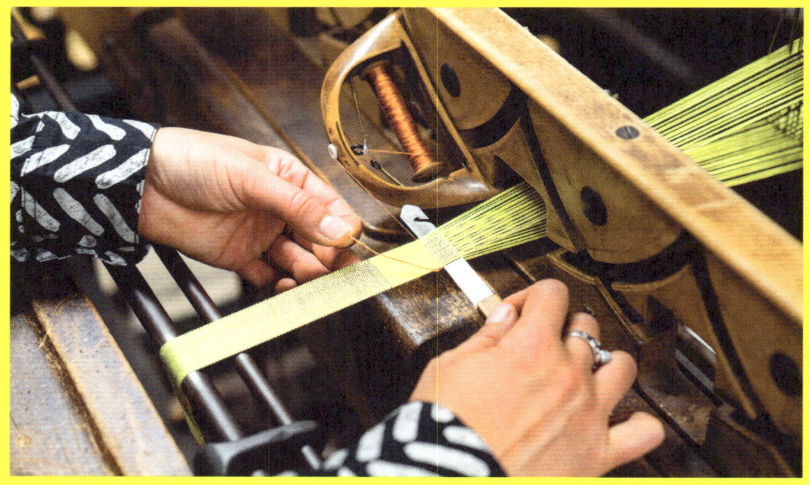

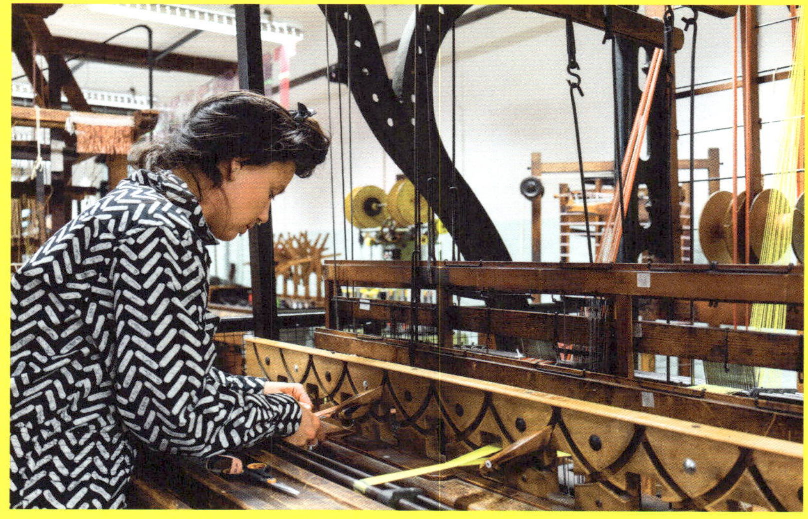

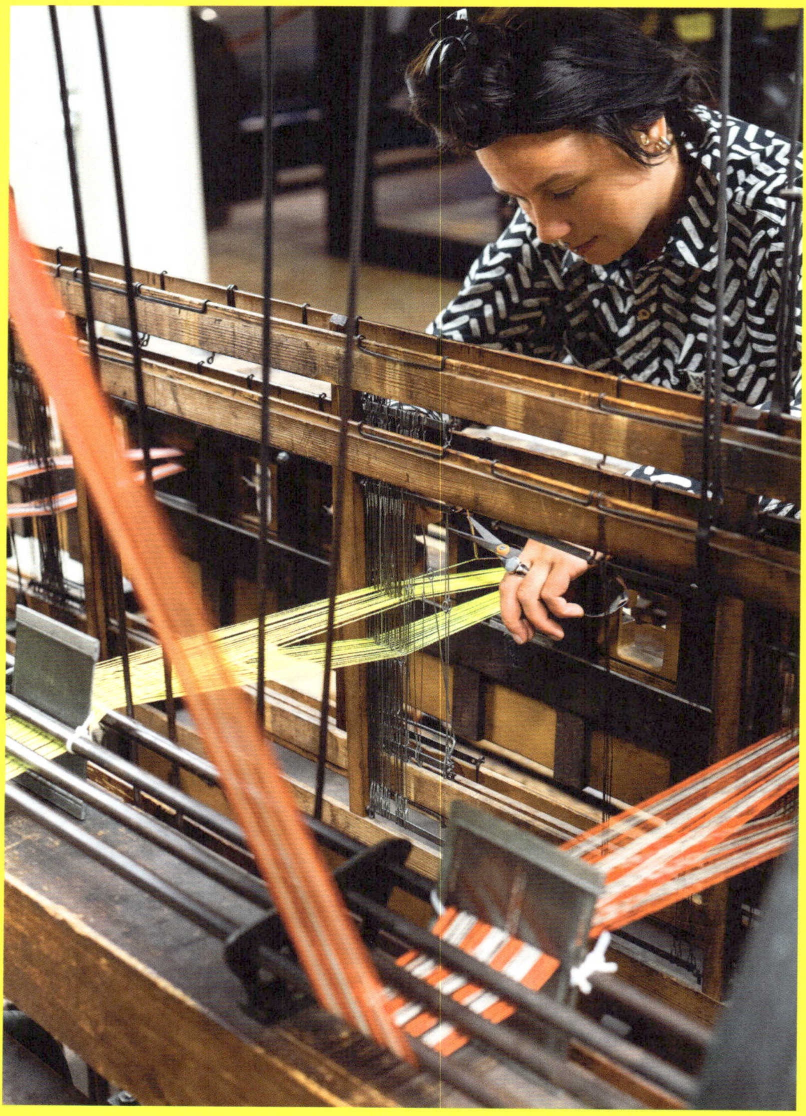

Changing the colour of the weft

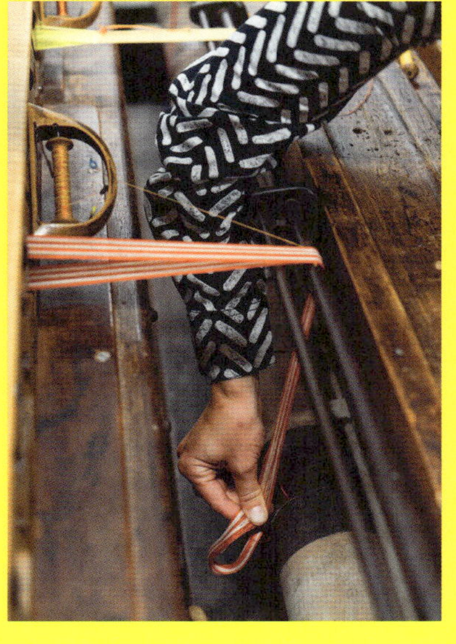

Checking the tension

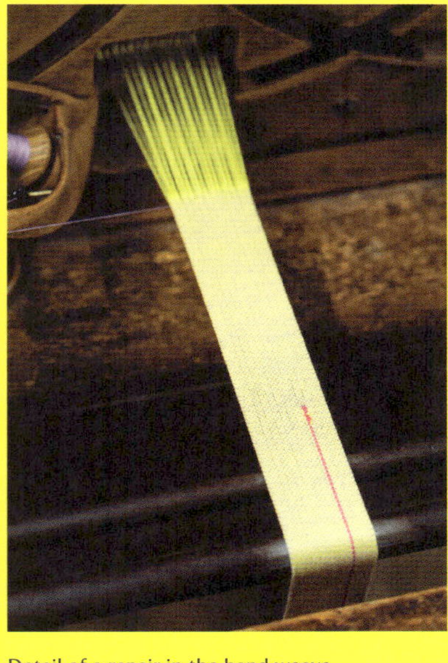

Detail of a repair in the band weave

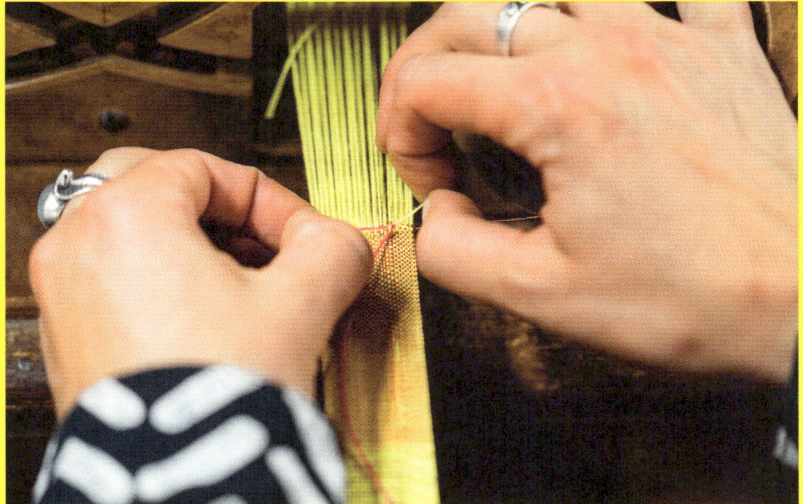

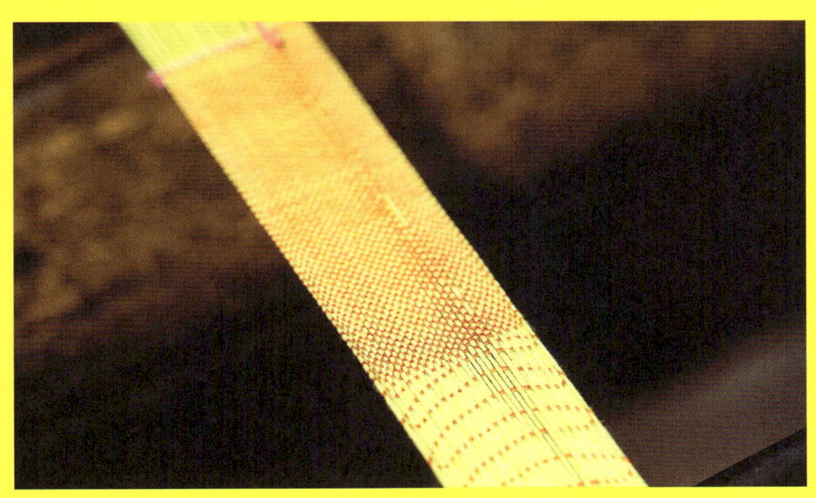

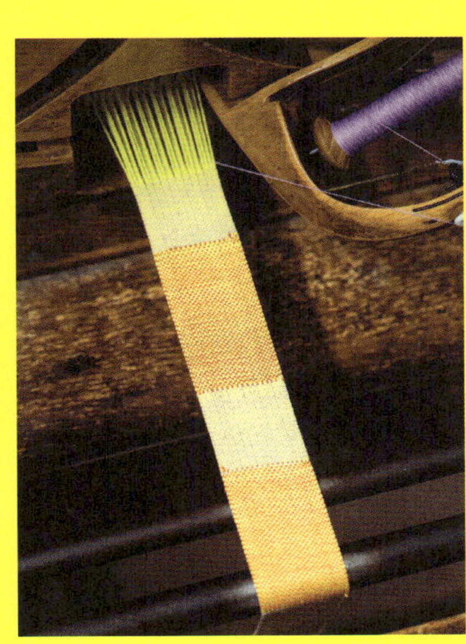

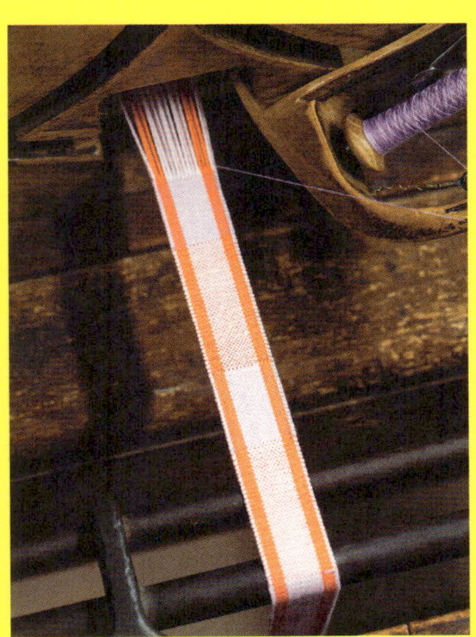

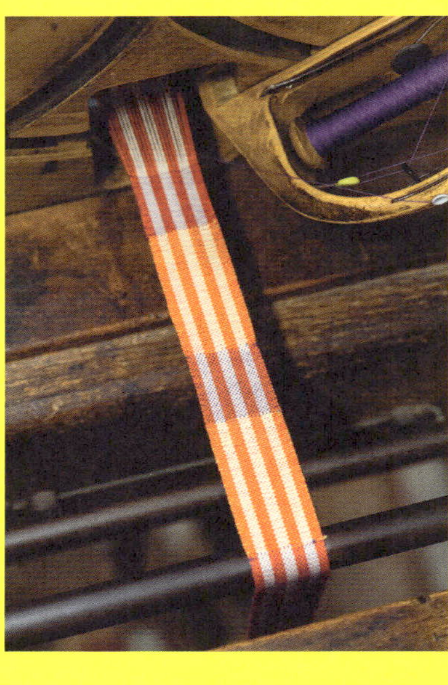
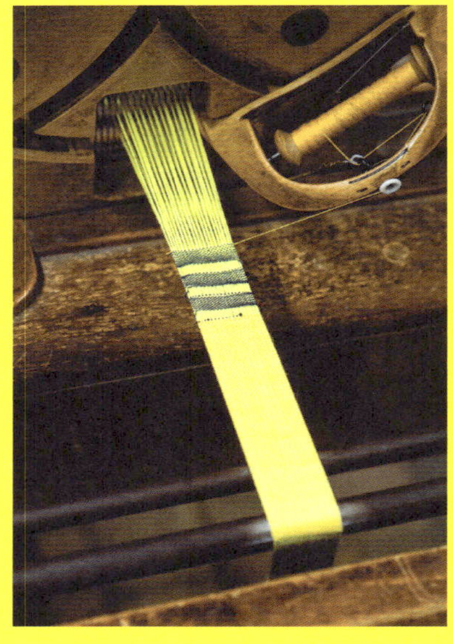
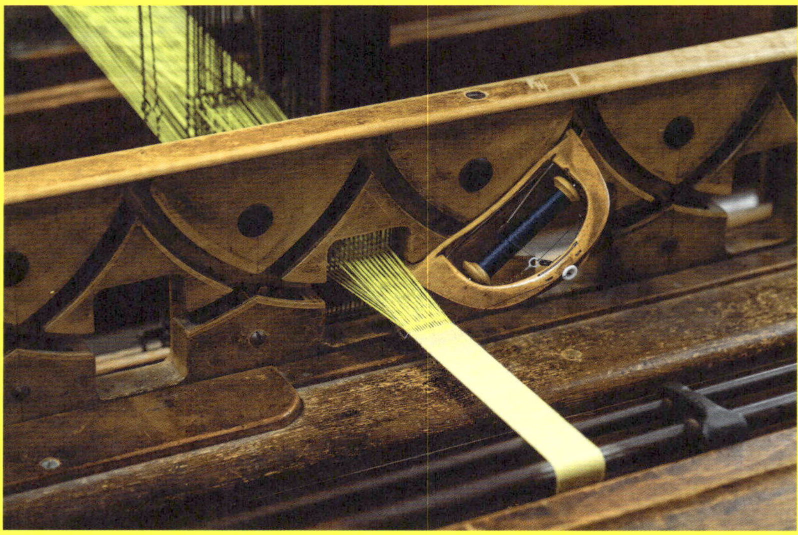

Details of the band weave on the loom

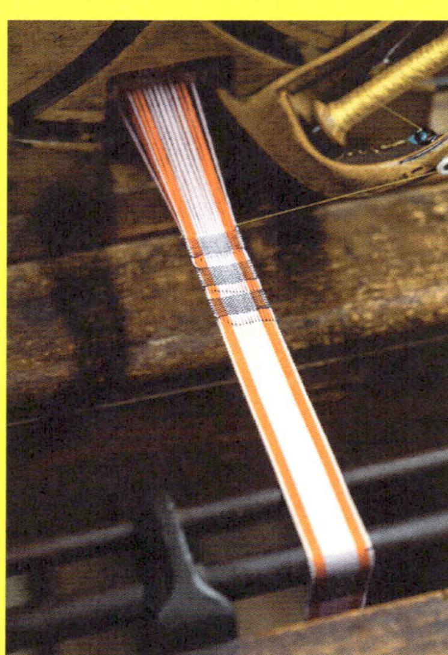
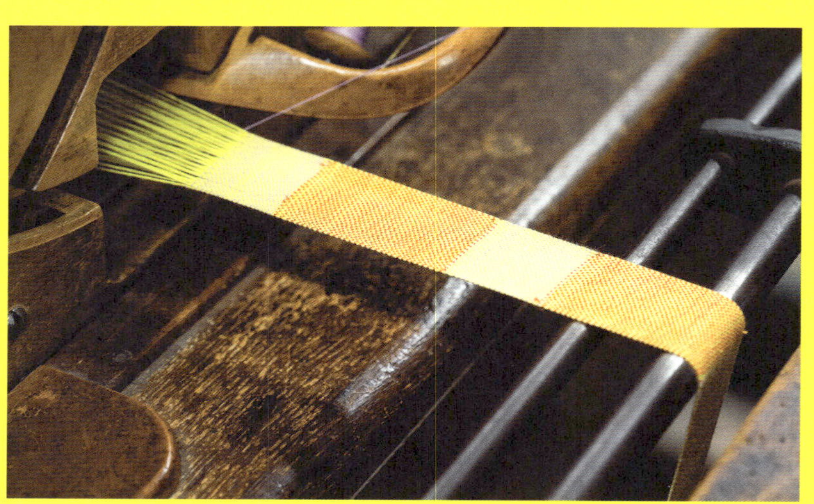

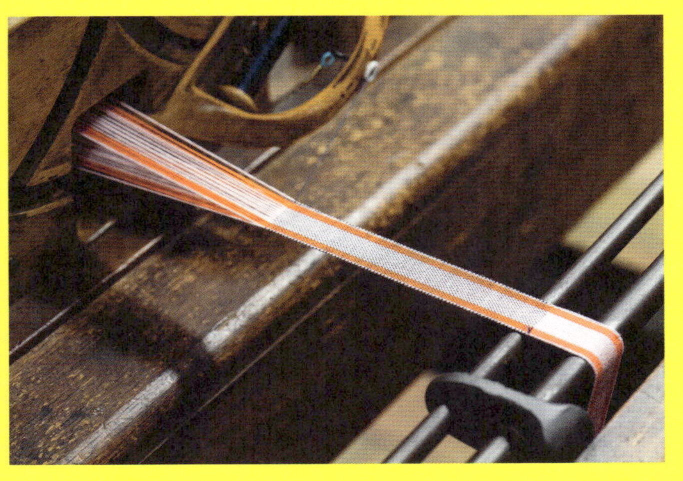

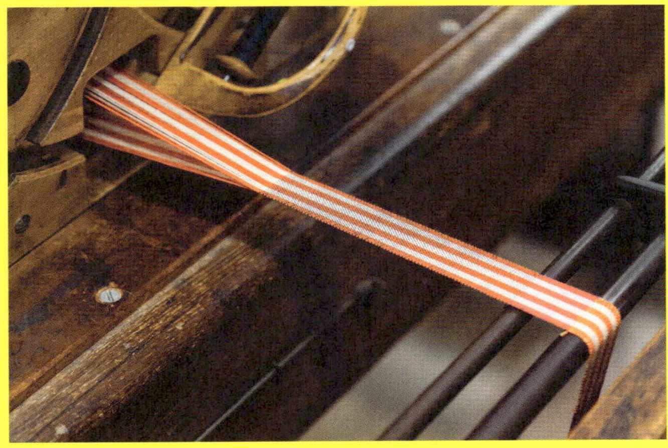

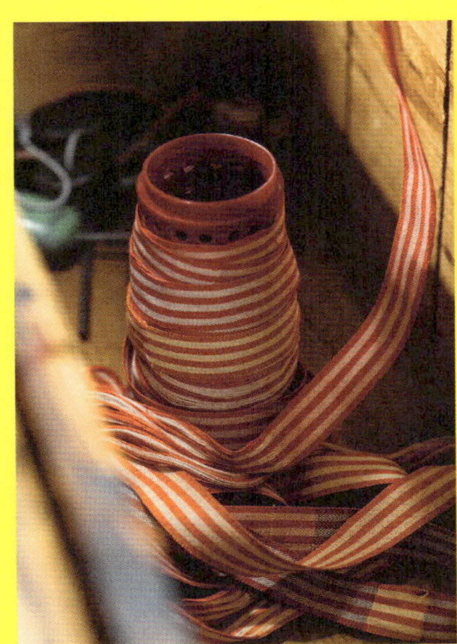

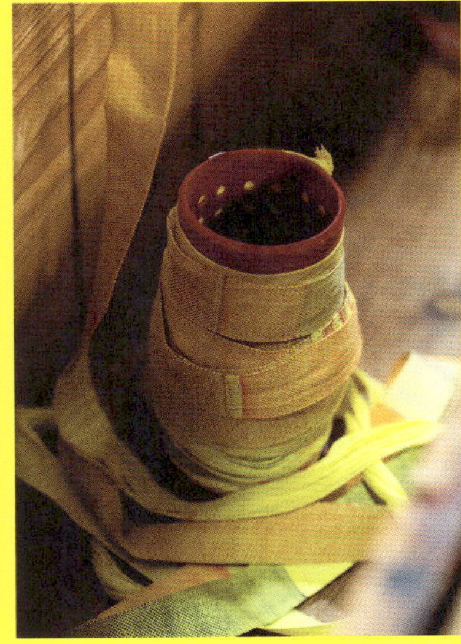

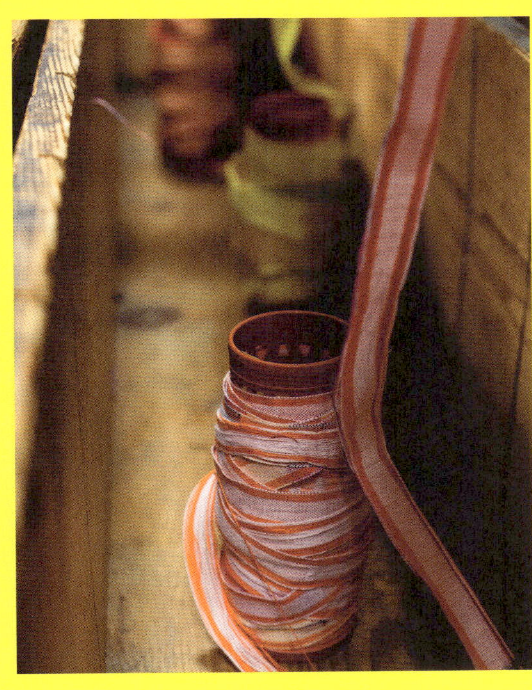

Cones of the finished band
weave for *small wares & hard
wares* (2021)

Hardware Production at Swarf, Norfolk with Sam Fish July 2021

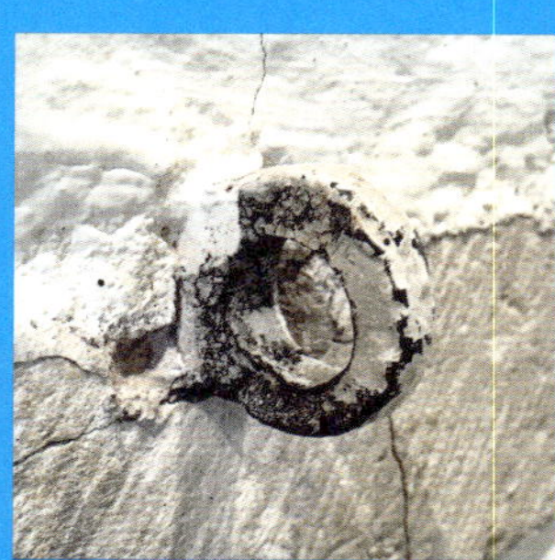

Wrought iron bolt hole at Vleeshal

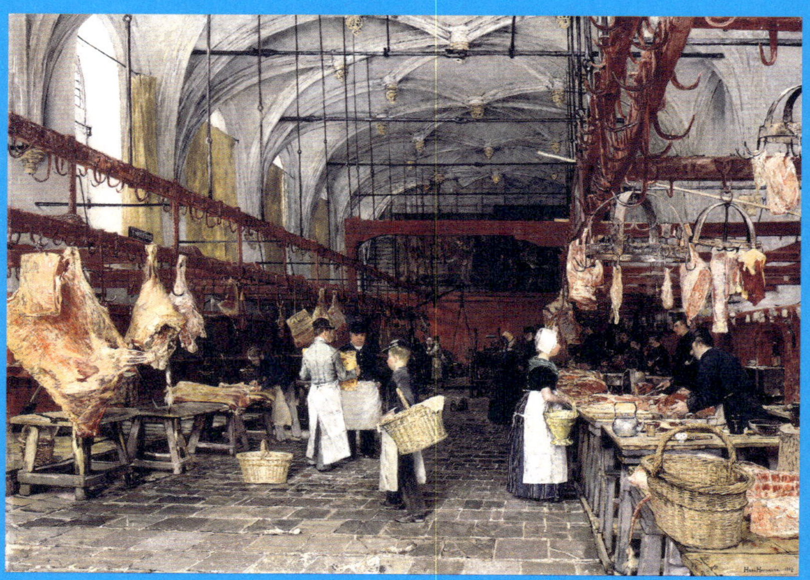

Historical hardware in the Vleeshal space when it still operated as a meat market
Hans Herrmann, *Fleischhalle in Middelburg* (1887)
Oil on canvas, 89.5 × 124 cm

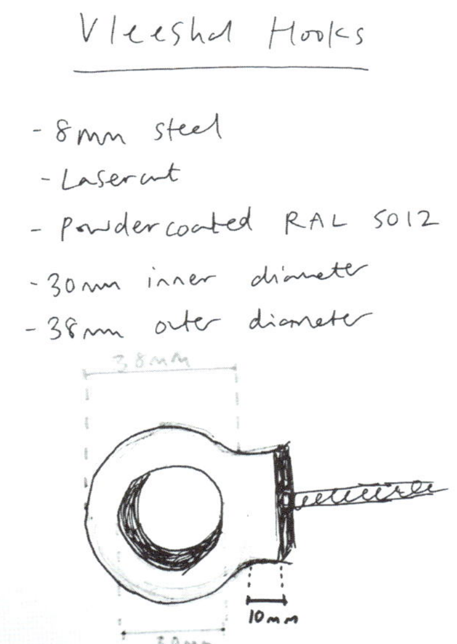

Katie's sketch for the hooks

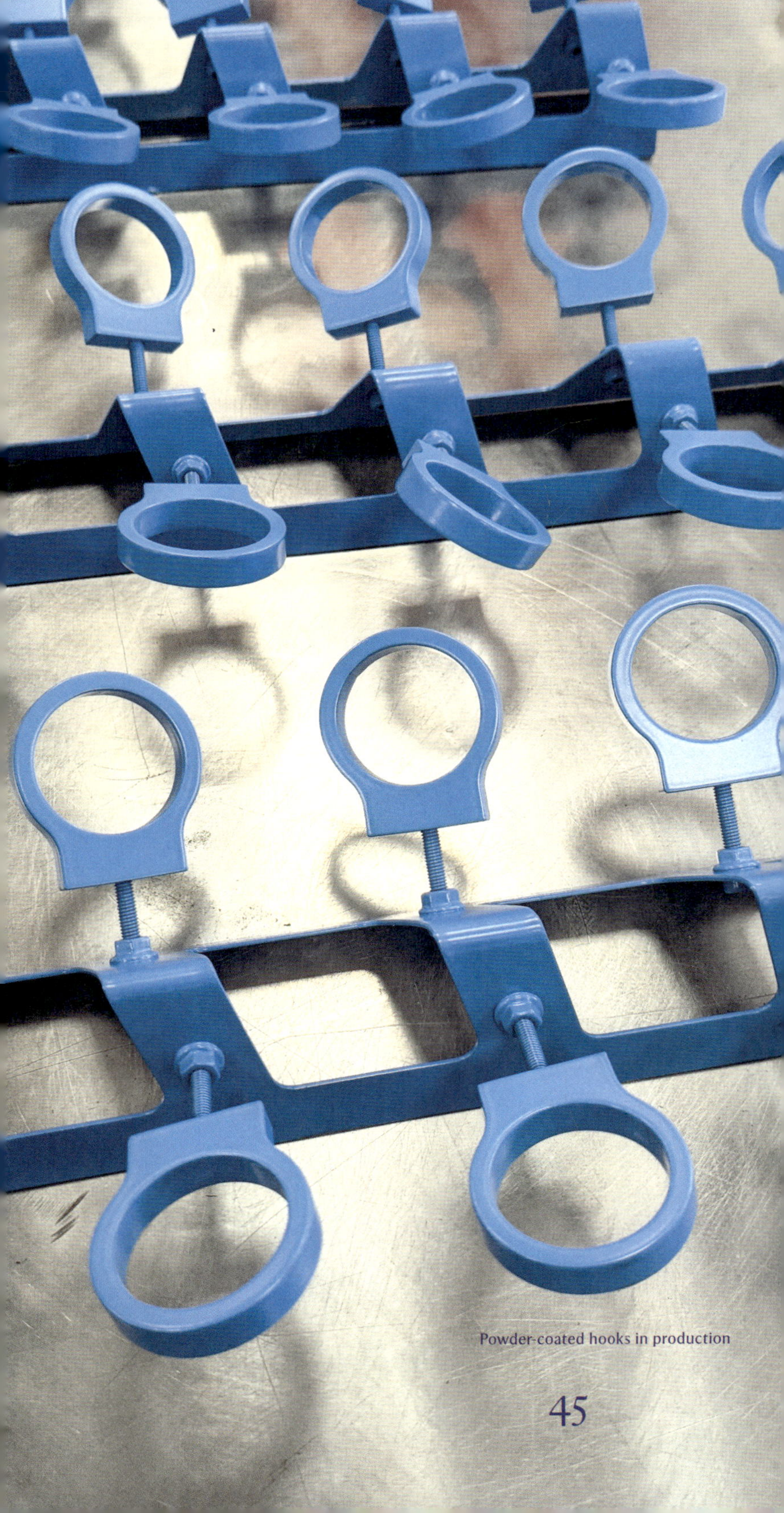

Powder-coated hooks in production

Sam holding the finished hook

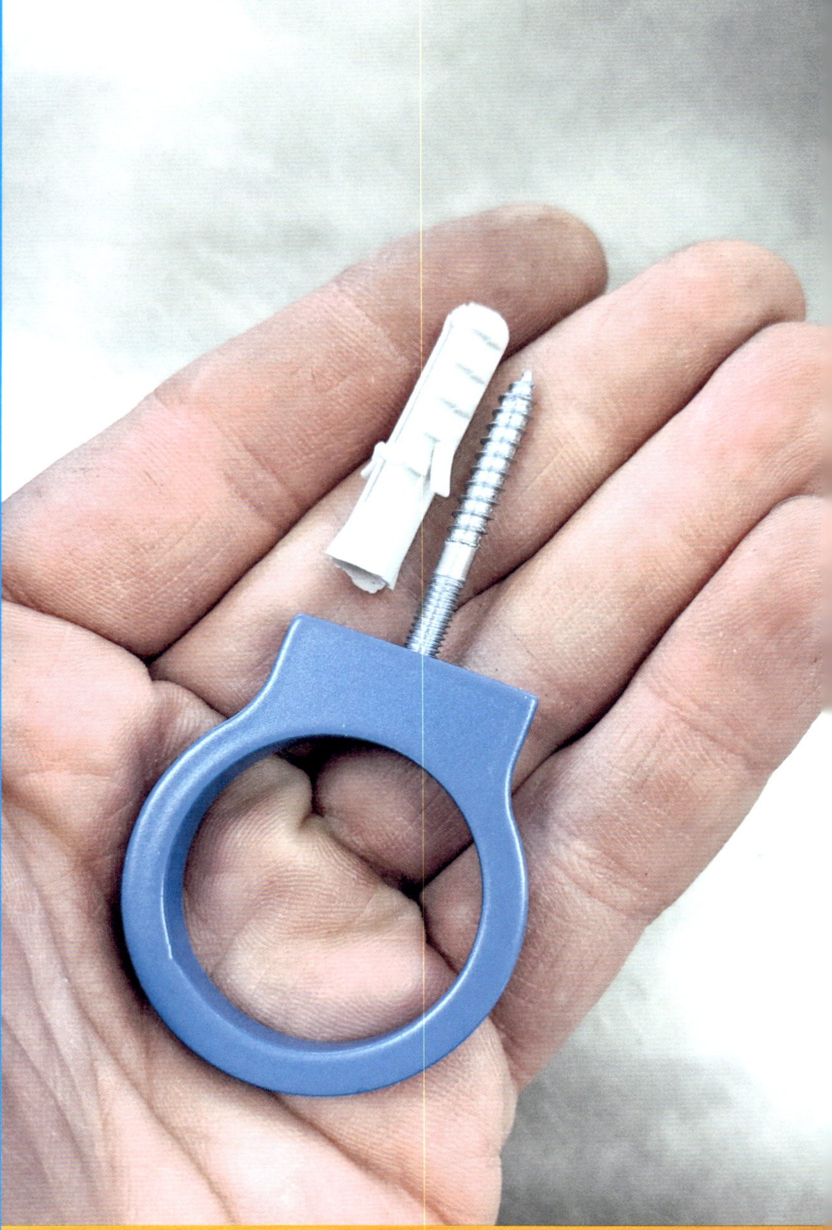

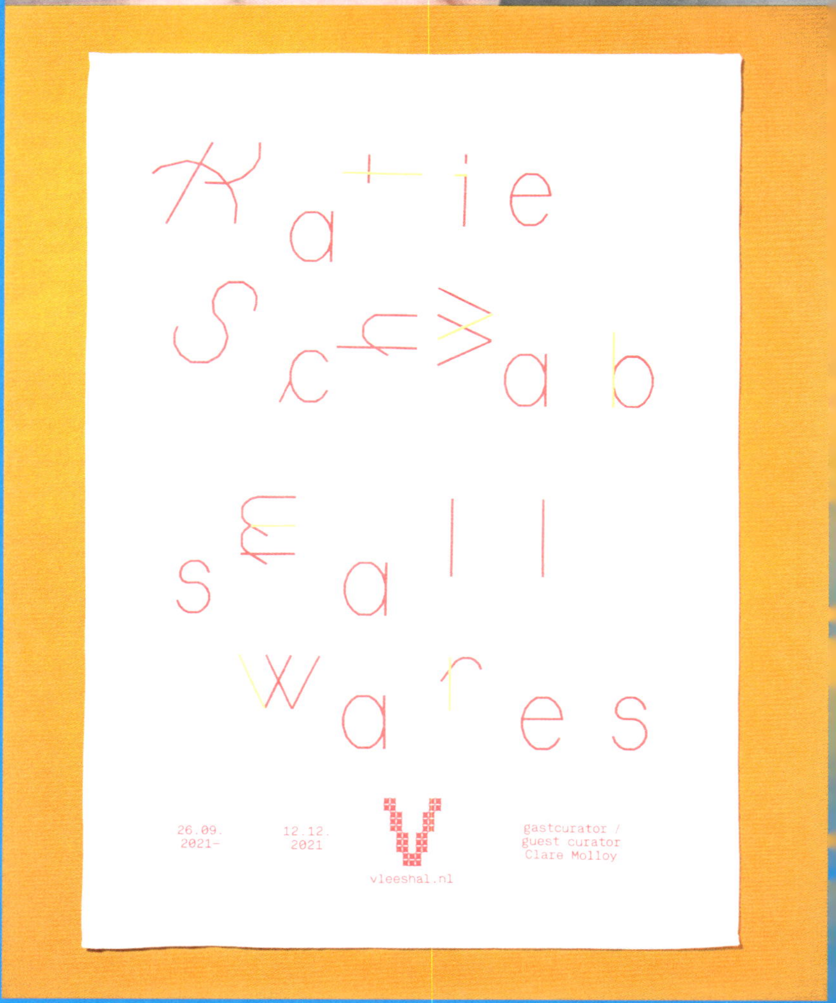

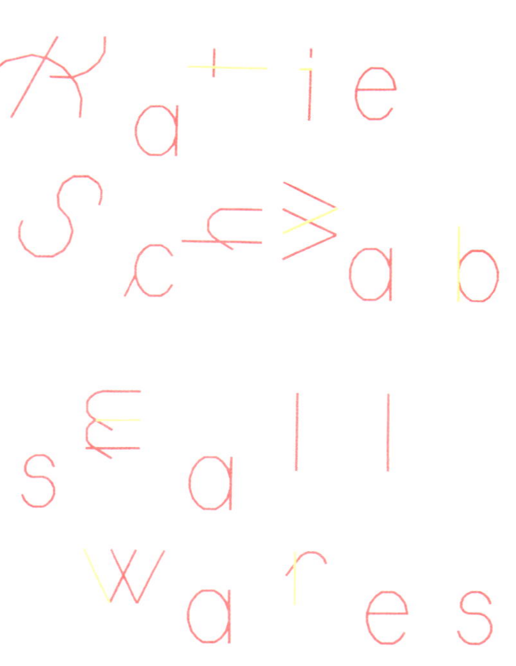

Katie Schwab
small wares
26.09.
2021–
12.12.
2021
vleeshal.nl
gastcurator /
guest curator
Clare Molloy

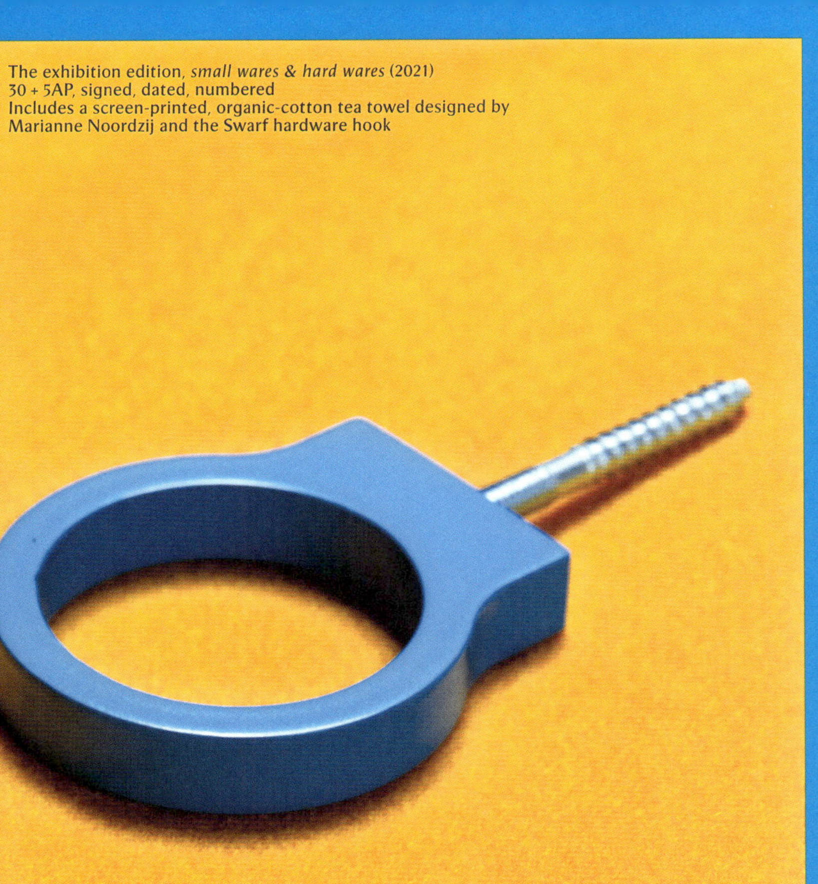

The exhibiton edition installed at Vleeshal

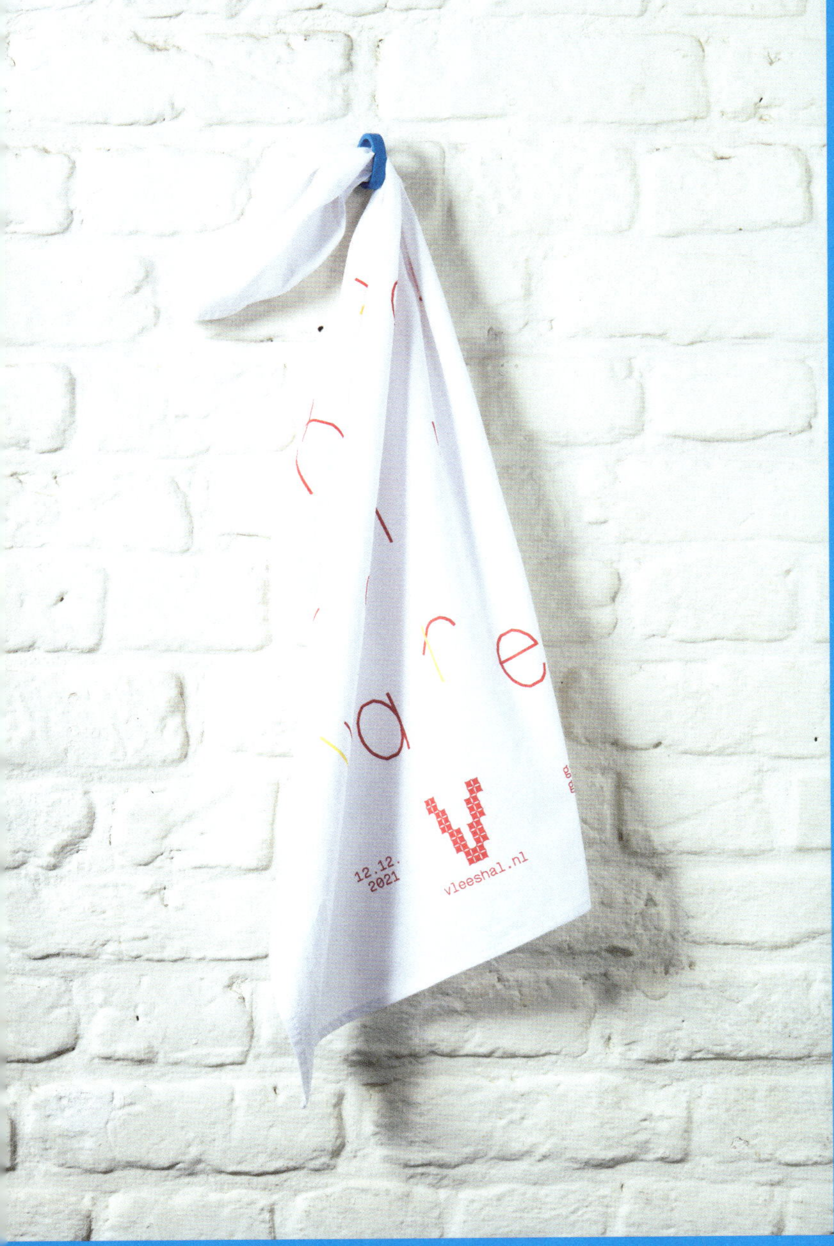

embossed vibrations

m. patchwork monoceros

the curtain shifts, ushers me in

guiding my shoulders through their
thread bearing doorway

healed and adorned

the entrance altar to reviving the worn out

making sure to exchange a moment

of tactile intimacy with each offering in this hall

my fingers stretch, skating lightly

over the embossed vibrations in

primary shades

cool, cream, brickwork, revealing

little evidence of the raw russet

landscape underneath

meets my back and outstretched arms

my head tips up

eyes trail the sways   of running ribbon

                    rows across rows

                    leapfrogging the cerulean hooks

          steel lily pads cradling the weight of the weft

a lost shard of stained glass

its crystalline edges long worn smooth

with time and tumble

I hold it to my lips, gifting it a secret,

then cast it skyward

high enough to find

the scaffolded curve of the ceiling

when it shatters against the load-bearing stone

what falls before me is a soft, vivid curtain

passageways in emerald, muted coral and canary

patient and aloft in the alcoves

not twinning but siblings

related in design and construction

unique in pattern and palette, they beckon

come friend, rest and wonder

mending fents into flags of soft and woolen repose

reseeding that which we are wont to waste

ankles dangling or tucked safely shut away

knees knocking the edges of enclosure

watching the wares from the places where objects of value reside the pendulum of tension and ease

that swings across the lifetime

of a strand of cotton
a cell of silk, a tuft of linen
a lesson in how to fall without harm

from binding together under the spindle and twist

to weaving crossways fortified

by sailing through the eyes of the loom

steps traced back along splintered checkerboard tiles

a darning of scars and vestiges.

Stoplappen: Dutch Darning Samplers

Rosalie Sloof

As a young girl, I was fascinated by a darning sampler that hung on the wall of my grandmother's living room. The fact that it was framed made it seem like a painting to me. I could also clearly read the name of the person who had made this particular piece of needlework: a Dutch girl named Cornelia Bonnema in 1731, when she was just thirteen years old. It was this family heirloom that sparked my curiosity and led me into the world of textile research. Of all of the many samplers I have encountered since, I have never come across anything quite like this intriguing piece.

Darning samplers – or *stoplappen* as they are called in Dutch – are textiles that ignite the imagination. Darning samplers have always been the modest sisters of their figurative counterparts, *merklappen*. However this publication offers *stoplappen* a chance to take centre stage, through the art of Katie Schwab. She celebrates the almost lost art of these often anonymous women of mending that inspired her to make a new series of work.

From the seventeenth century to the beginning of the twentieth century, learning needlecraft formed an essential part of young girls' education in the Netherlands. Samplers were studies with which the stitches for mending clothes and household textiles were taught. Although some darning samplers exist on cotton muslin, most darning samplers were created on modest pieces of off-white linen and worked into using coloured silks so that mistakes in the stitching were easily seen and learnt from.

Stoplappen were the second stage in an embroidery education; they followed on from *merklappen*, decorative samplers

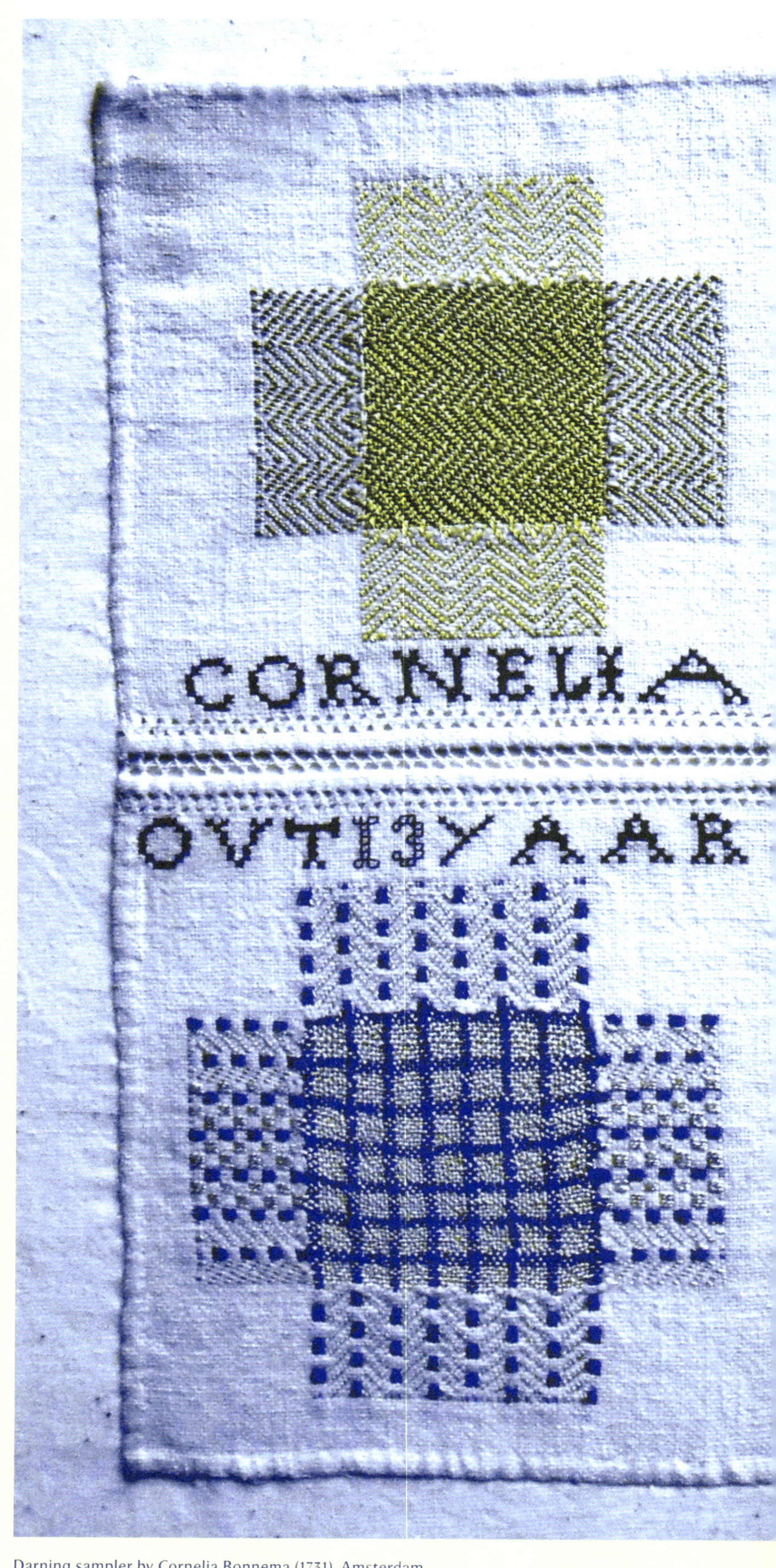

Darning sampler by Cornelia Bonnema (1731), Amsterdam
Linen, silk, 25.5 × 25.5 cm
Cornelia Bonnema out 13 yaar anno 1731 [Cornelia Bonnema 13 years old anno 1731]

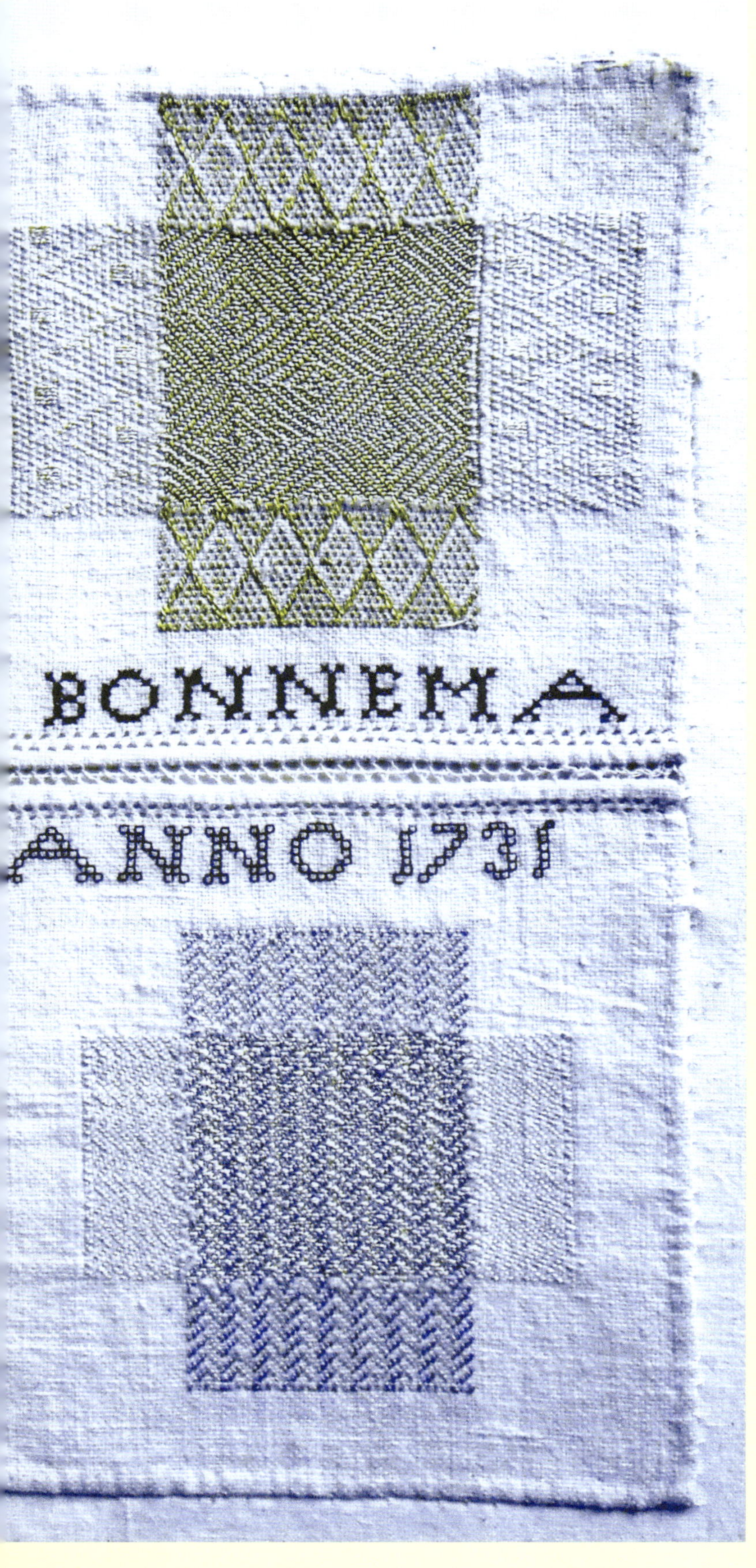

embroidered with alphabets, motifs and borders, which girls would start making between the ages of ten and twelve. Creating a darning sampler started with mending a simple tear but it also required some careful planning, often grouping the darns around a central motif, measuring and counting the threads to create a balanced composition. Girls of thirteen and fourteen learnt to repair square-cut holes with all kinds of weaves and weaving patterns. With the help of their teacher, who was most likely also the person who made the cuts in the fabric, girls worked on a set of eight or nine different darns arranged in a strict grid pattern. Others emulated the *horror vacui* approach – Latin for "fear of empty space" – of their first figurative sampler and added even more darned squares.

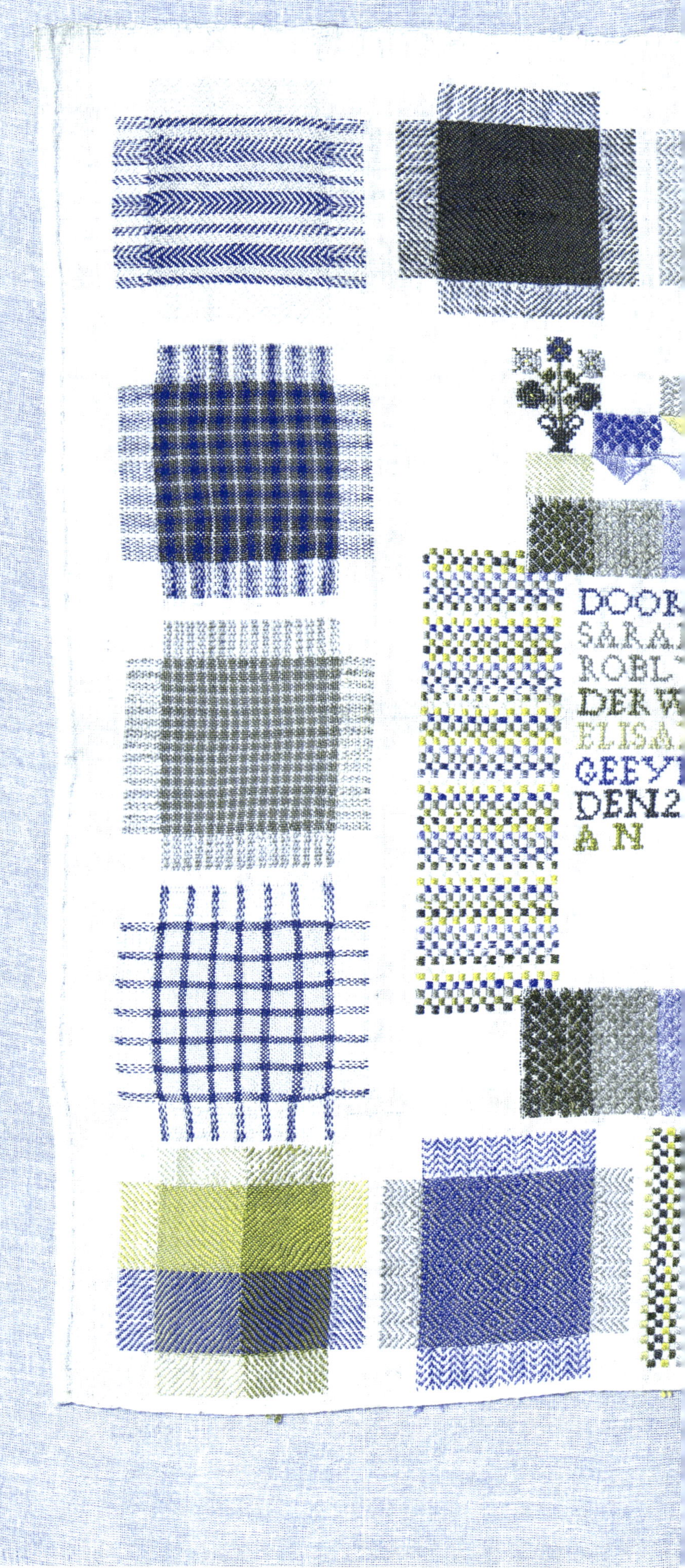

Darning sampler by Sara Johanna Roblyn (1775), Middelburg
Linen, silk, 51 × 49.5 cm
Door myn gedaan Sara Johanna Roblyn door onderwys van Maria Elisabeth
Hendrick geeyndigt den 21 July anno 1775 [Done by me Sara Johanna Roblyn
taught by Maria Elisabeth Hendrick finished the 21st of July anno 1775]

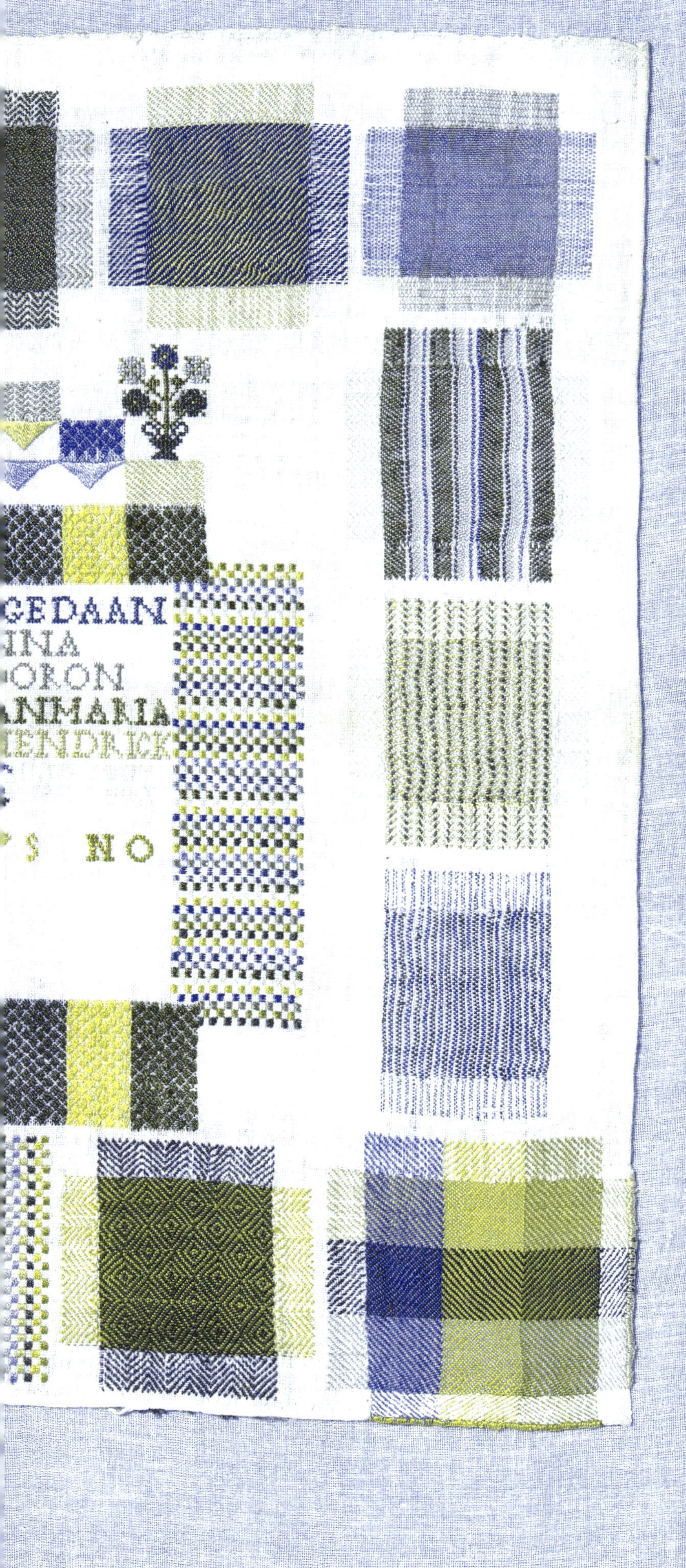

GEDAAN
INA
ORON
NMARIA
ENDRICK
S NO

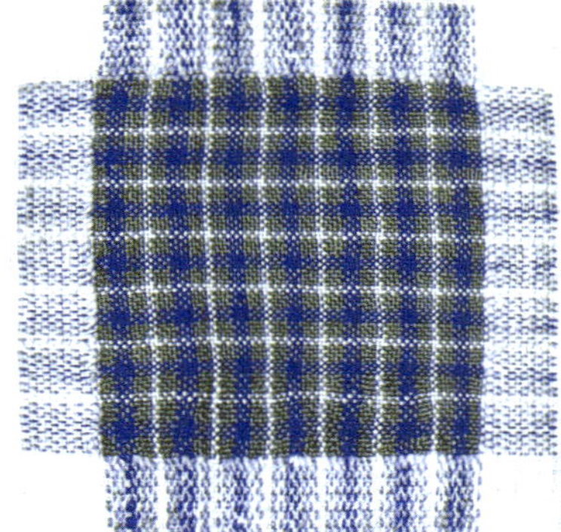 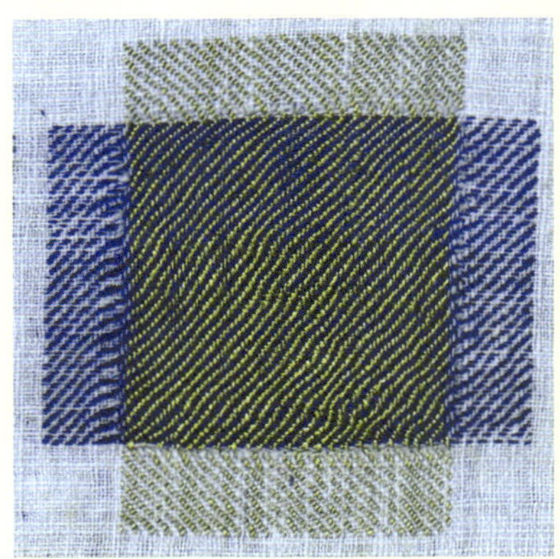

Details from Sara Johanna Roblyn's darning sampler (from left to right): repairs created using plain-weave gingham [*bontje*], basic twill, herringbone twill and diamond-twill techniques

Starting with repairs in plain weave binding, the simplest darns were those worked in one or two colours with the same number of warp and weft threads. Variations show striped or checked patterns resembling the popular check gingham cottons imported from Asia, referred to in Dutch as *bontjes*, they were frequently used as lining fabric in eighteenth-century gowns. Girls then continued with more complex twill-weave patterns, in which the binding points of the threads created characteristic steep diagonal lines in many variations such as herringbone and diamond twills.

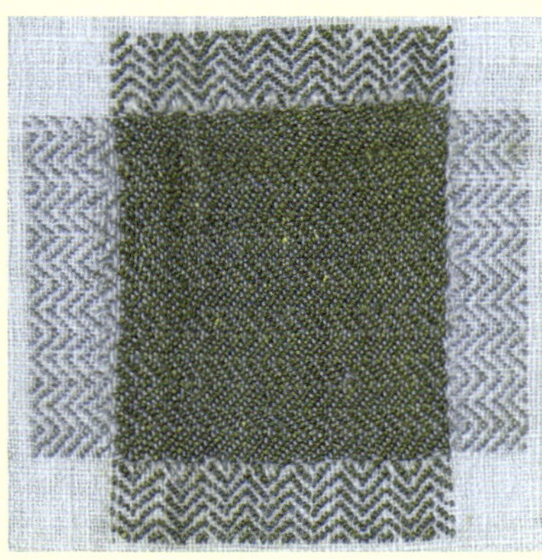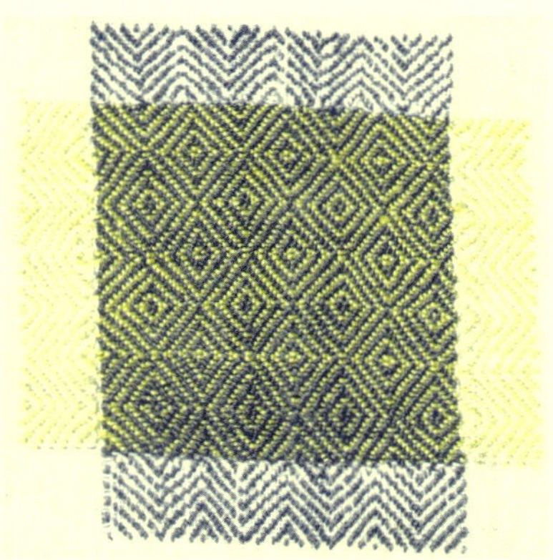

Advanced pupils showed their skills creating difficult darns in satin weave with decorative floral patterns suited for the repair of fine linen or silk damask. A highly employable skill as merchant families wanted their fine textiles, particularly damask tablecloths, to be invisibly mended when they suffered wear and tear. Subsequently, the girls expanded their stitching skills by moving on from darning square holes to right-angle tears and corner darns in which repairing a selvedge – meaning the edge of a woven fabric – could also be practised. Then they progressed to darns for knitwear, renowned for their difficulty as they had to retain flexibility and durability simultaneously. A few girls even received lessons in repairing needle lace. Most girls added only their initials to their linen samplers; their skilled teachers remained anonymous. However, a group of expertly crafted samplers that were made in the city of Middelburg, in the southwest of the Netherlands, were uniquely different.

In the eighteenth century, the city of Middelburg prospered as one of the country's leading ports. It hosted the Zeeland Chamber, an important office of the VOC [Dutch East India Company], second only to Amsterdam. Well-to-do families that had made their fortunes in the colonial grain or spice trades either sent their daughters to special French schools or arranged for private tuition at home, which created a flourishing market for needlework classes. Friendly competition between local teachers boosted the level of craft that was achieved, and 1715 to 1815 was the "golden age" of Middelburg darning samplers. What makes the Middelburg samplers unique is that as well as adding their own names to the samplers, the full names of their teachers – Sara de Troi, Maria Letellier and Adriana de Vroe, among others – were also preserved for posterity. The Middelburg *stoplappen* are the only pieces in the Netherlands to eschew anonymity in favour of naming makers and teachers alike.

What further distinguishes the Middelburg samplers is a central area created in darning stitch, which is reminiscent of a stepped gable house or motifs representing a city building. The darns that are placed around this central motif are rather large, colourful and well-executed. This central frame is filled with a true sampler-ID in cross-stitched lettering, starting with the phrase: *Door mijn gedaan* [Done by me], followed by the name of the girl, her teacher and the date of completion. Some girls also included a starting date, revealing that it sometimes took over a year to finish a darning sampler. This formula stayed the same until 1815. It forms a unique and remarkably individual statement added to such a useful piece of needlework, initially meant as a work of reference and tool for learning. Moreover, the full names of the girls have become an invaluable resource for archival research into pupils and their families. Around 125 names of girls taught by more than twenty teachers from Middelburg have been cross-stitched on these samplers, which are preserved in collections held across the world.

Learning darning skills was not just the preserve of the privileged; such skills were acquired by girls of all class backgrounds and, in particular, needlework was a staple of what was taught in orphanages across the Netherlands. In Middelburg, for instance, girls living at the *Burgerweeshuis* [the city's Civic Orphanage] were expected to become proficient in mending. During the same period that the Middelburg samplers were made, girls at the Civic Orphanage of Amsterdam also created a series of samplers, many of which have survived. The patrons of this orphanage valued the skill of sampler making and regularly urged the girls to persist and finish their work. In fact, girls were not allowed to leave the orphanage unless they had completed their darning sampler. This set-up proved useful as several of these girls would go on to find work in the households of wealthy merchant families in the city. These samplers, many of which were treasured by families, served as tokens of their makers' abilities.

Embroidered names on samplers have become an invaluable resource for archival researchers looking into the later lives of pupils and their families. Cornelia Bonnema, for example, was the daughter of a shipping broker. The Bonnema family originated from the province of Friesland, but Cornelia was baptised in Amsterdam. She lived in the city centre, close to a brewery on one of the docks, which today is opposite the Central Station. Looking at the great number of Dutch samplers that have survived, these useful pieces of needlework were clearly important to their makers as a personalised selection of darning patterns and techniques – important enough to be passed down for generations. By practising their darning skills, girls in the Netherlands created a fascinating record of fabrics and colours at a time when clothing and textiles were carefully crafted, repaired and valued. The almost lost art of repair that the darning samplers record reminds us that a more sustainable world is not so far away: all we have to do is set our minds and hands to it.

Further reading on Dutch samplers

Gieneke Arnolli and Rosalie Sloof. *Letter voor Letter: Merklappen in de opvoeding van Friese meisjes.* Zwolle: Waanders Uitgevers and Leeuwarden: Fries Museum, 2004.

Clare Browne and Jennifer Wearden. *Samplers from the Victoria and Albert Museum.* London: Victoria and Albert Museum, 2002.

Eef de Jonge-Everaert. *"Door mijn gedaen": De geschiedenis van de Zeeuwse merk- en stoplap.* Middelburg: VZM/BPMZ, 1995.

Berthi Smith-Sanders. *Merk- en stoplappen uit het Burgerweeshuis Amsterdam: Ik heb een letter niet goed op de stofdraad geborduurd.* Venlo: Smith-Sanders, 2013.

Joke Visser and Walter van de Garde. *Oefenstof: Merklappen en andere vrouwelijke handwerken 1600–1920.* Eindhoven: Lecturis, 2013.

Online resources

Dealer of Dutch darning samplers, "Ex Antiques." https://www.exantiques.nl

"TRC Needles by The TRC Digital Encyclopaedia of Decorative Needlework." https://trc-leiden.nl/trc-needles

Threads of Resilience: Build, Rebuild, Wear and Repair

Ann Coxon

Since 2020, resilience is a notion that has gained increasing pertinence. Faced with the enormous challenges of a global pandemic – as well as climate emergency, mass migration, inequality and injustice – governments, policymakers, educators, health workers, academics and community leaders have turned to the concept of resilience in their search for new approaches to individual and collective wellbeing. Defined as both the capacity to recover quickly from difficulties and the ability to spring back into shape, resilience is also a textile quality.

In her essay of 1957 "The Pliable Plane: Textiles in Architecture," Anni Albers refers to "the specific quality of textiles in regard to flexibility, pliability, and their high degree of performance relative to their weight ..."[1] These are precisely the qualities that make textiles so resilient. Beyond (or possibly preceding) their role as decorative objects, textiles can be used to provide shelter, to insulate, strengthen, bandage, bind and repair. Woven structures, as Albers conjectures, have more in common with built structures than might be supposed: "If the nature of architecture is the grounded, the fixed, the permanent, then textiles are its very antithesis. If, however, we think of the process of building and the process of weaving and compare the work involved, we will find similarities despite the vast difference in scale."[2]

RVNT [BEEF] carved into the floor of Vleeshal

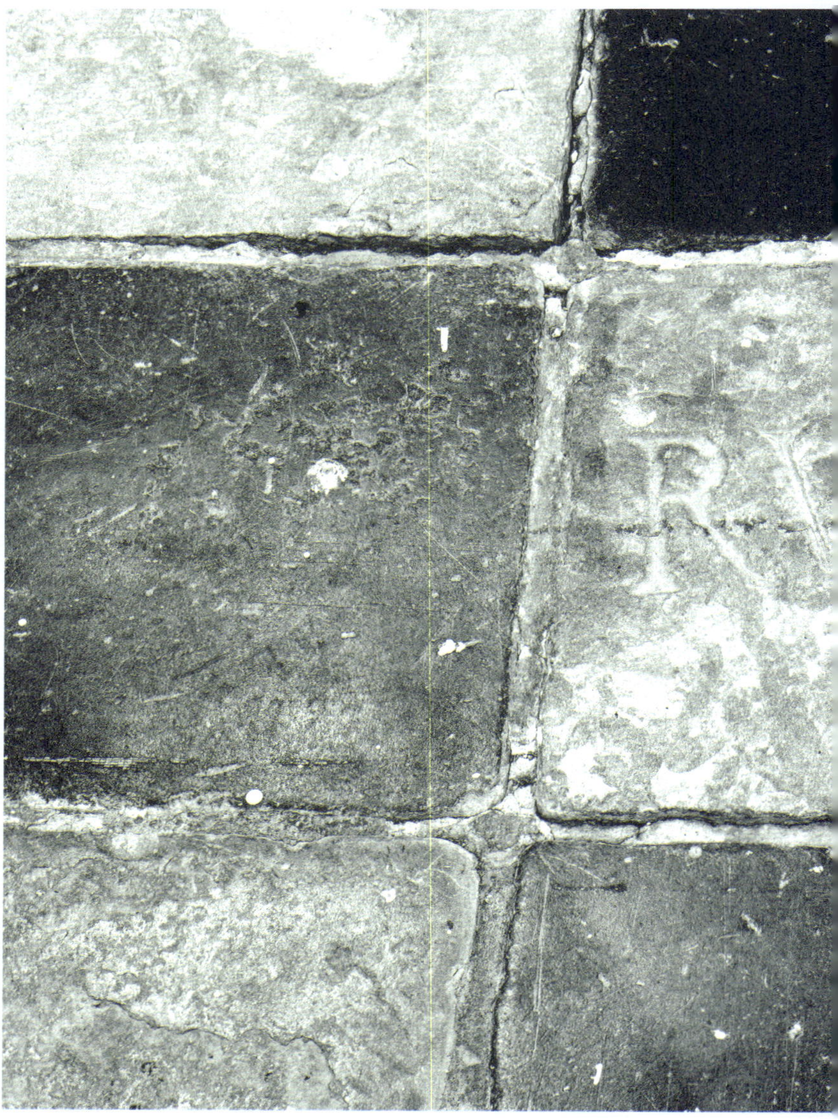

As if taking up Albers' suggestion of finding similarities, Katie Schwab's exhibition *small wares* explores the processes of building, weaving and stitching, uncovering material memories and the ways in which both buildings and textiles demonstrate their resilience. Schwab responds to the site of the late-Gothic Vleeshal building with its history as a meat market, its wartime destruction and post-war rebuild. She also takes in the wider history of textile production in the Zeeland area of the Netherlands where Vleeshal is located. Schwab's research led her to the collections of the Zeeuws Museum, Middelburg and the TextielMuseum, Tilburg where she looked at darning samplers, jacquard looms, and woven ribbons and braids. While these archival settings provided her with rich stories about the history of the area, she was also drawn to the small details of the Vleeshal building itself, following its clues like a detective piecing together her own evidence: flagstones in the floor with mysterious letters carved into them; the scar-like holes in the walls; the wrought iron bolt holes; the colours of the glass window panes. Interestingly the word "clue" comes from the Germanic, Middle English *clew*, meaning a ball of yarn. The artist asks not just what these textile archives and architectural details reveal about their history, but also how they resonate with us in the present. Her resulting interventions draw attention to the specific depth of the Vleeshal walls, the height of the ceiling, the texture of the brickwork surfaces, the wear and tear of the curtain. But they also raise broader questions about materials, categories and techniques, blurring boundaries between past and present, art and craft, architecture and textile, resilience and repair.

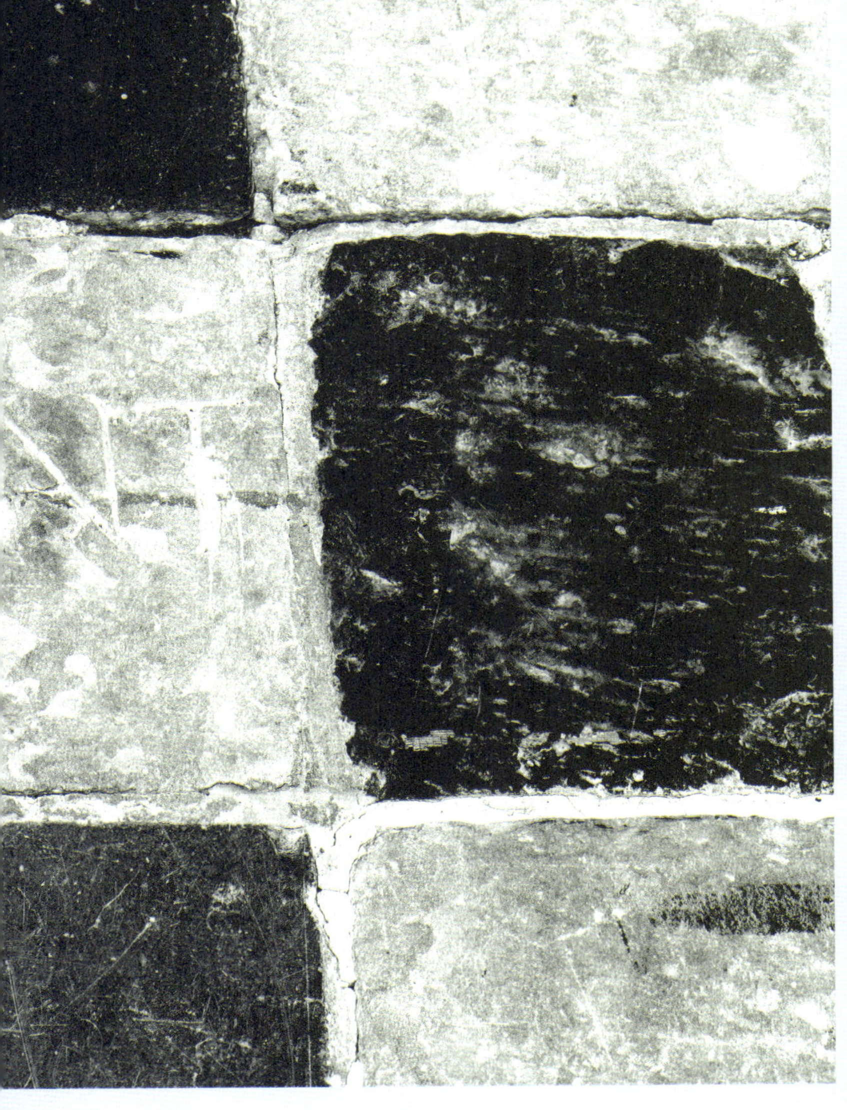

Warp and weft threads – the basic, structural components of woven fabric – run through Western histories of architecture. Anni Albers was doubtless aware of German architect Gottfried Semper's mid-nineteenth-century treatises on style and architecture in which he set out to demonstrate that textile materials and techniques, particularly knotting, plaiting and weaving of fibres, form the historical and stylistic basis of architectural design.[3] Enclosing walls, according to Semper, have their origins in weaving. The first walls, he suggests, were constructed from wicker as pens for animals. The relationship between woven textiles and walls is played out in the Western world through the history of tapestry. In the mediaeval period, tapestry was used to insulate and to decorate castles and fortresses with their expanses of stone wall. Tapestries could be made to the dimensions of the space for which they were intended, but they could also be rolled up and moved from place to place. In this way, they became like portable walls, recalling the earlier, woven enclosures outlined by Semper. Reflecting, not only on this mediaeval history of textiles, but also on earlier periods of human migration and settlement (like Semper before her), Albers refers to the "nomadic nature" of textiles and their ability to provide portable dwellings such as tents or yurts. "Shelter," she states, "is perhaps the most vital use, besides clothing, that has been made of this pliable, quasi two-dimensional material."[4]

Albers' woven, hanging room-dividers and curtains – commissioned to filter light and to create privacy in modernist glass and concrete buildings – and her "pictorial weavings" paved the way to the New Tapestry, or Fiber Art as it was known in the US, of the 1960s and 1970s, in which textiles came off the wall and out into space as sculptural and environmental artworks. At this time, new approaches by textile artists including Magdalena Abakanowicz and Jagoda Buić from Eastern Europe, Lenore Tawney, Sheila Hicks and Claire Zeisler from North America, pushed the "wall hanging" into three dimensional form, making ambitious artistic statements with woven, twisted and knotted fibre. Departing from traditional tapestry techniques, Lenore Tawney and Magdalena Abakanowicz gathered critical acclaim in the early 1960s for their hanging, woven pieces, which reached up to six metres in height, grazing the ceilings of the spaces in which they were exhibited. One can see similarities here with Katie Schwab's rectangular patch-worked hanging, *strength study* (2021), which reaches down from the vaulted ceiling to hover just above the stone floor in the cavernous Vleeshal. But the title of Schwab's work and its means of construction also tell of a different story, calling to mind another history of textiles in art quite different from the grand architectural, sculptural and environmental ambitions of the New Tapestry or Fiber Art artists.

The 1960s and 1970s saw a parallel development in art practice using textiles associated not with the tradition of the tapestry workshops, but with domestic craft. Feminist artists shone a spotlight on the previously unseen and uncelebrated, centuries-long labour of women in the home. Artists such as Miriam Shapiro, Judy Chicago and Faith Wilding employed stitching, quilting and crochet techniques to make art from what was previously relegated to the realms of hobbyist craft. As the curator and writer Lucy Lippard puts it, "Women are raised with an exaggerated sense of detail, which extends from body to house to the objects it contains … On a historical level, the quilt can be seen as a symbol of the feminist resurrection of our foremothers'

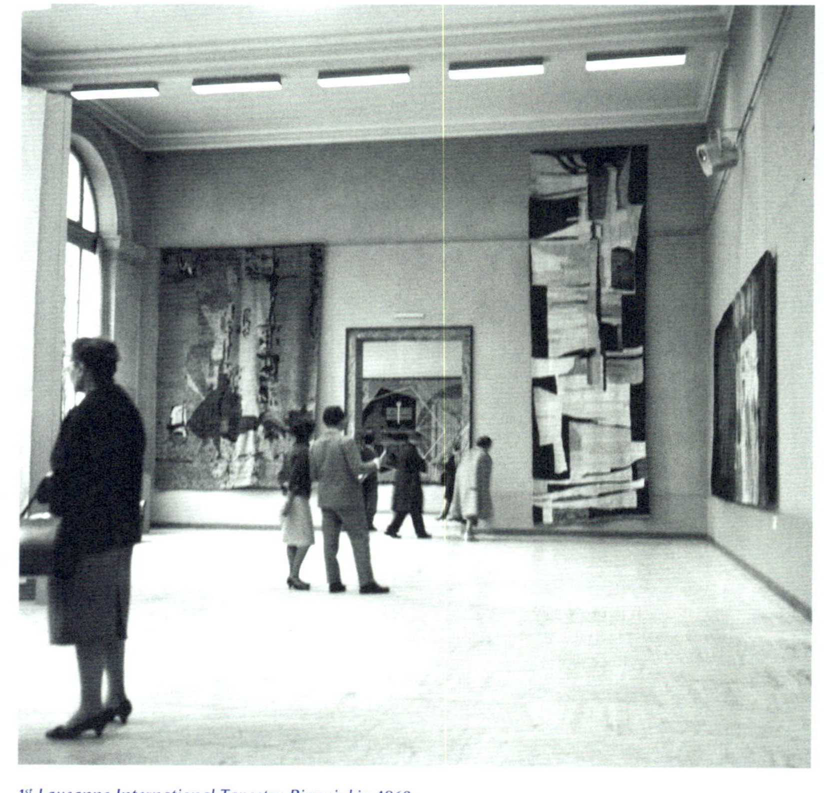

1st Lausanne International Tapestry Biennial in 1962
Exhibition view with works by Jolanta Owidzka, Magdalena Abakanowicz and Wojciech Sadley

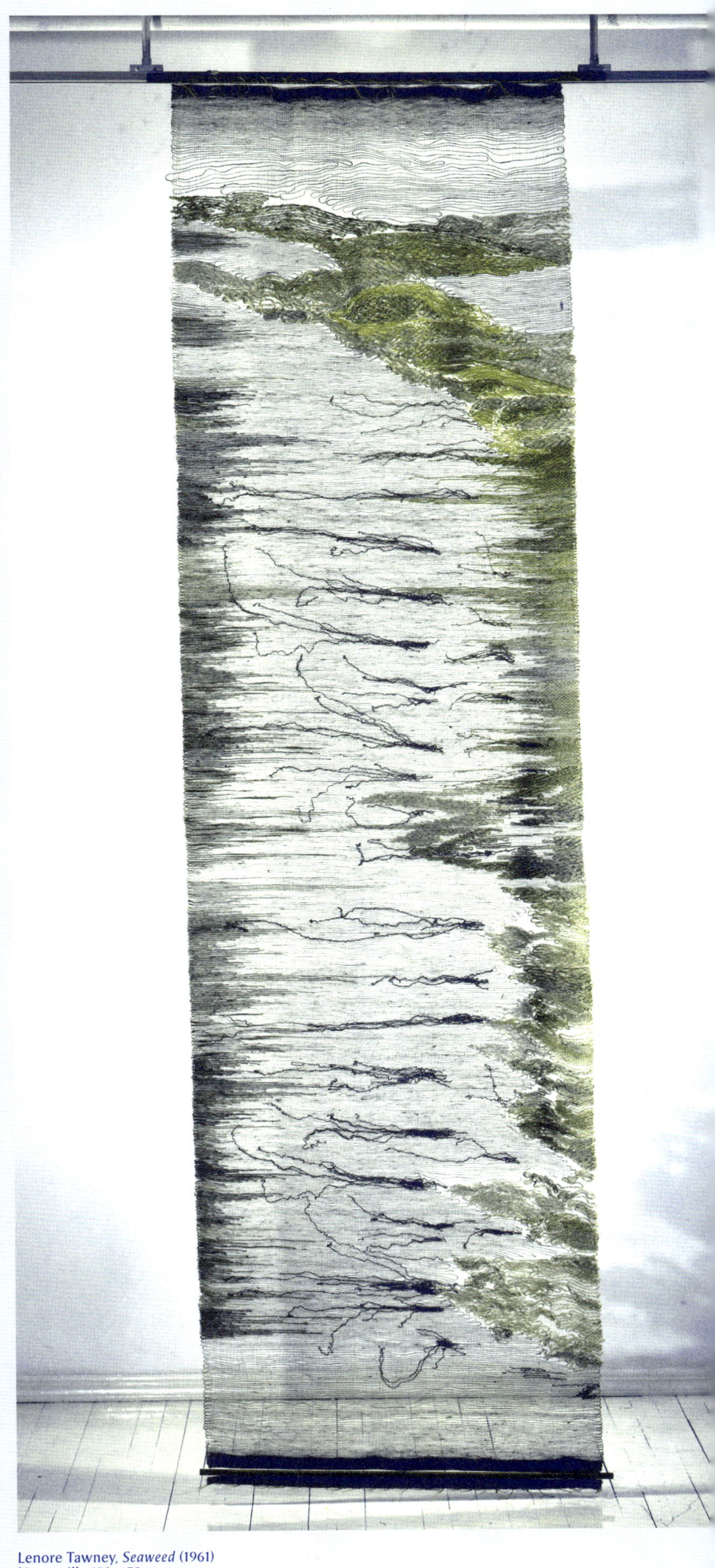

Lenore Tawney, *Seaweed* (1961)
Linen, silk, 120 × 32 cm

lives … Rehabilitation has always been woman's work. Necessity is the mother, not the father, of invention."[7]

The first decades of the twenty-first century have seen a revival of interest in domestic textile practices. International art galleries and museums have expanded their reach to include the creative endeavours of those who may not refer to themselves as artists. The quilts of Gee's Bend, Alabama, for example, have recently come into the collection of the Tate Gallery, London. Though these quilts have been, and will continue to be, seen alongside canonical, twentieth-century modernist abstract painting, their attraction lies not only in their improvised use of geometry and colour, but also in their testament to the creativity born of necessity. Found, used, worn materials, sometimes dirty, frayed and fading, speak of poverty and hardship, and the quilts pre-dating the 1960s are documents that reverberate with the meaning of resilience.

Katie Schwab's *strength study* is made up of patched-together pieces of bias binding, a notion or small ware (terms for little textile articles like ribbons, buttons, threads and more) commonly used in dress-making. It is made from thin strips of cloth cut on the bias, meaning diagonally, against the grain of the perpendicular warp and weft threads, giving it elasticity. Bias binding can be used to strengthen and neaten garments, especially on the edges of hems, seams or armholes, where they may be subject to wear-and-tear and likely to fray. Schwab has spoken of her attraction to the coloured threads used in Dutch darning samplers, colours echoed in the glass panels of the Vleeshal windows and consequently in her choice of bias strips. Her hanging textile, catching the light, takes detailed work and presents it on an architectural scale. Textiles, she reminds us, are not only used to decorate and soften an interior space. They also have an inherent strength which lies in their very structure and build: the crossing of warp and weft, the cutting on the bias, the stitching of the pieces, the lightness of the fabric, its tensile, pliable, resilient properties. Schwab's *small wares* are both nomadic and site-specific. They are tailor-made for the building, yet they can be moved, re-positioned and repurposed – individual artworks ready to be exhibited elsewhere. Piecing together the histories of the site through small details, the artist reflects on what it means to build and rebuild, to wear and repair. Created in a period when COVID-19 forced so many to shelter at home and to reflect on questions of inner strength, these *small wares* are made up of many resilient threads.

Notes

1. Anni Albers, "The Pliable Plane: Textiles in Architecture," in *Anni Albers: Selected Writings on Design*, Brenda Danilowitz, ed. (Middletown, Connecticut: Wesleyan University Press, 2000), 46.

2. Ibid., 44.

3. See also: Gottfried Semper. *Style in the Technical and Tectonic Arts; or, Practical Aesthetics* (Los Angeles: Getty Research Institute, 2004) And: Gottfried Semper. *The Four Elements of Architecture and Other Writings* (Cambridge: Cambridge University Press, 2011).

4. Albers, *Selected Writings*, 46.

5. Anni Albers referred to her "pictorial weavings" as being made "to no other end than their own orchestration, not to be sat on, walked on, only to be looked at." In this respect, she felt the need to assert their status as art, not craft or design. Katie Schwab's *small wares* includes *alcove cushions* (2021), made in the name of art, but distinctly designed to be sat on. This may demonstrate the extent to which artists have been freed from the rigid categories of art, craft and design since Albers made her statement in 1959.
Anni Albers, "Pictorial Weaves," in *Anni Albers: Pictorial Weavings* (Cambridge, MA: MIT New Gallery: 1959). Exhibition catalogue. Cited in *Anni Albers*, eds., Ann Coxon, Briony Fer and Maria Müller-Schareck, (London: Tate Publishing, 2018), 13. Exhibition catalogue.

6. Magdalena Abakanowicz drew critical acclaim and attention to Poland's radical weaving production when she first exhibited her woven textile, *Composition of White Forms* (1962), a work measuring 615 cm in height, at the 1st *Lausanne Tapestry Biennial*. At this time Lenore Tawney was also becoming known in the US for her tall, free-hanging, open-warp woven forms.

7. Lucy R. Lippard, "Up, Down, and Across: A New Frame for New Quilts," in *The Artist & The Quilt*, ed. Charlotte Robinson, (New York: Knopf), 32.

small wares
Vleeshal,
Middelburg
26 September
–
12 December 2021
Exhibited Works

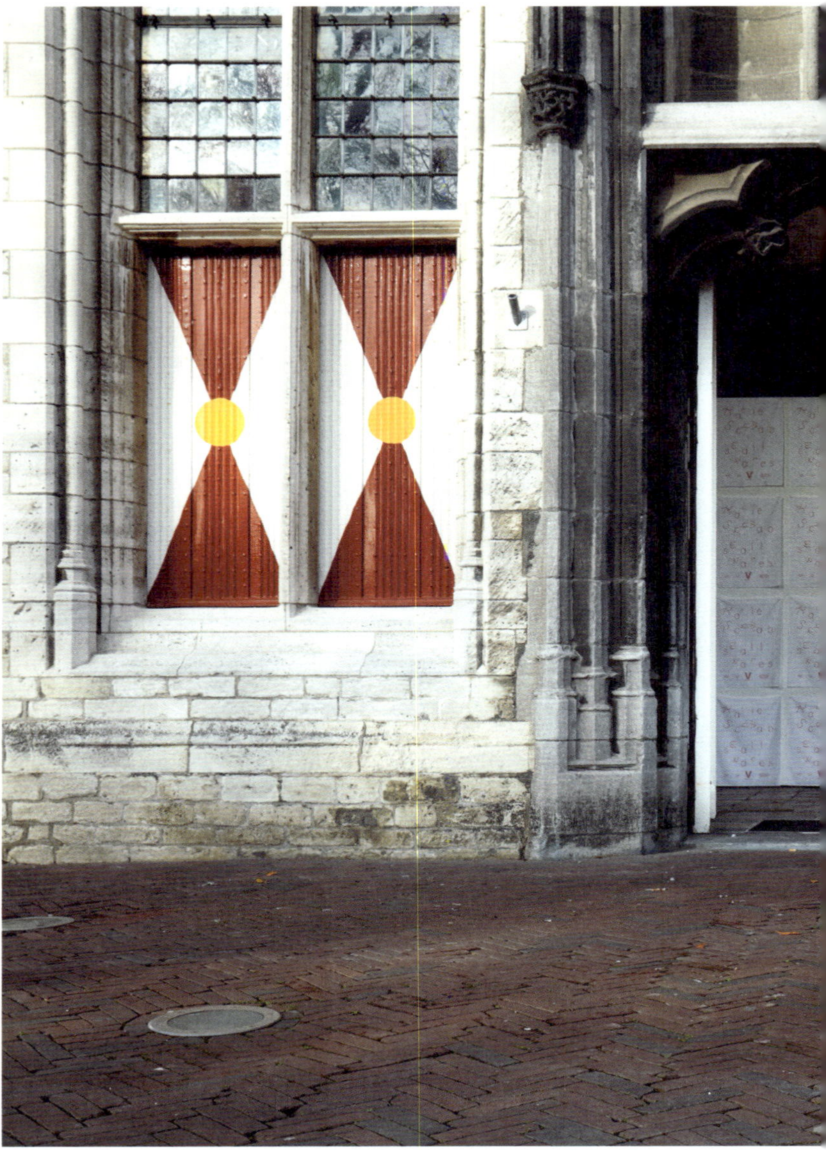

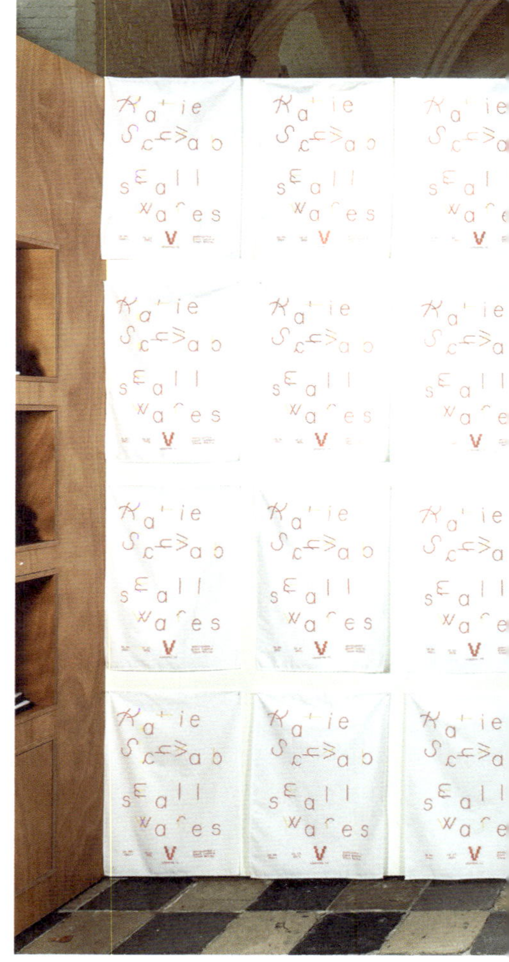

small wares entrance wall
with screen-printed, organic-
cotton tea towels, designed by
Marianne Noordzij

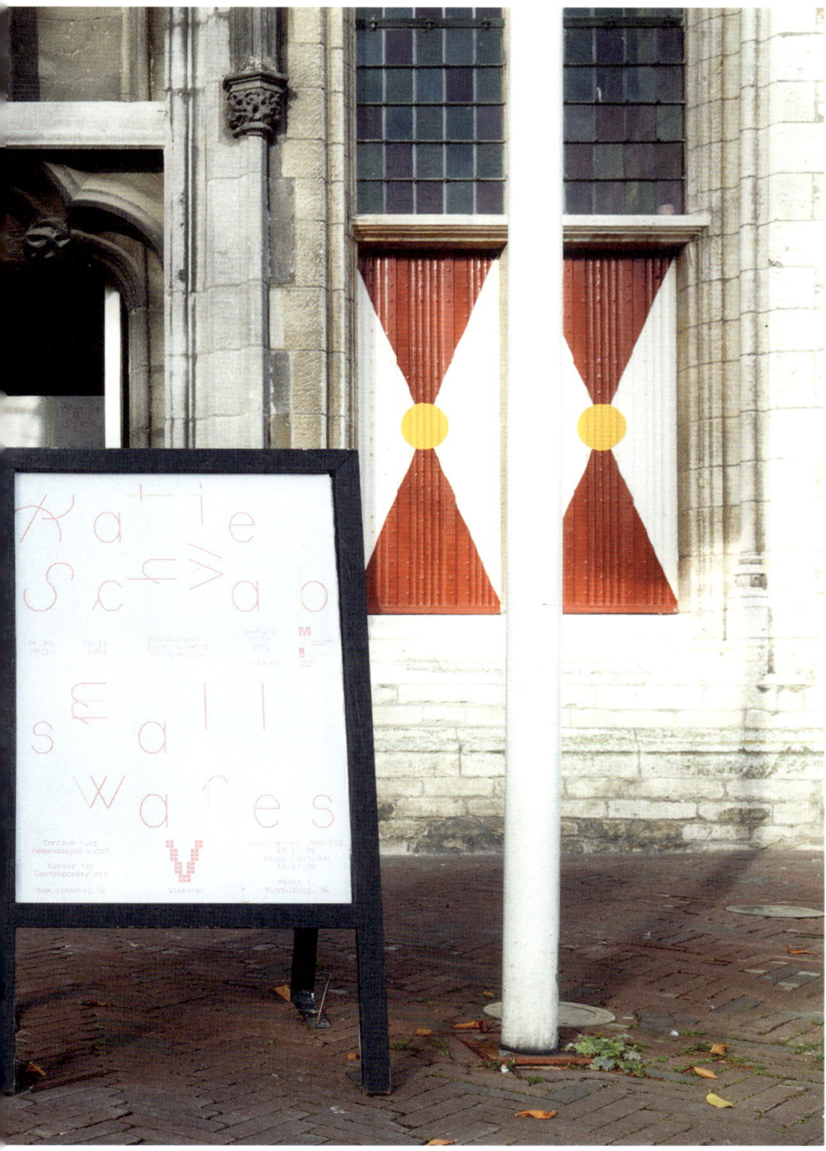

Exhibition poster outside Vleeshal, designed by Marianne Noordzij

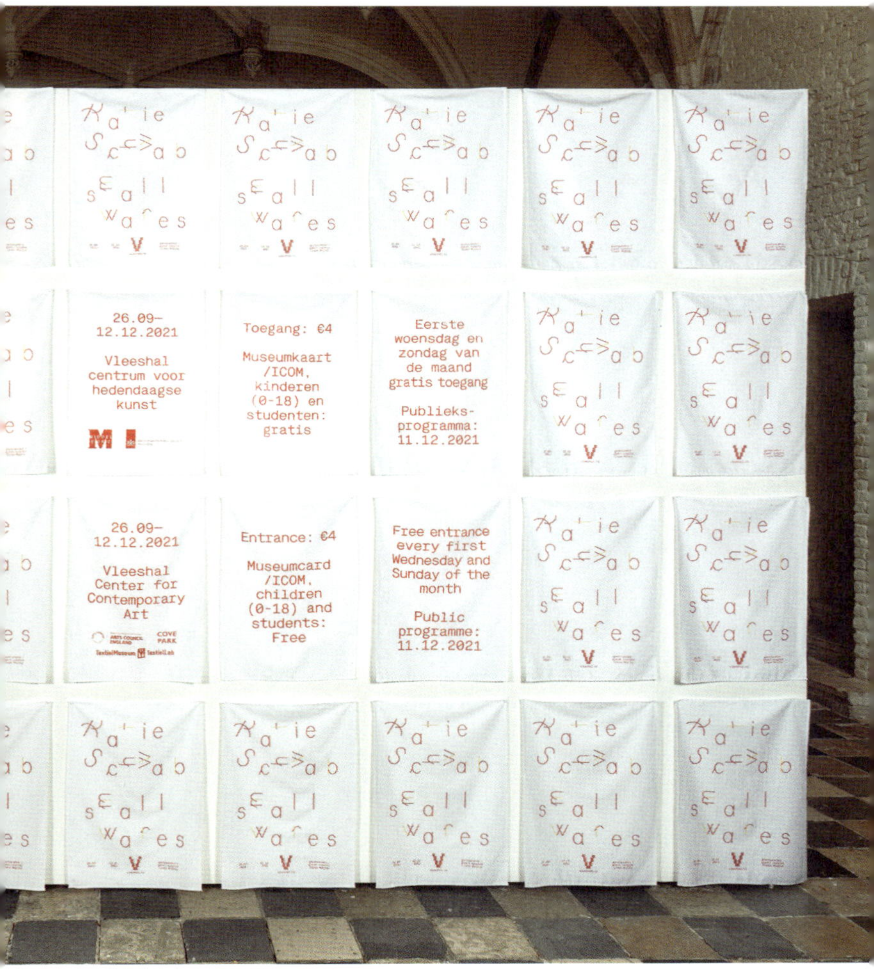

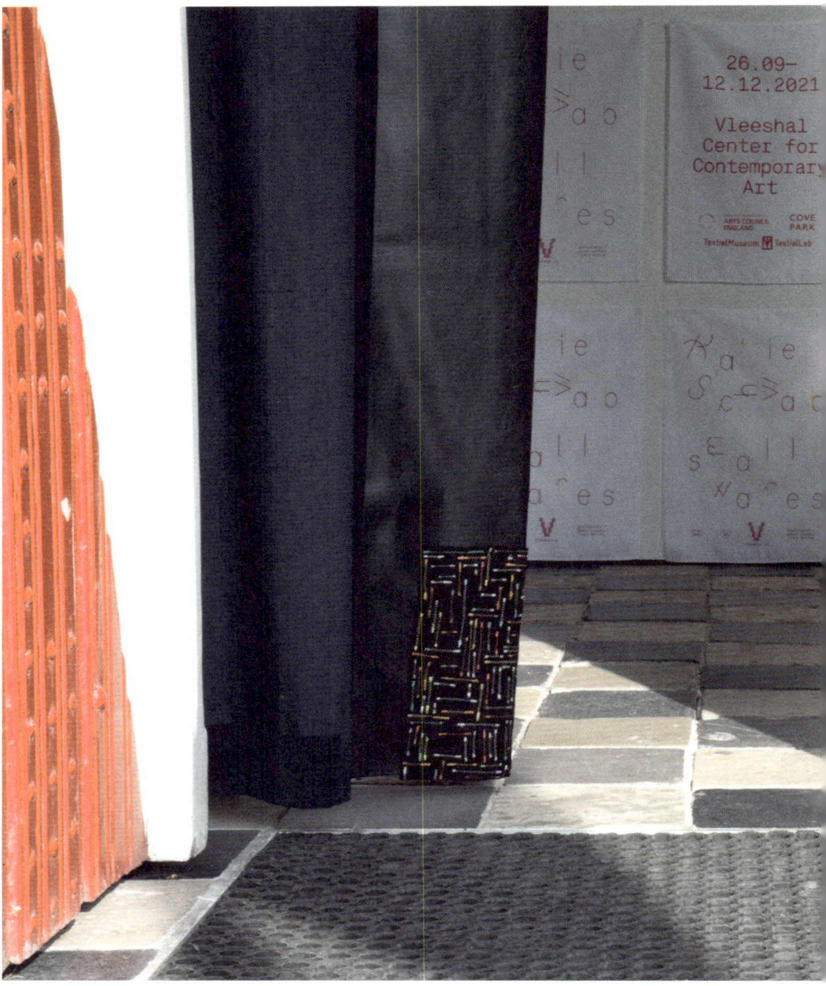

patches (2021)
Wool offcuts, polyester thread, 40 × 34 cm and 30 × 10 cm

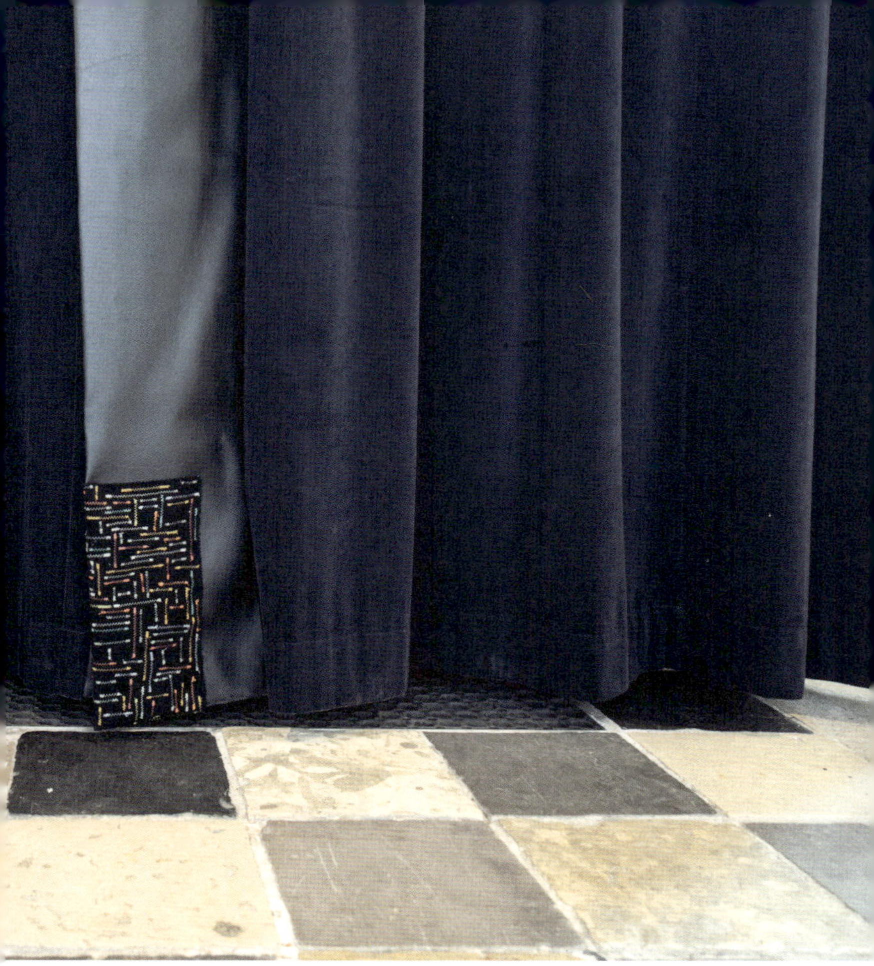

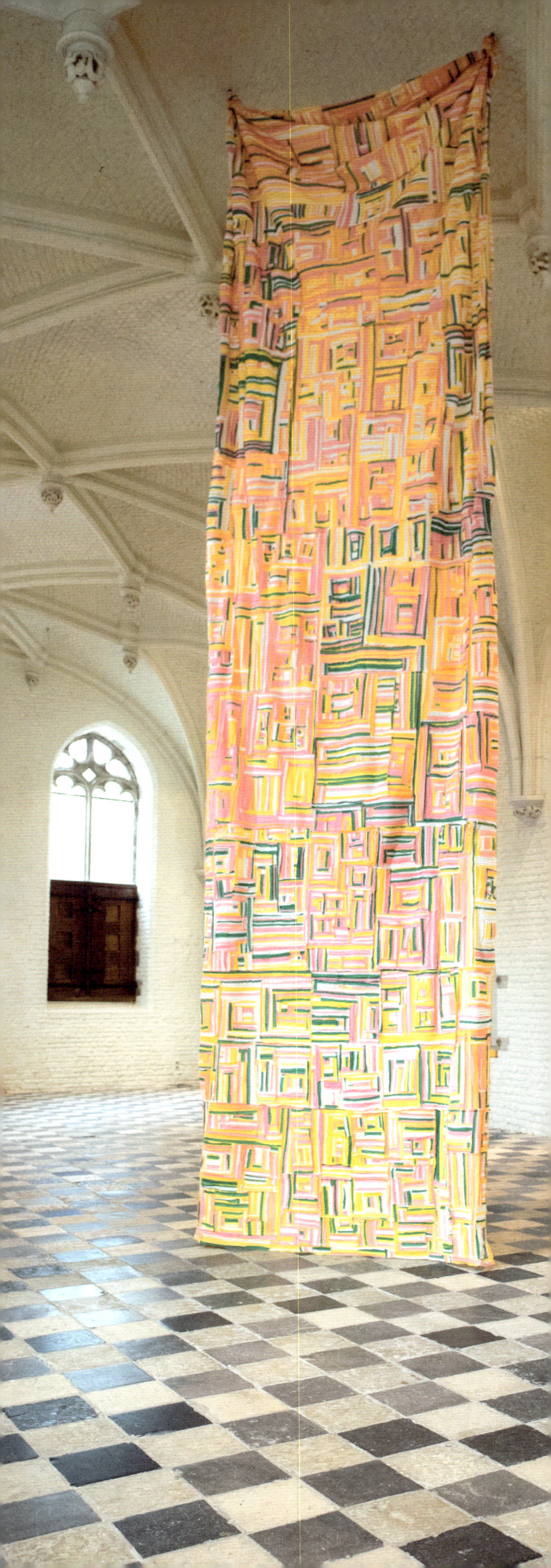

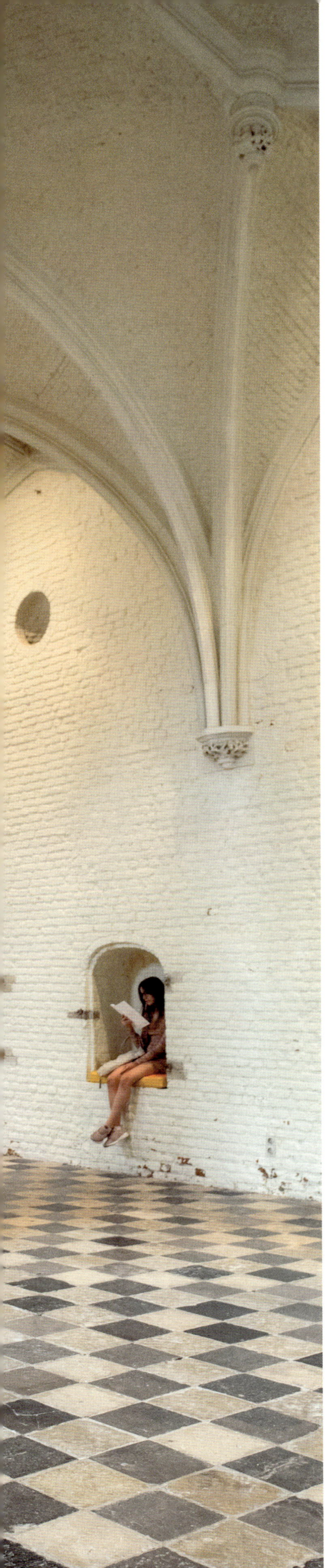

strength study (2021)
Cotton bias binding, polyester thread, powder-coated steel, 740 × 246 cm

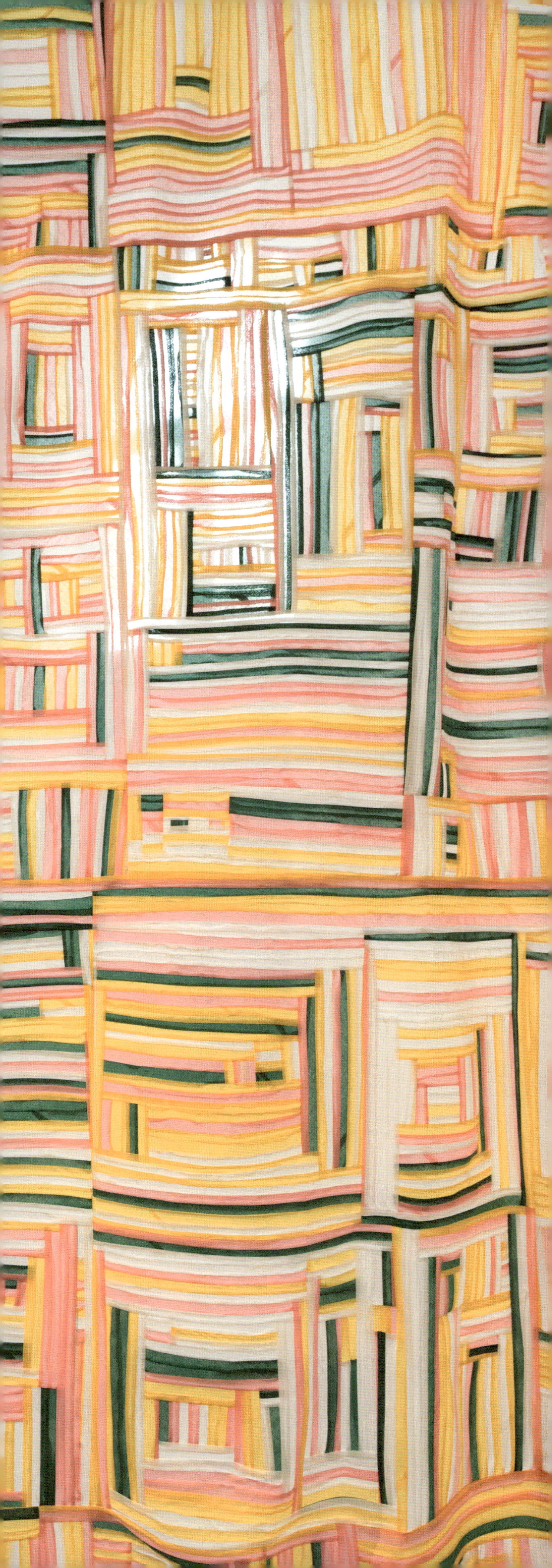

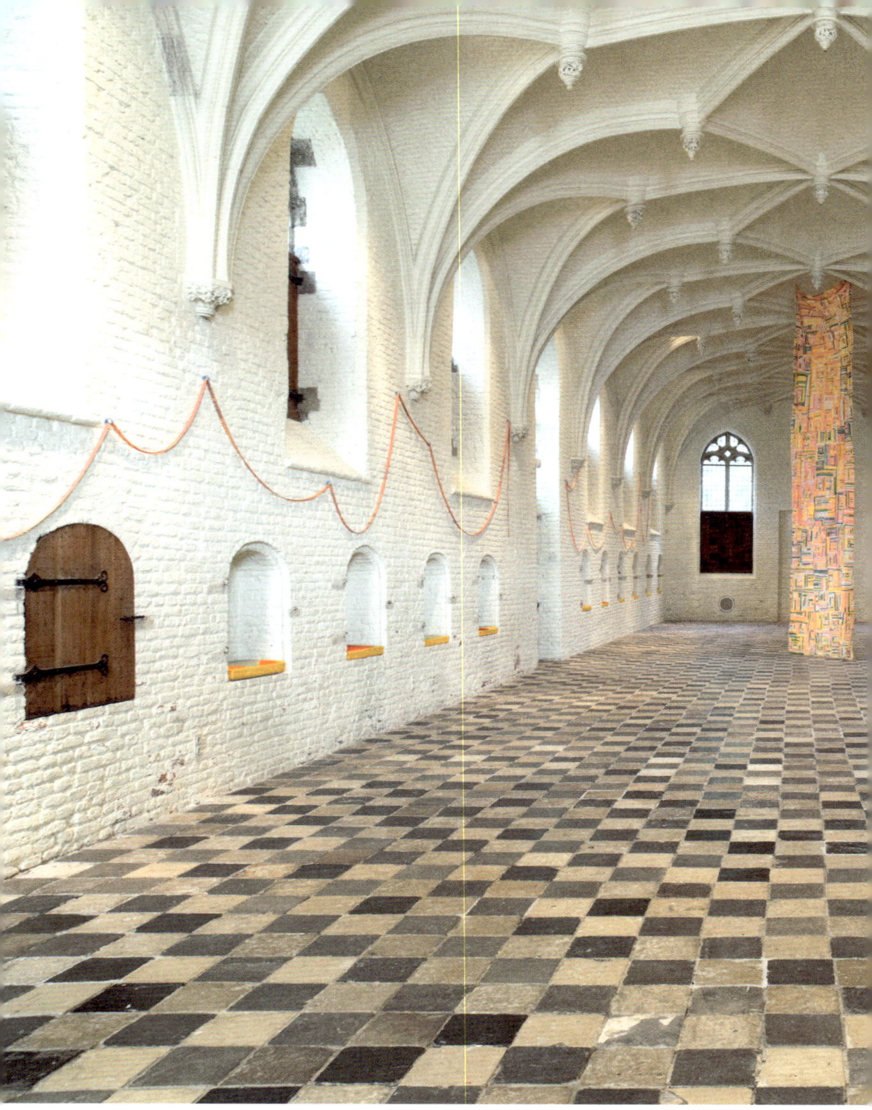

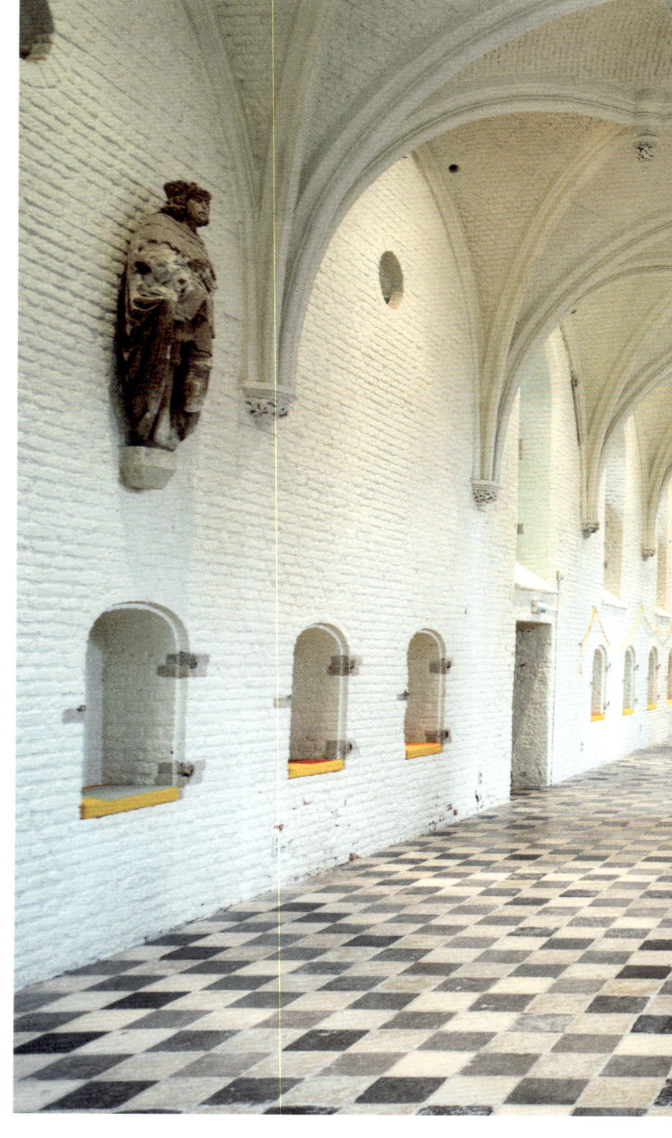

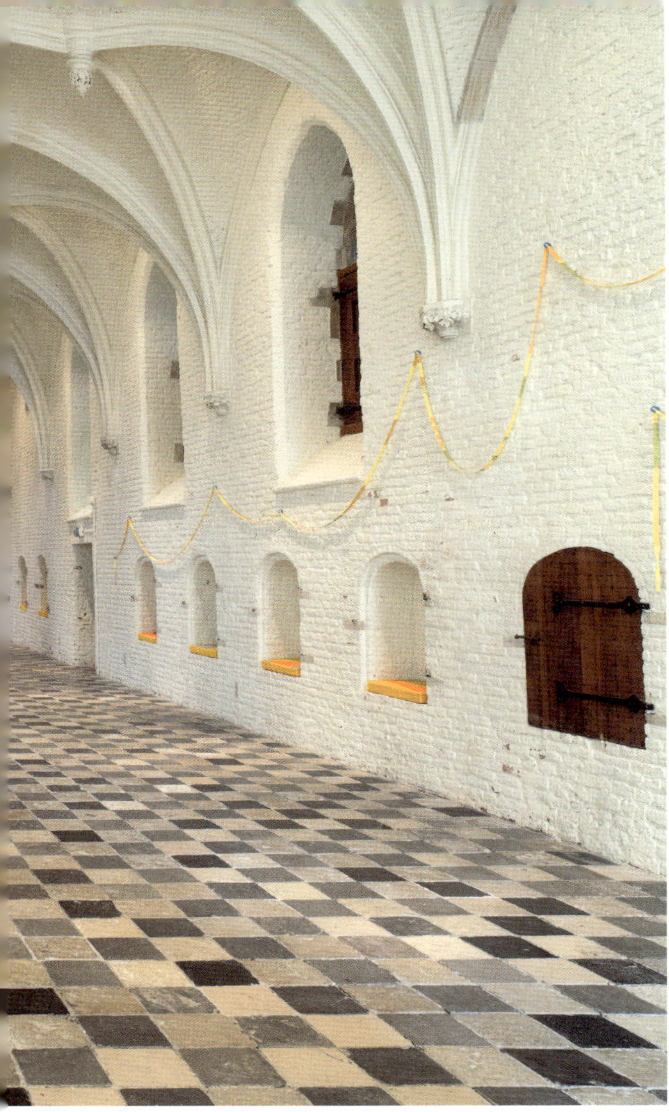

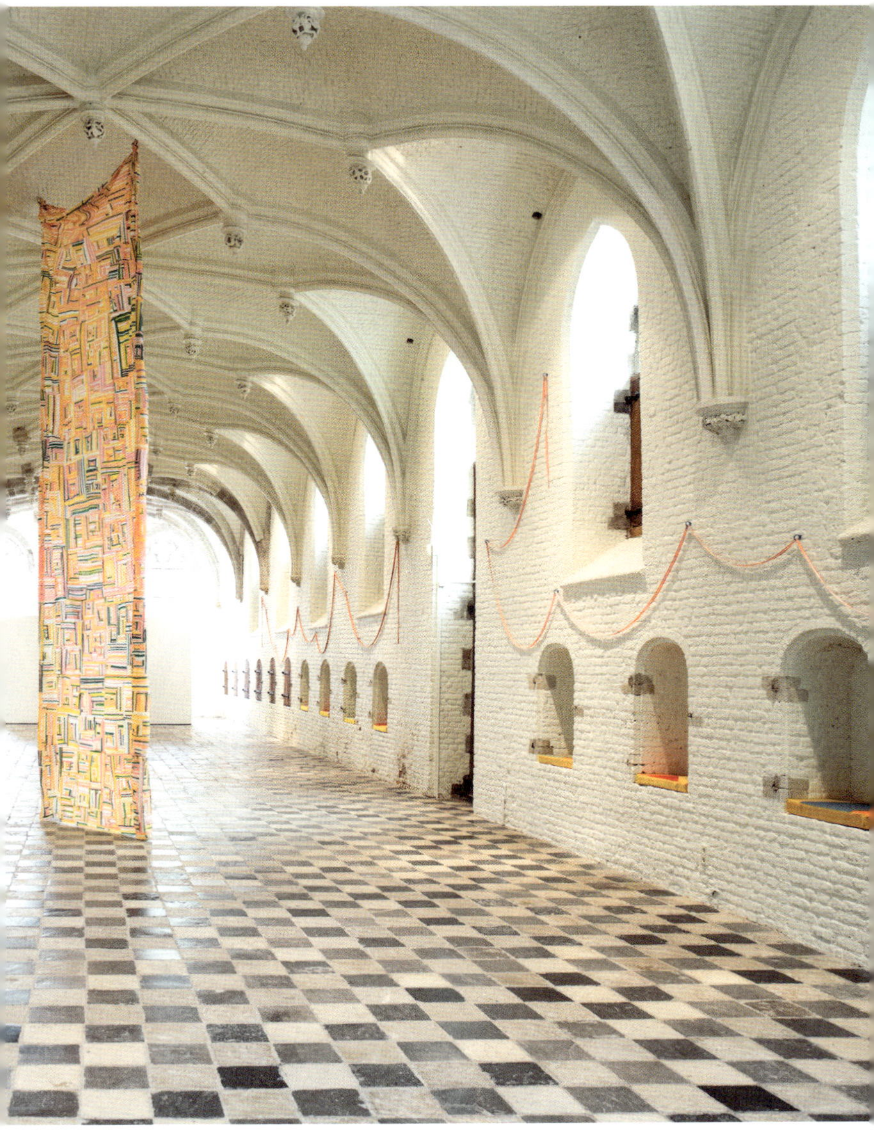

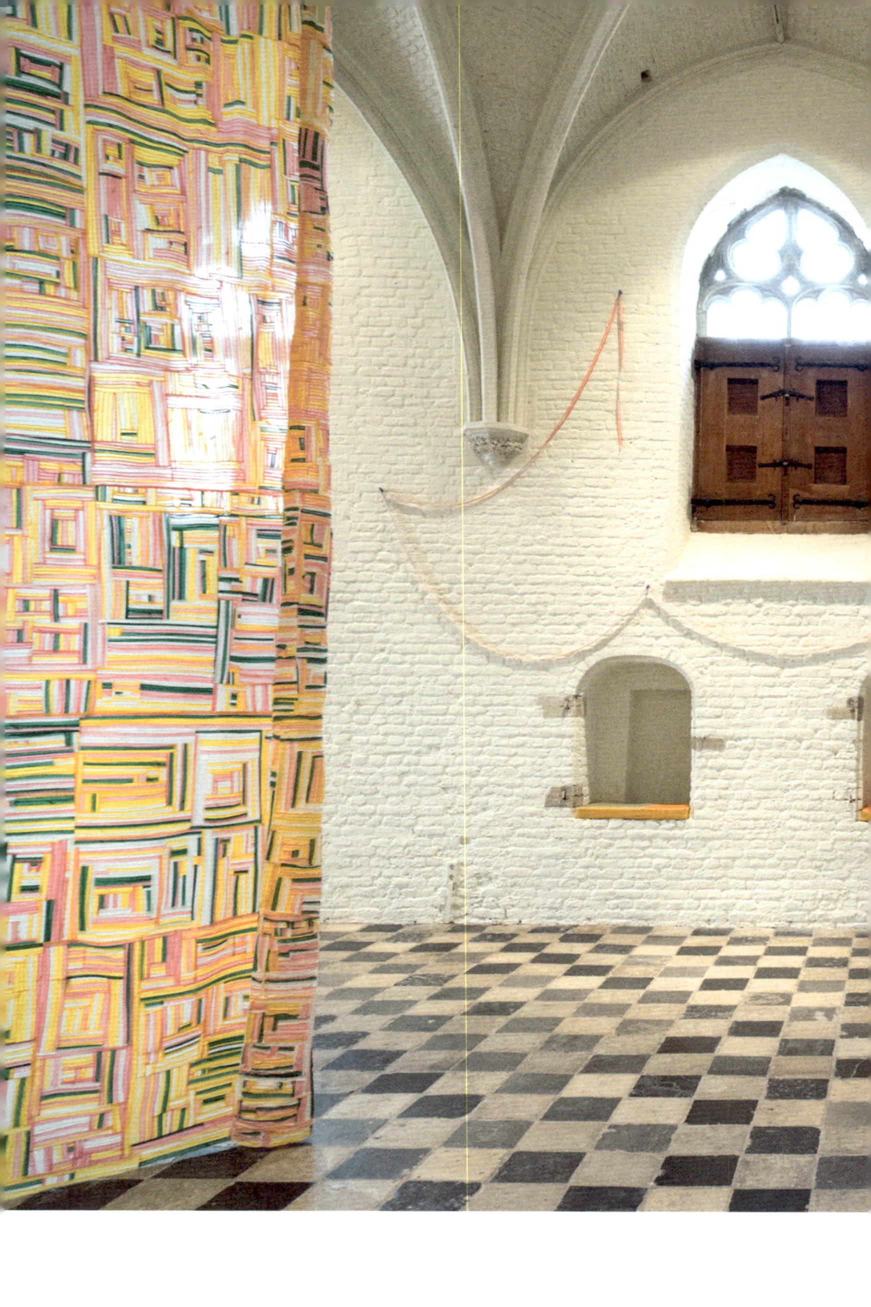

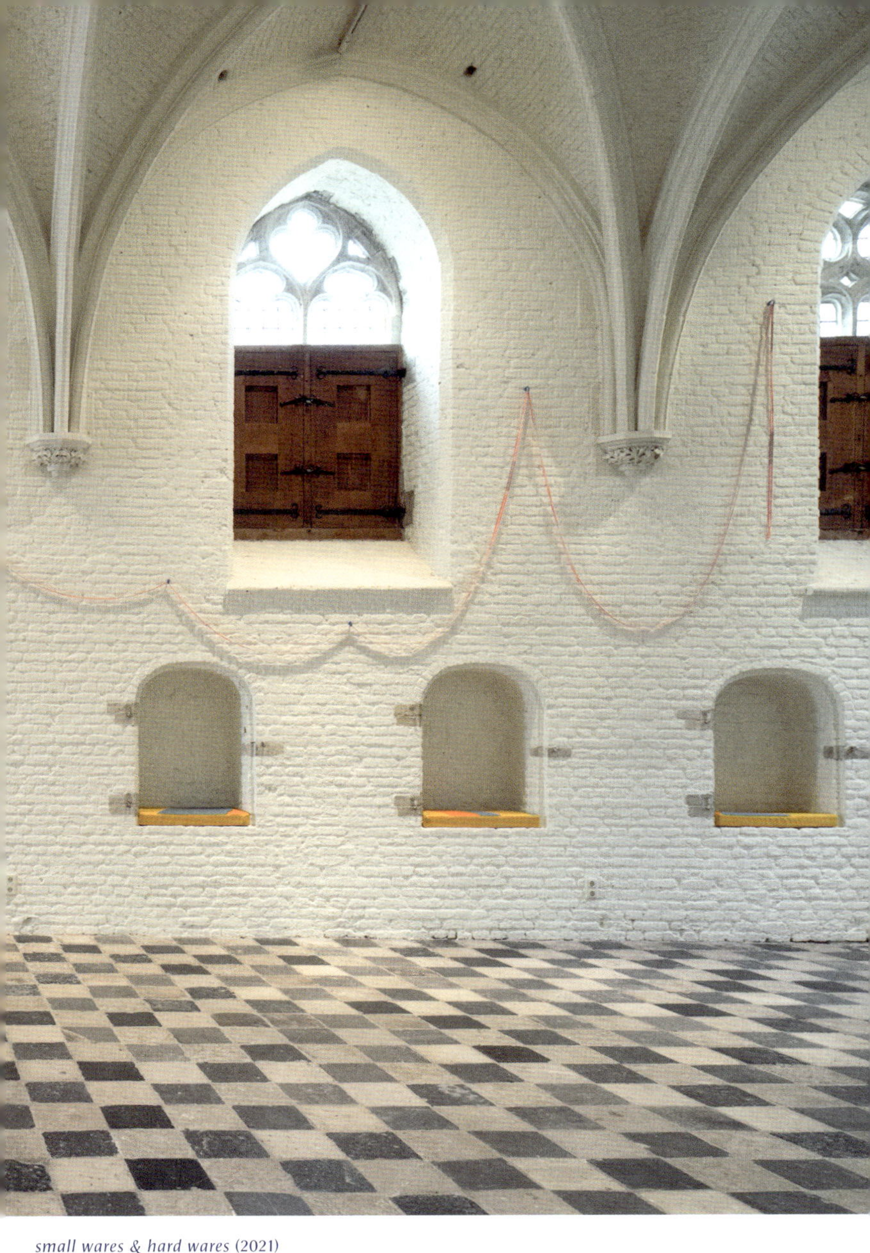

small wares & hard wares (2021)
Cotton, silk, linen, powder-coated steel, dimensions variable
Band weave made with Veva van der Wolf at TextielLab, Tilburg
Hardware hook made with Sam Fish at Swarf, Norfolk

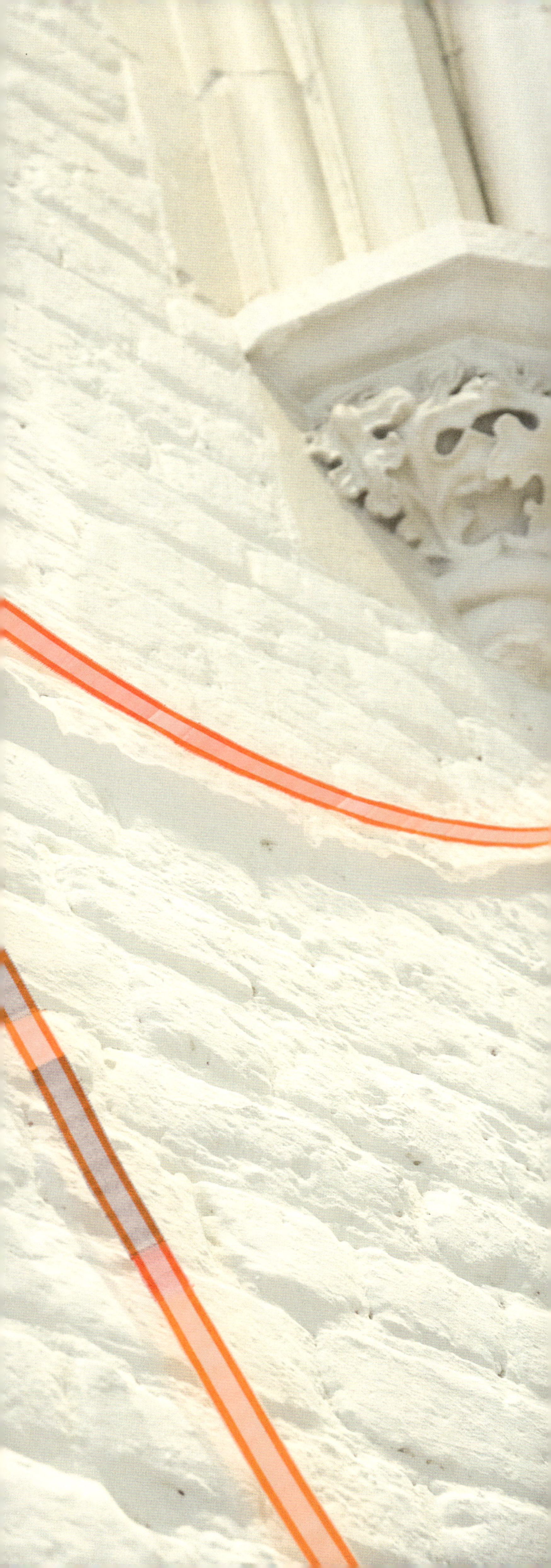

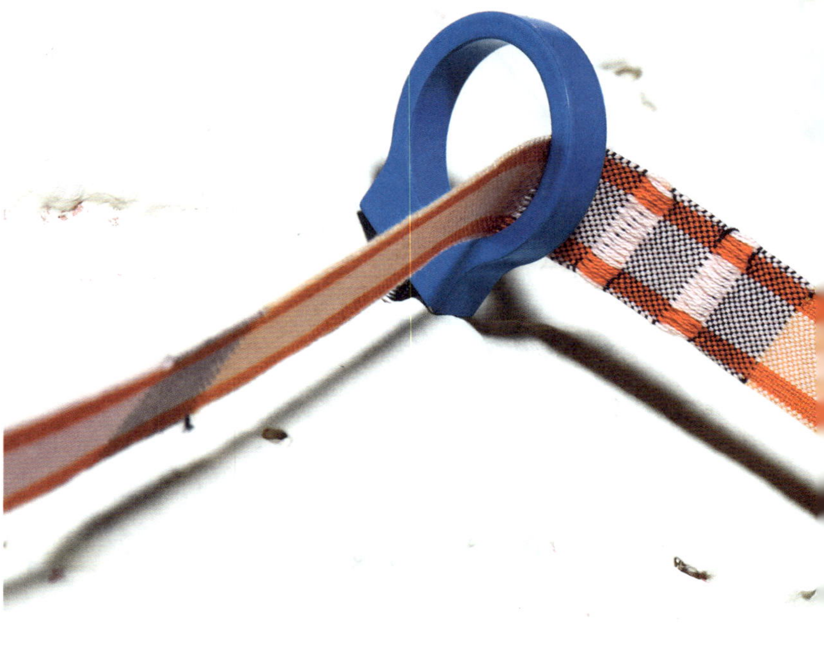

small wares & hard wares (2021), details

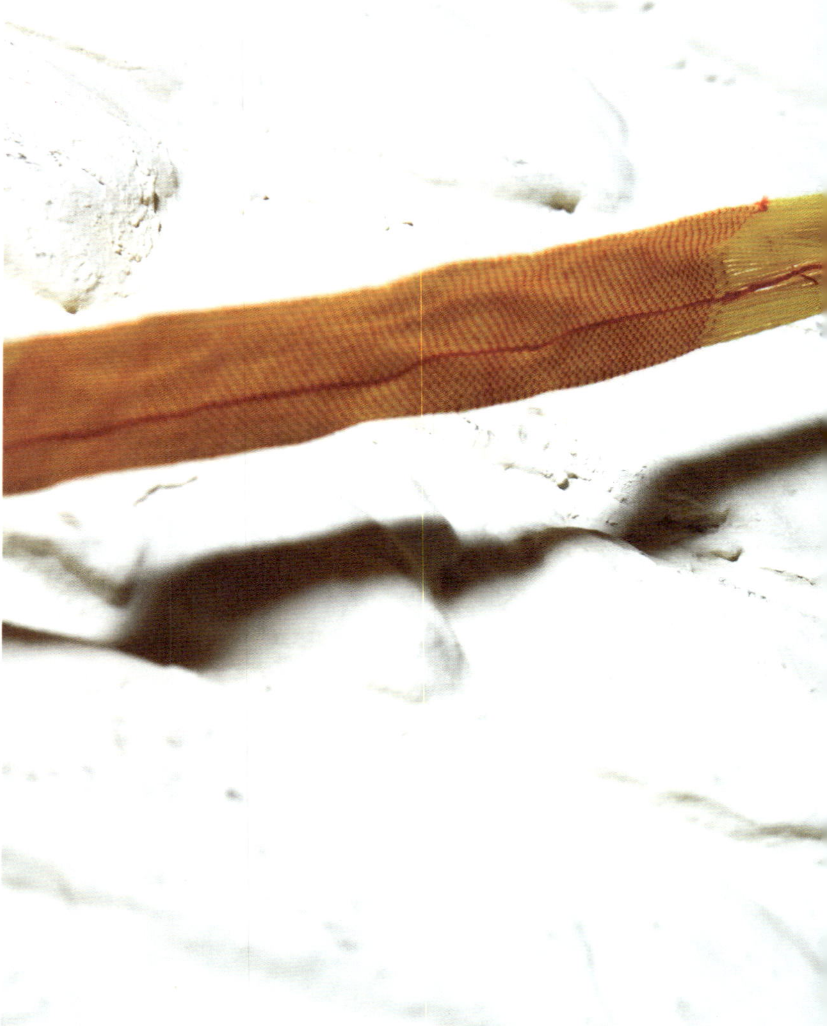

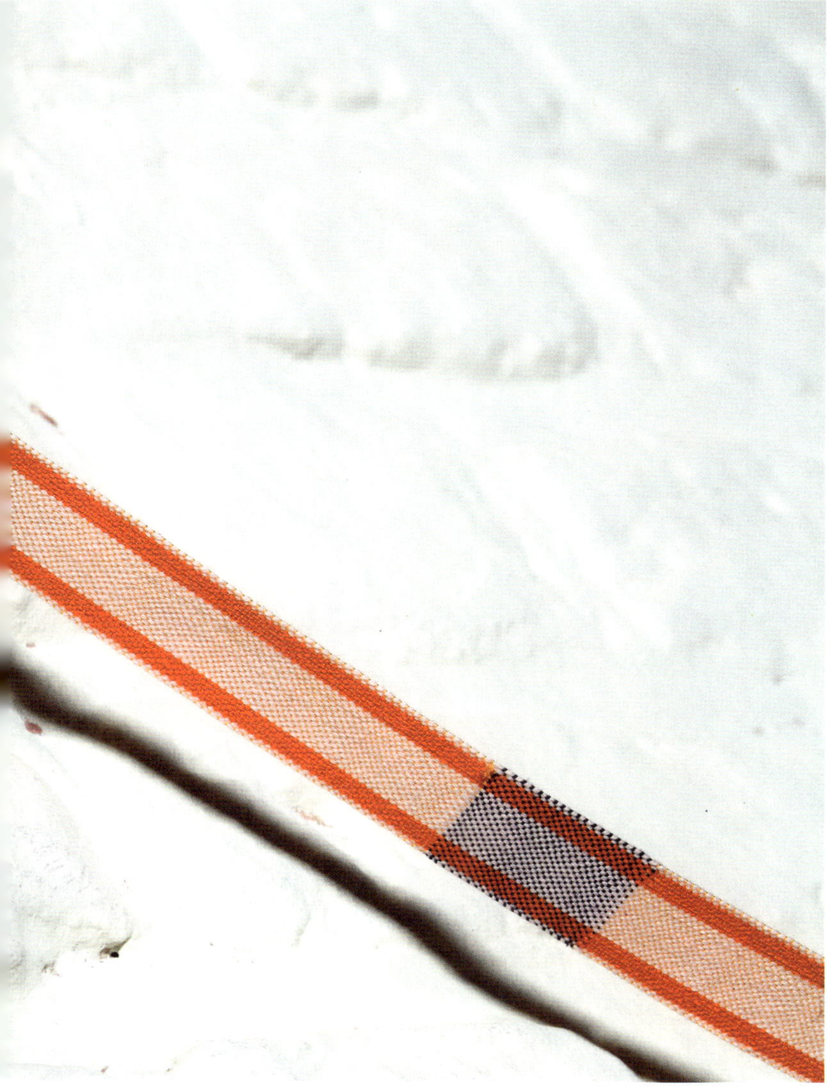

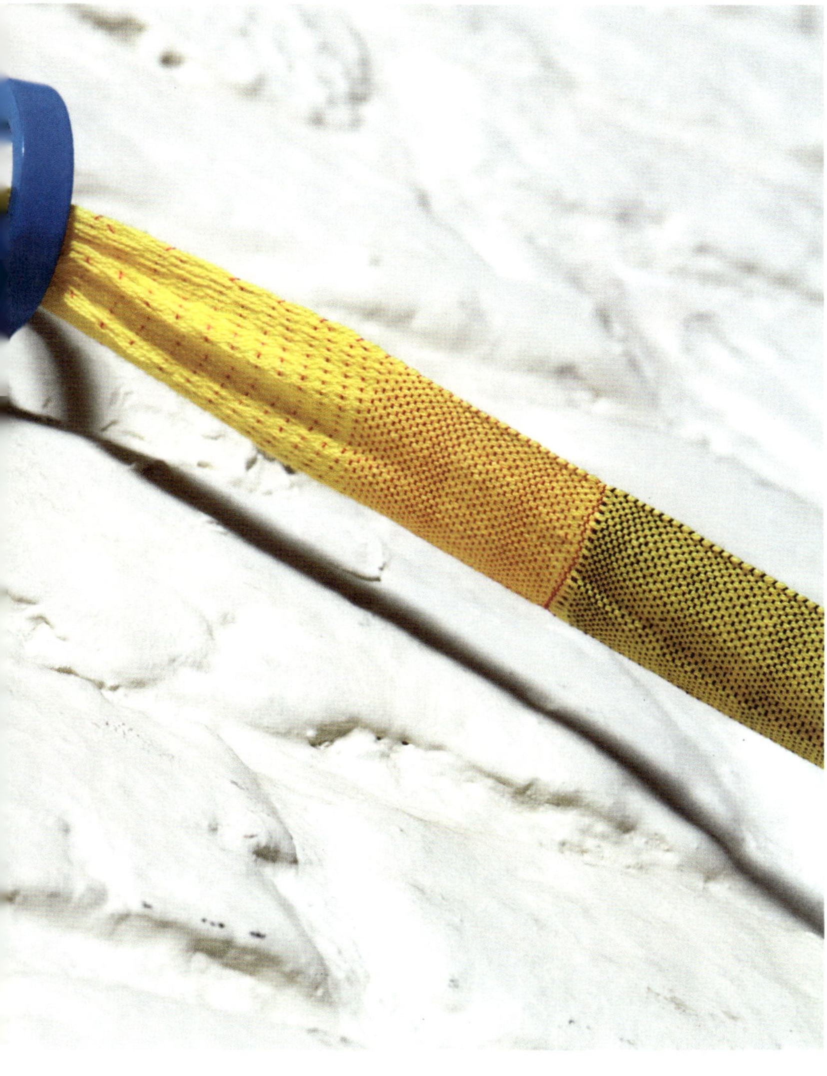

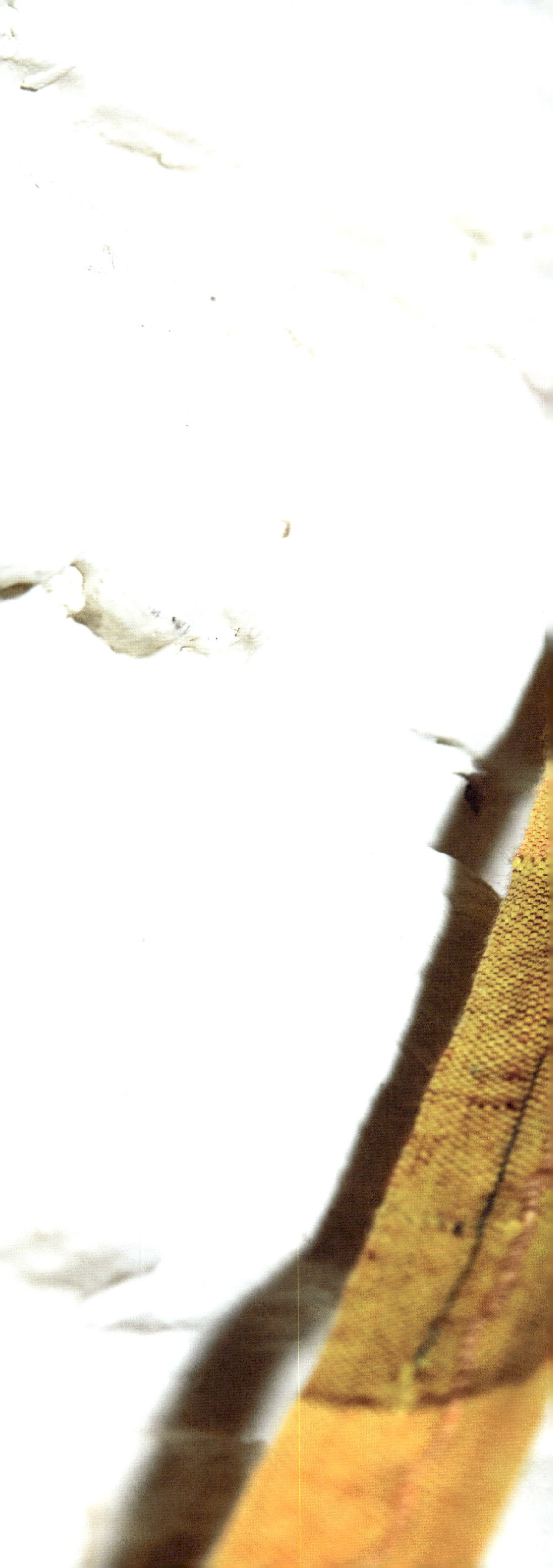

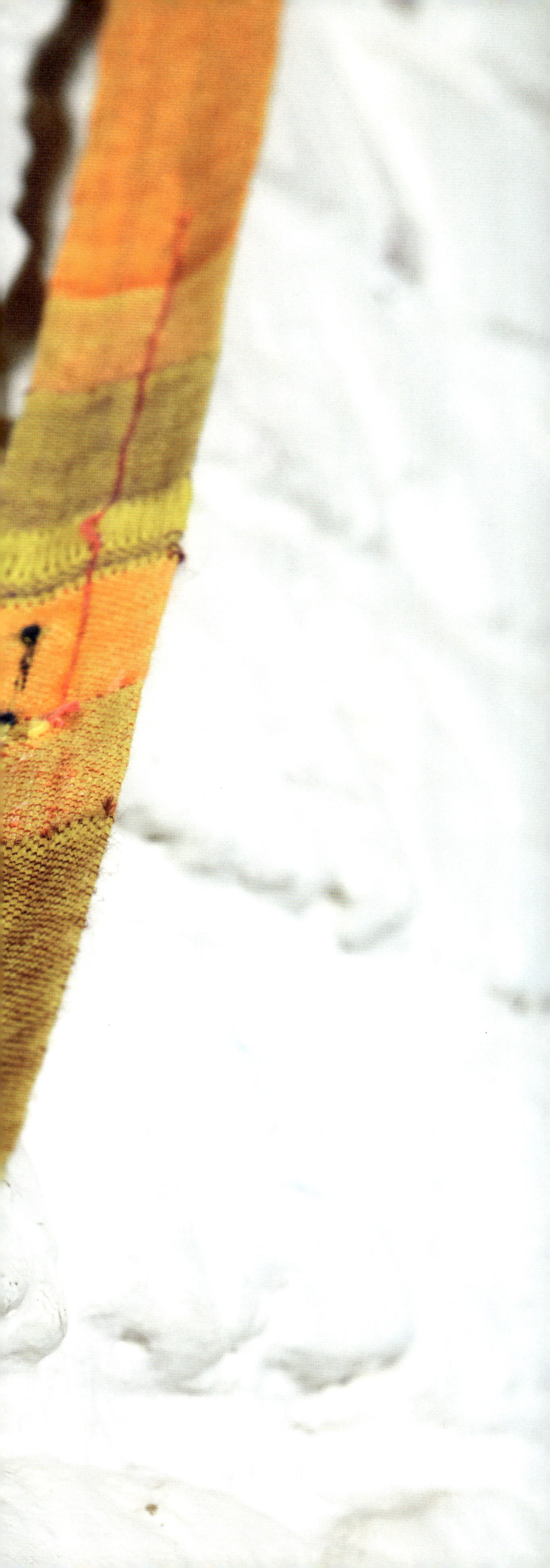

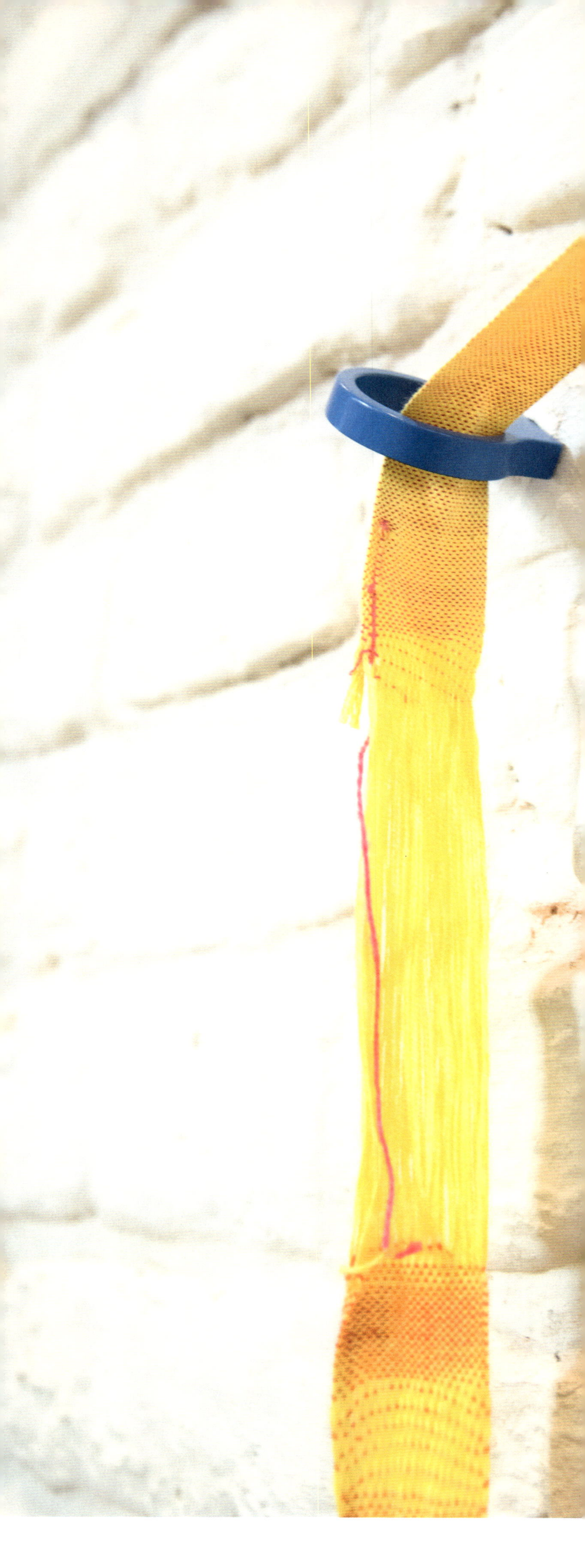

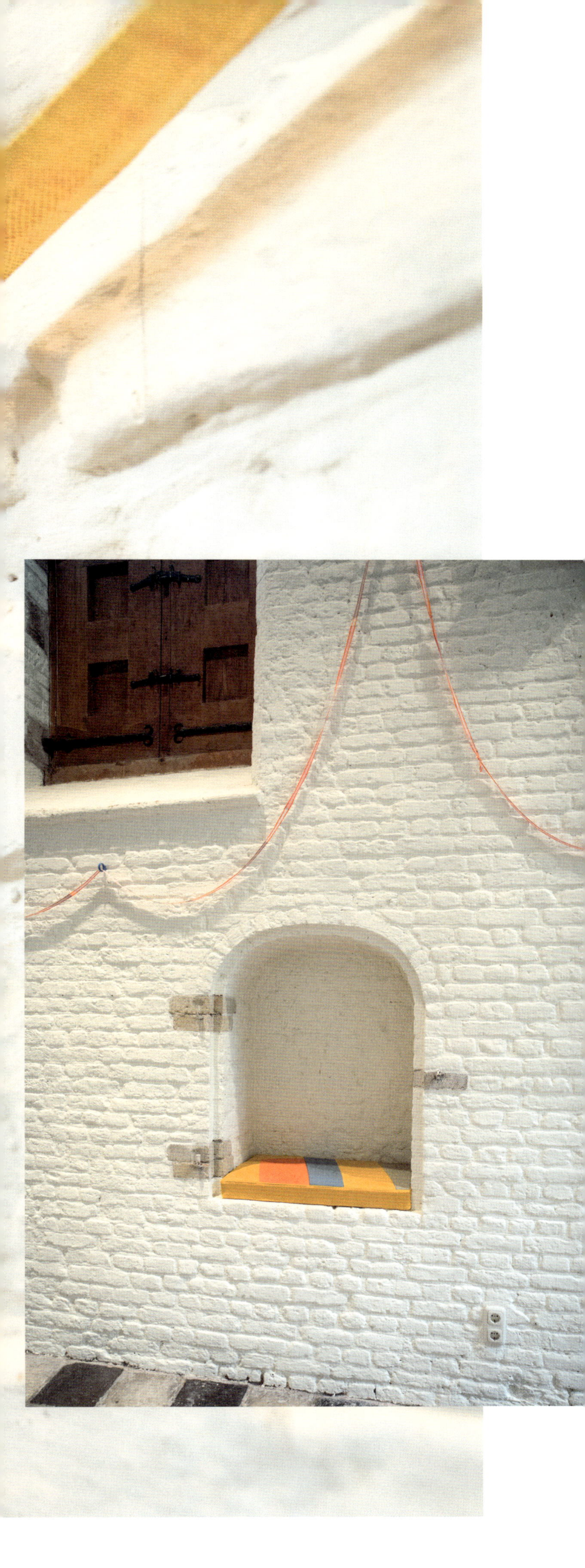

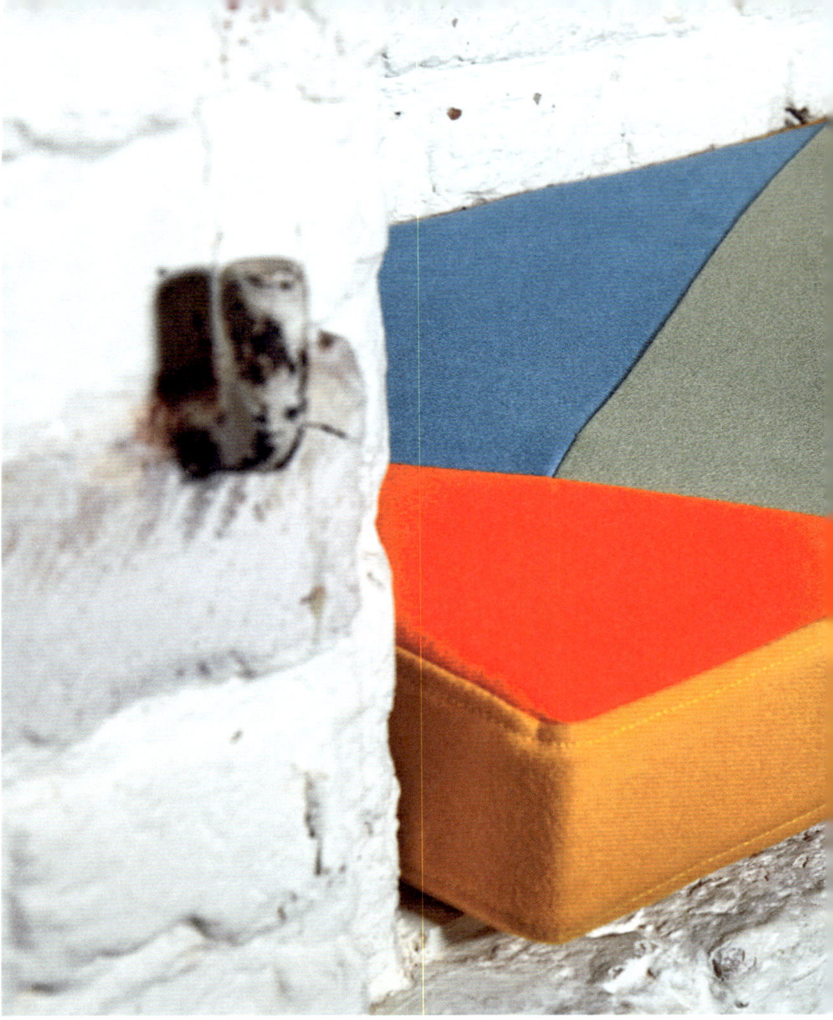

20

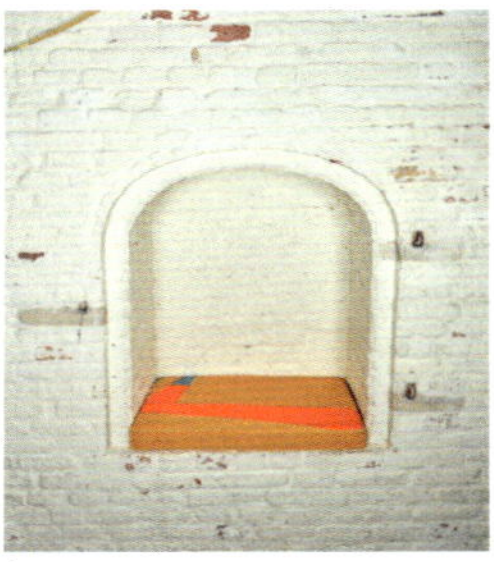

1

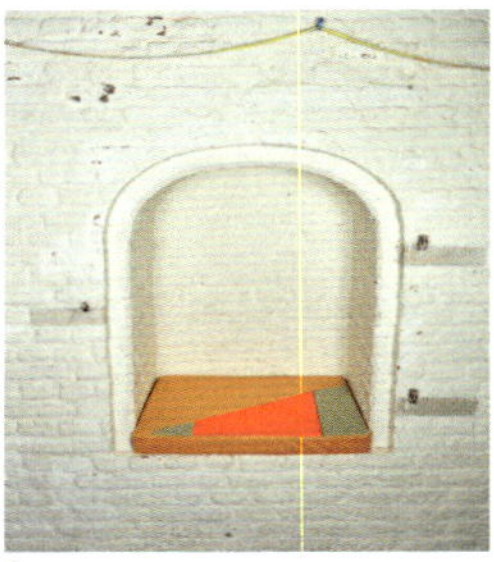

2

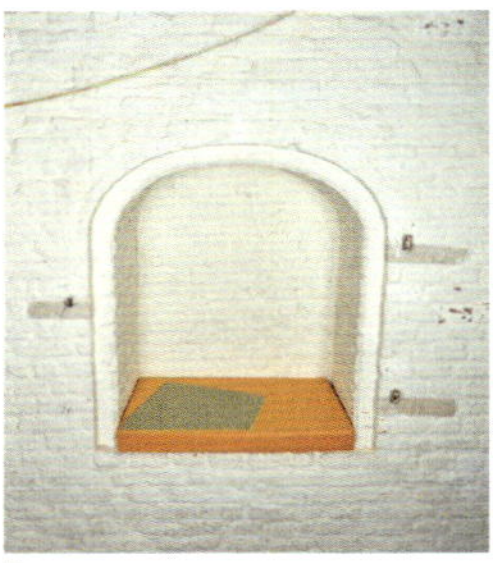

3

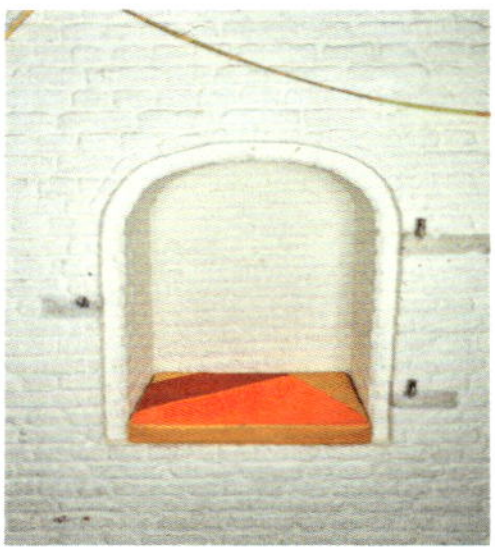

4

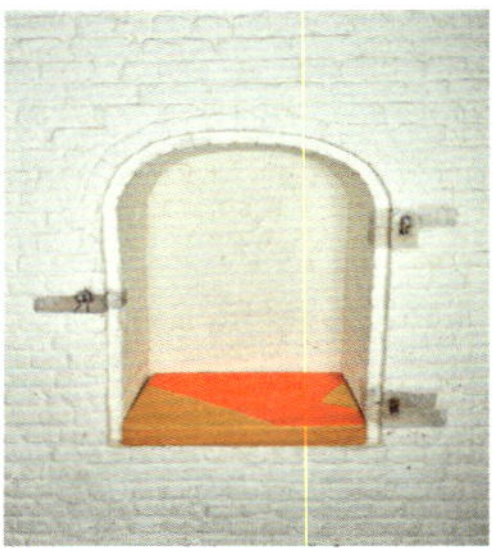

5

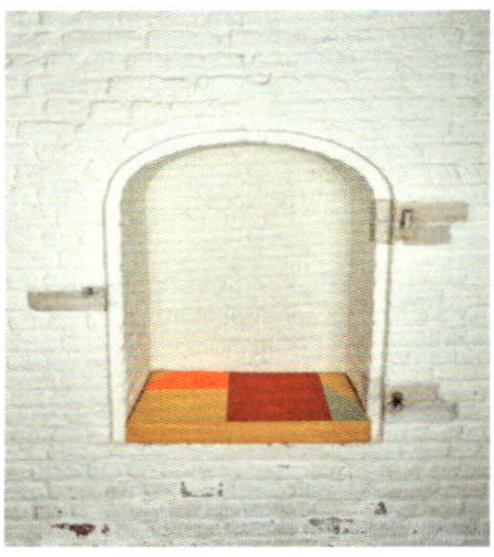

6

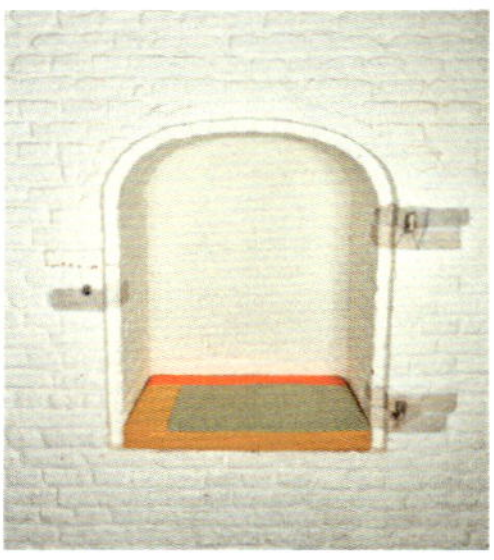

7

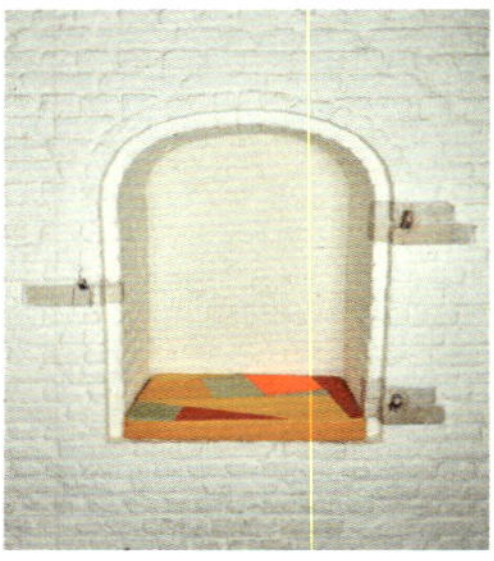

8

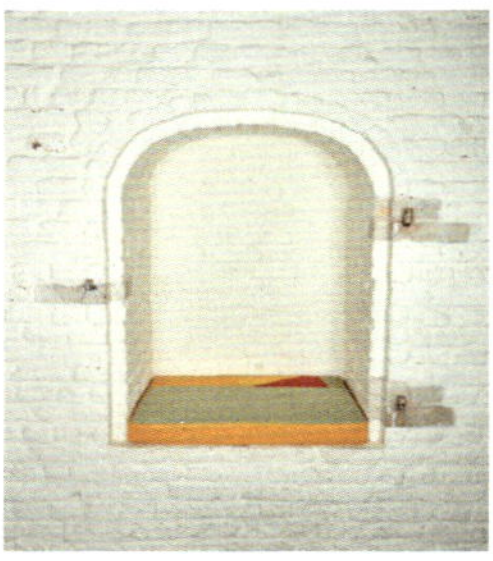

9

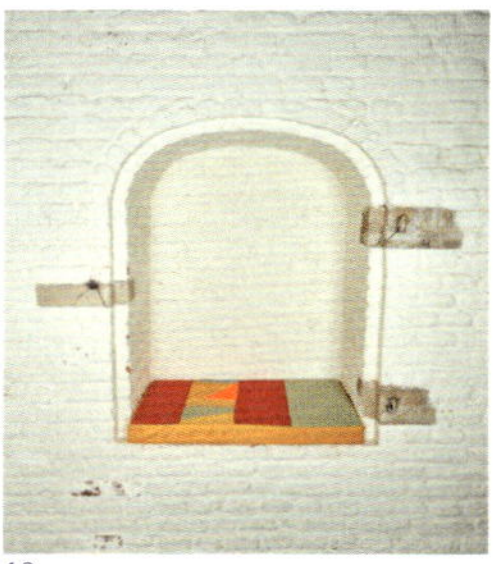

10

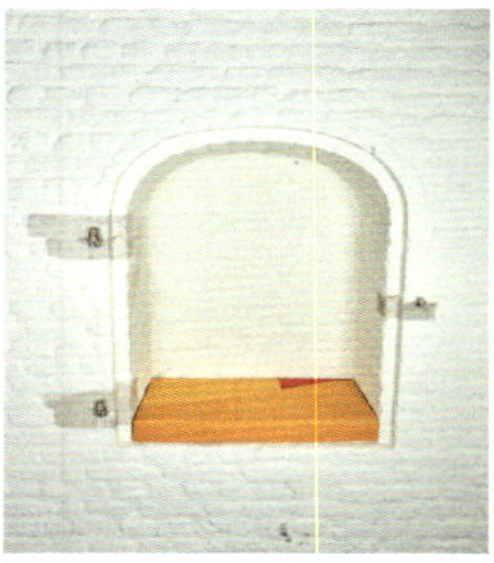

11

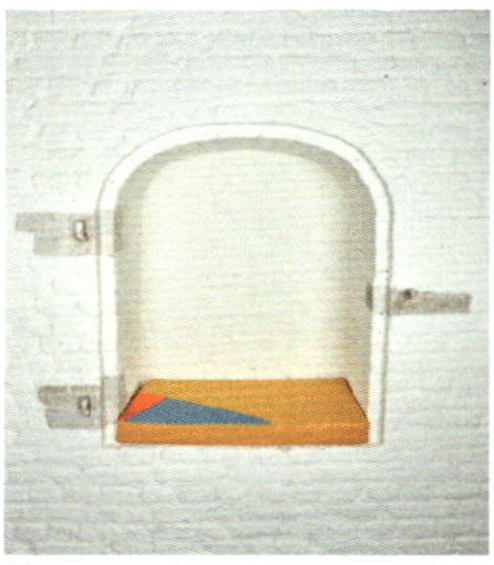

12

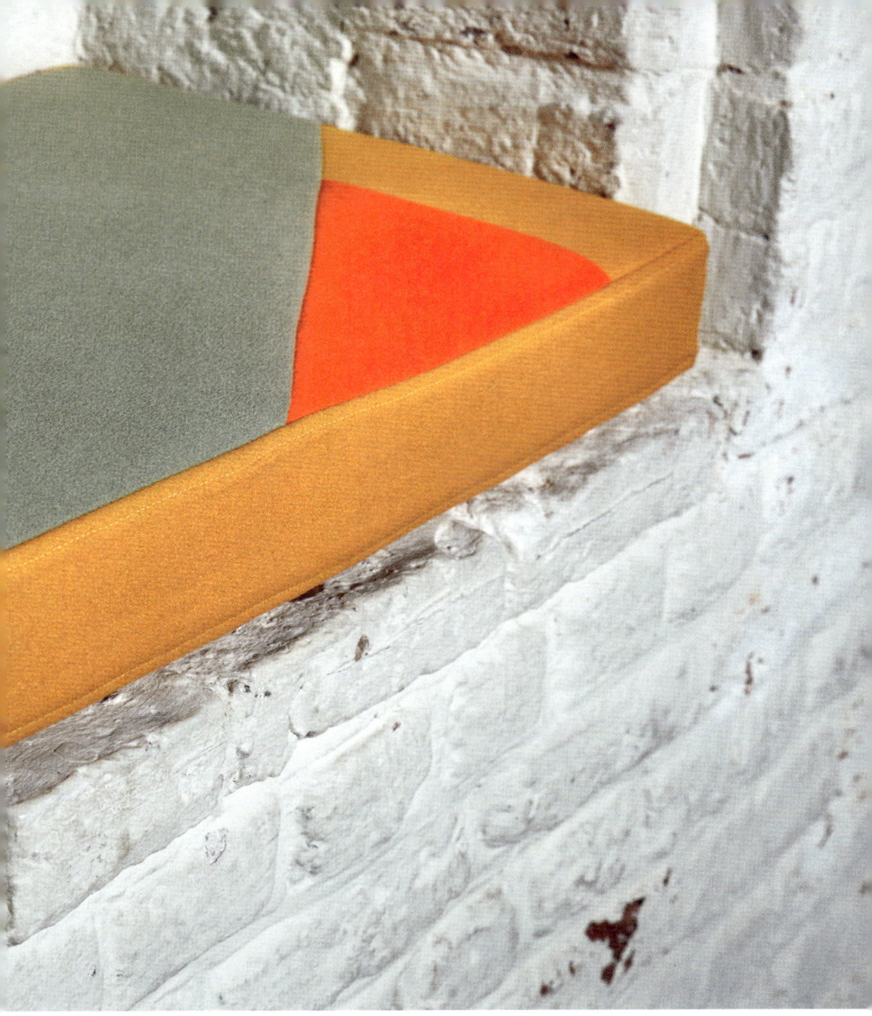

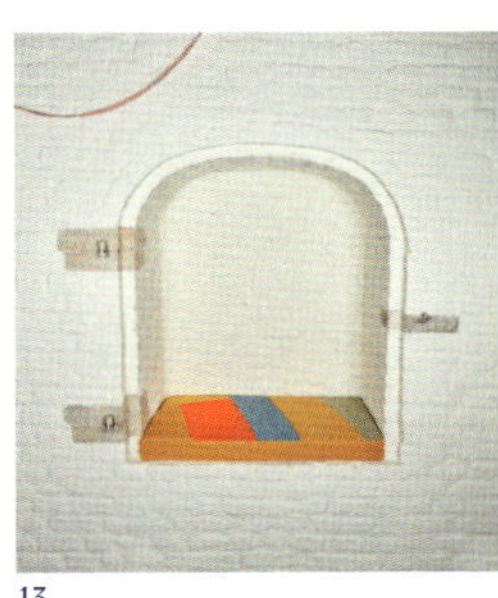

13

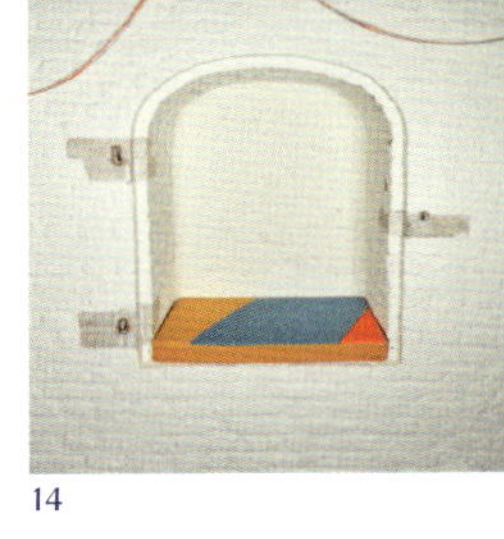

14

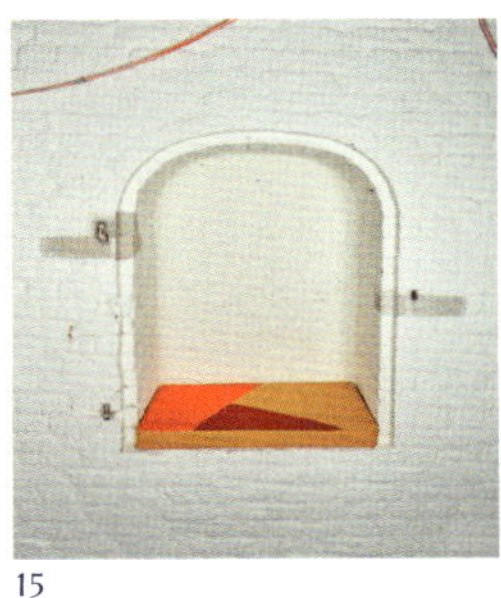

15

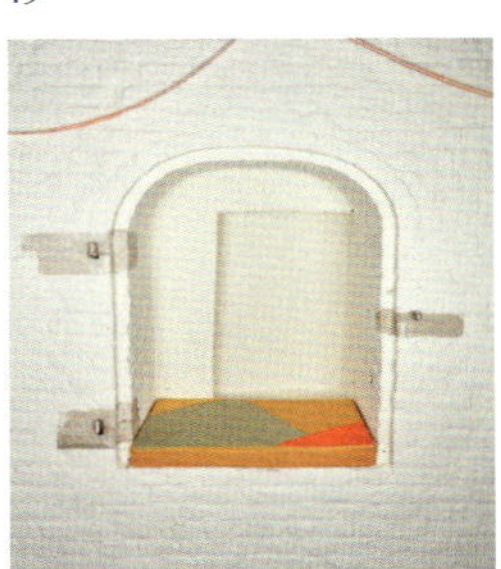

16

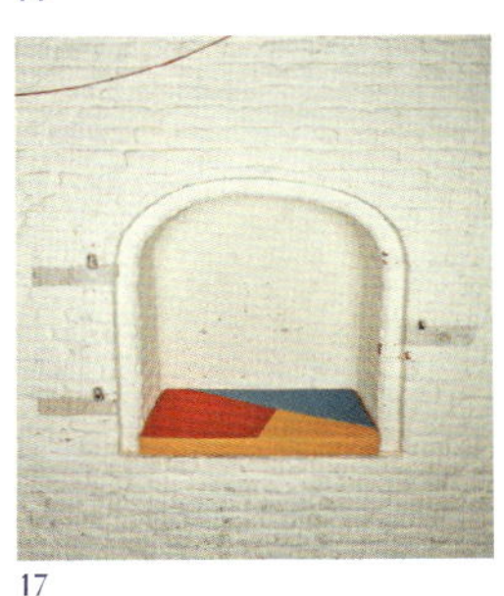

17

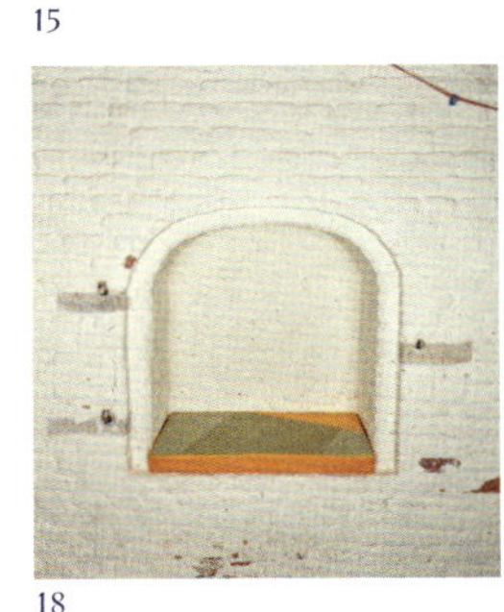

18

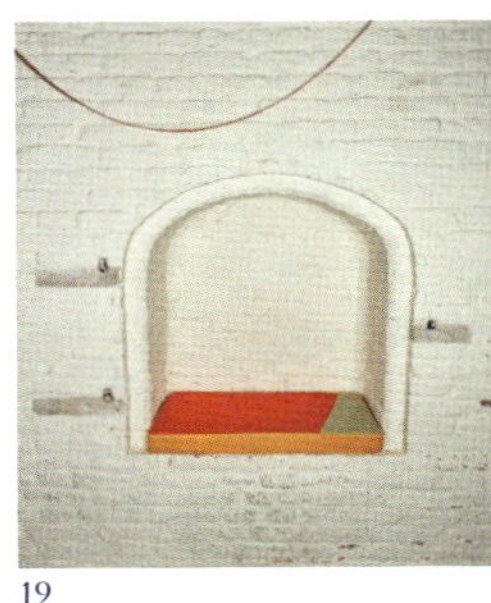

19

alcove cushions (2021)
Broadcloth, polyester thread, foam
20 alcove-sized cushions

Dimensions: width front × width back × depth × height
1–10 installed on the east of the exhibition space
11–20 installed on the west of the exhibition space

1.   77 × 75 × 42 × 8 cm
2.   78 × 75 × 43 × 8 cm
3.   77 × 76 × 43 × 8 cm
4.   77 × 76 × 42 × 8 cm
5.   79 × 78 × 47 × 8 cm
6.   77 × 77 × 46 × 8 cm
7.   78 × 77 × 45 × 8 cm
8.   78 × 77 × 45 × 8 cm
9.   76 × 74 × 44 × 8 cm
10. 77 × 78 × 45 × 8 cm
11. 78 × 78 × 41 × 8 cm
12. 77 × 78 × 43 × 8 cm
13. 79 × 77 × 42 × 8 cm
14. 77 × 76 × 43 × 8 cm
15. 77 × 77 × 43 × 8 cm
16. 77 × 77 × 43 × 8 cm
17. 77 × 75 × 37 × 8 cm
18. 75 × 75 × 37 × 8 cm
19. 79 × 76 × 38 × 8 cm
20. 78 × 78 × 38 × 8 cm

Exhibition invitation and booklet designed by Marianne Noordzij

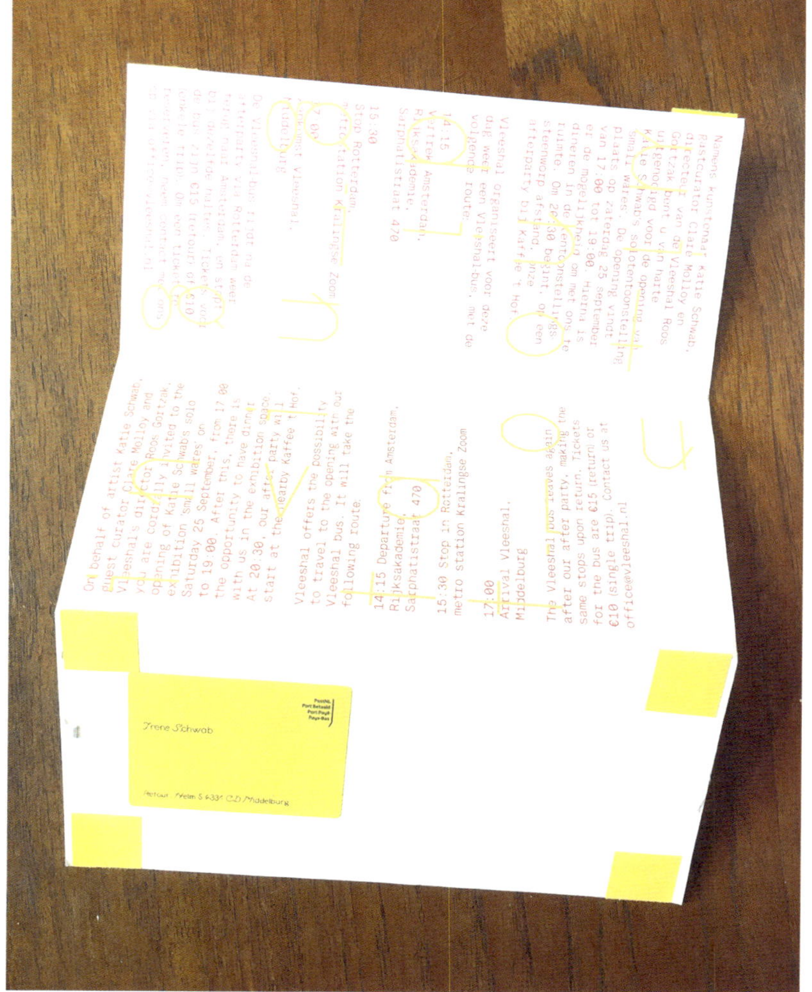

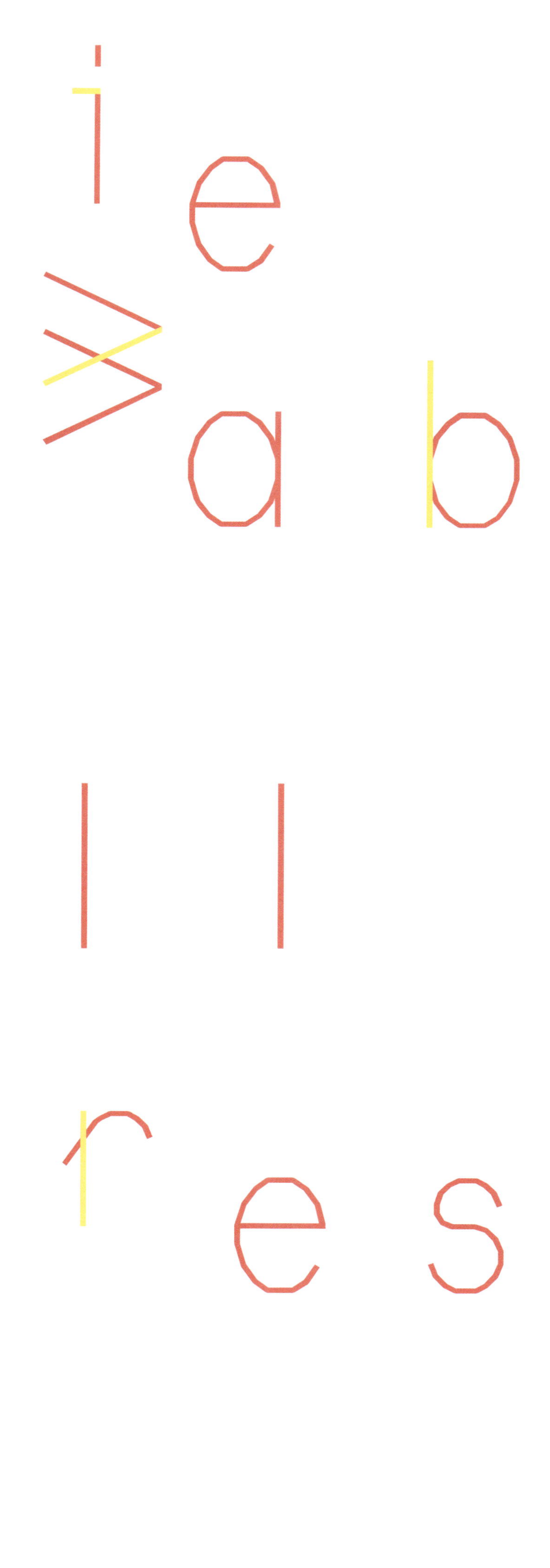

3   *strength study* (2021)
Cotton bias binding, polyester thread, powder coated steel
740 x 246 cm

Directly above Vleeshal there used to be a cloth market (*lakenhal*). *strength study* descends from the vaulted ceiling, alluding to this former space of textile trading. *strength study* is constructed from bias binding, a small ware that is cut at a 45° angle for durability, and is often used for hemming. In *strength study* bias binding is freed of its concealed supporting role. Both the front and back of the work can be seen and its construction is on display. *strength study* was created using domestic tools: scissors, a ruler, an iron, threads and a sewing machine. It was pieced together in an improvised pattern, using an intuitive logic akin to the process of quilt making.

When researching the Vleeshal's history of repair, Schwab encountered a photograph of the war damaged façade being held up by wooden scaffolding. This image influenced the proportions of *strength study*, a vertical textile at architectural scale. Light passes through the geometric gauze-like patterns, drawing a parallel to the sun passing through Vleeshal's leaded windows. The subtle yellow and rose hues of the stained glass inspired the work's palette.

Rebecca Lewin; Catherine Long; Alix de Massiac; Gunnar Meier; the Molloys; Franziska Mueller Schmidt; Geeske Pluijmers; Nanda Runge; Maki Suzuki, Åbäke; Michiel Vermet; Veva van der Wolf, TextielLab; and the women and girls behind the darning samplers.

small wares is dedicated to the strength of Irene Schwab.

4   *patches* (2021)
Wool offcuts, polyester thread
30 × 10 cm, 40 × 34 cm

In autumn the Vleeshal's entrance is cloaked in a heavy curtain. Katie Schwab has patched the tears on the bottom of this hardworking textile using zigzag techniques that prevent a fabric from fraying. *patches* is a study of the zigzag machine-stitch and the saw toothed cuts made by pinking shears. *patches* acknowledges and strengthens that which has been torn, damaged or simply worn-out.

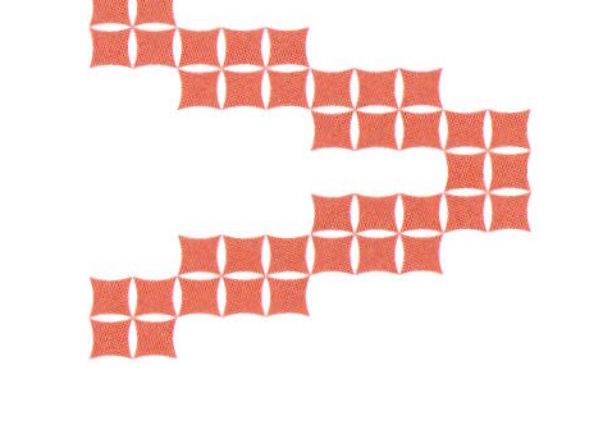

Vleeshal, Center for
Contemporary Art

Markt 1, Middelburg, NL
www.vleeshal.nl
open: Wed—Fri 13—17:00
Sat—Sun 11—17:00

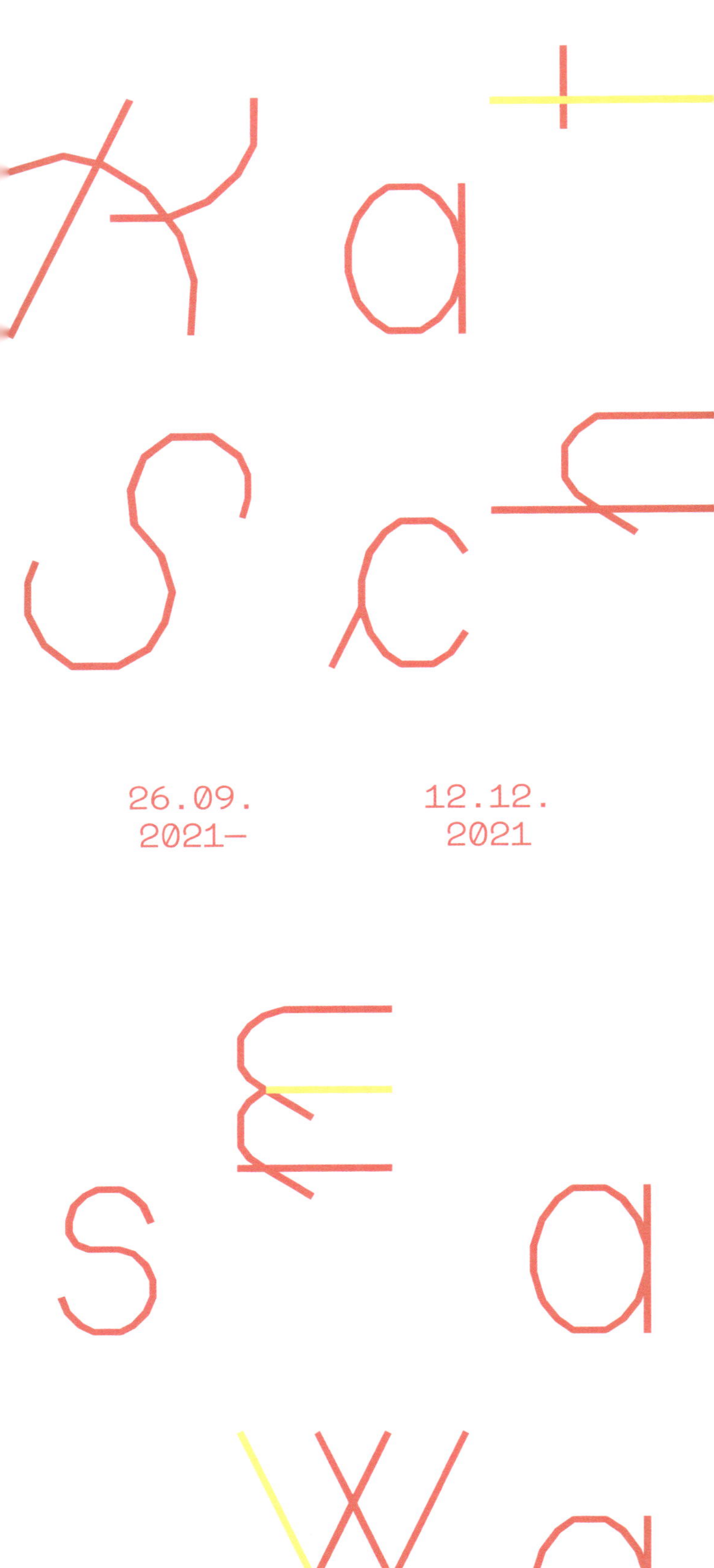
Kat
Sch
26.09.
2021–
12.12.
2021
s
a
w
guest curator
Clare Molloy
public
programme
11.12.
2021

INTRODUCTION
Ribbons, looms and 18th century Dutch
darning samplers are the starting
points for *small wares*, the solo
exhibition by Katie Schwab (*1985,
London, UK). "Small wares" is the
trade term for narrow textiles used
for reinforcing seams and preventing
fabrics from unravelling. These
unassuming articles, which often
remain invisible and yet lend a
garment strength, are referenced in
Schwab's new body of work.

The ability to repair textiles by
hand was once commonplace across the
Netherlands. In the aftermath of
industrialisation this has become an
increasingly rare skill. Schwab's
research into hand-sewn repair techniques focused on darning samplers
(*stoplappen*) in archives in Zutphen,
Leeuwarden and the Zeeuws Museum,
Middelburg. Created by young girls,
these embroidered linen cloths
document methods of invisible mending
rendered in brightly coloured threads.

Alongside the importance of textile
histories, another key reference is
the Vleeshal site, a late-gothic
building that was severely damaged by
a fire during WWII. During its postwar
reconstruction, the architectural
rubble was encased in wood and concrete to create the Vleeshal's new
foundations. The building's former
trauma was transformed, becoming its
source of strength. Taking this
hidden history as a metaphor and a
methodology, *small wares* is a subtle
examination of invisible strength and
processes of repair.

EXHIBITION EDITION
Katie Schwab's practice operates at
the intersections of art, craft and
design. For Vleeshal she has created
small wares & *hard wares* (2021),
an exhibition edition of 30. Each
signed edition consists of a custom
hook, made in the UK with SWARF, and
a screen printed organic tea towel
designed by Marianne Noordzij from
Werkplaats Typografie, Arnhem. The
edition objects function together
and apart, and are ready to be used
in everyday life. The edition is
available at Vleeshal and via the
online shop.

cm each

cushions
vitation for
small wares
usual vantage
itting inside
ou are welcome
the woollen
The choice of
cknowledges the
that has con-
Netherlands and
e the 14th cen-
JK exported wool
Lands, where it
d woven into

alcove cushions
are made from broad-
cloth, a wide woollen
fabric created by Hainsworth
in Yorkshire, who handle the
entire production from
fleece to fabric. The sides
of *alcove cushions* are cut
from golden-ochre broadcloth.
The cushion tops have been
sewn from off-cuts known
as "fents", commonly considered a waste product by
the textile industry. Schwab
sees their value and restores
their status. She has pieced
the fents together diagonally,
creating abstract patterns
in sage, blue, orange and red.

teel

giant darning cloth, the three ribbons of
ross the walls. Katie Schwab wove this small
van der Wolf at the TextielLab in Tilburg.
om 1880, the ribbons incorporate a myriad
on and linen. The weft of the ribbons
ured repair stitching on Dutch darning
t pinks of the warp make reference to the
lant-dye madder, which was historically
nk and navy threads trace repairs to places
production process.

across the wall follows a specific score:
es in the masonry. Kees Wijker, Vleeshal's
the "scars of Vleeshal". Having installed
1990s, he has an embodied knowledge of
sanded down or left open. Intrigued by
Schwab created bespoke blue hardware
er coated steel hooks were developed with
coves' wrought iron bolt-holes.

Brattinga and Marianne Noordzij,
Werkplaats Typografie; Filip
Caranica; Peder Clark; Jim Hayman,
Cotton Smiles; Marieke De Jongh,
Musea Zutphen; Edwards Upholstery;
Jantiene van Elk, Wilma Kieboom and
Elles van Vegchel, TextielMuseum; Sam
Fish, SWARF; Jeffrey Graham, William
Gee; Hainsworth; Alexia Holt, Cove
Park; Karina Leijnse, Zeeuws Museum;

1   *alcove cushions* (2021)
     Broadcloth, polyester thread, foam
     20 alcove sized cushions, c. 77 × 43 × 8

         In shaping ex-   *alcove
      hibitions, Katie Schwab   are an i
     pays close attention to   you to vie
     the materials, histories and   from the u
     forms already present in   point of s
     the space, and carefully   the wall.
     considers the way the works   to sit on
     are encountered in relation   cushions.
     to the body. Built origi-   material a
     nally as a meat market, the   wool trade
     Vleeshal's thick walls and   nected the
     flagstones intentionally   the UK sin
     keep the space cool. The   tury. The
     word "RVND", meaning beef,   to the Low
     can still be found carved   was dyed a
     into the floor. The alcoves,   tapestries
     with their heavy oak doors,
     were used by the traders as
     cupboards to keep knives or
     money safely shut away.

2   *small wares & hard wares* (2021)
     Cotton, silk, linen, powder coated s
     Dimensions variable

         Treating Vleeshal's brickwork as a
          small wares & hard wares dance ac
         ware with passementerie expert Veva
          Created on a band-weaving loom fr
         of stripes and holes in silk, cott
          is informed by the brightly colo
         samplers. The vivid oranges and sof
          array of colours produced by the
         grown across the Zeeland region. Pi
          where the warp snapped during the

          The pattern that the ribbon take
         it only hangs from pre-existing ho
         head technician, calls these marks
         exhibitions in the space since the
         where the holes have been filled-in
          this layer of architectural repai
         for these holes. Laser cut and powd
         SWARF, their form nodding to the a

ACKNOWLEDGEMENTS

With thanks to:
Leandra Bos, Roos Gortzak, Hanna
Verhulst, Luuk Vulkers and Kees
Wijker, Vleeshal.

The artist's family and friends;
Gieneke Arnolli; Johanna van
Benthem and Reinier Salverda; Anniek

PUBLICATION
The first institutional publication on the artist's practice, *Katie Schwab*: *Sample Book*, is forthcoming, co-published by Vleeshal and Dent-de-Leone, edited by Clare Molloy and designed by transdisciplinary graphic design collective, Åbäke.

EDUCATION
There is a free educational activity for kids available at our desk. For more information on our educational workshops, please contact: educatie@vleeshal.nl

PRESS
For press requests, please contact Leandra Bos: leandra@vleeshal.nl

GUEST CURATOR
Clare Molloy

TEAM VLEESHAL
Director: Roos Gortzak
Management assistant: Hanna Verhulst
Assistant curator: Luuk Vulkers
Head technician: Kees Wijker
Marketing & communication: Leandra Bos
Hosts: Theresa Schipper (head), Lotte Dooms, Hannah Dupré, Ruth Hengeveld, Nick Koper, Auke van Laar, Ploen Mevis, Daphne de Reu, Suzan van de Ven, Maaike Wisse

GRAPHIC DESIGNER
Marianne Noordzij, Werkplaats Typografie, Arnhem

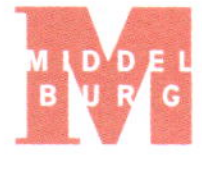
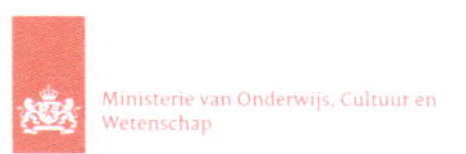

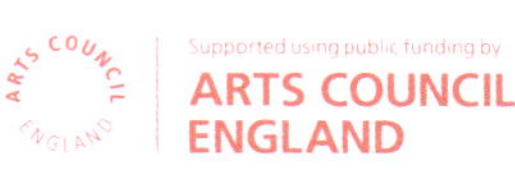

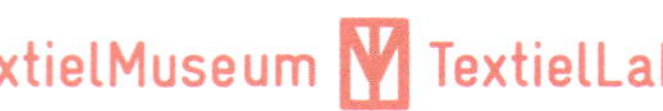

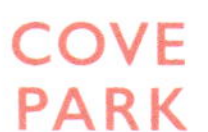

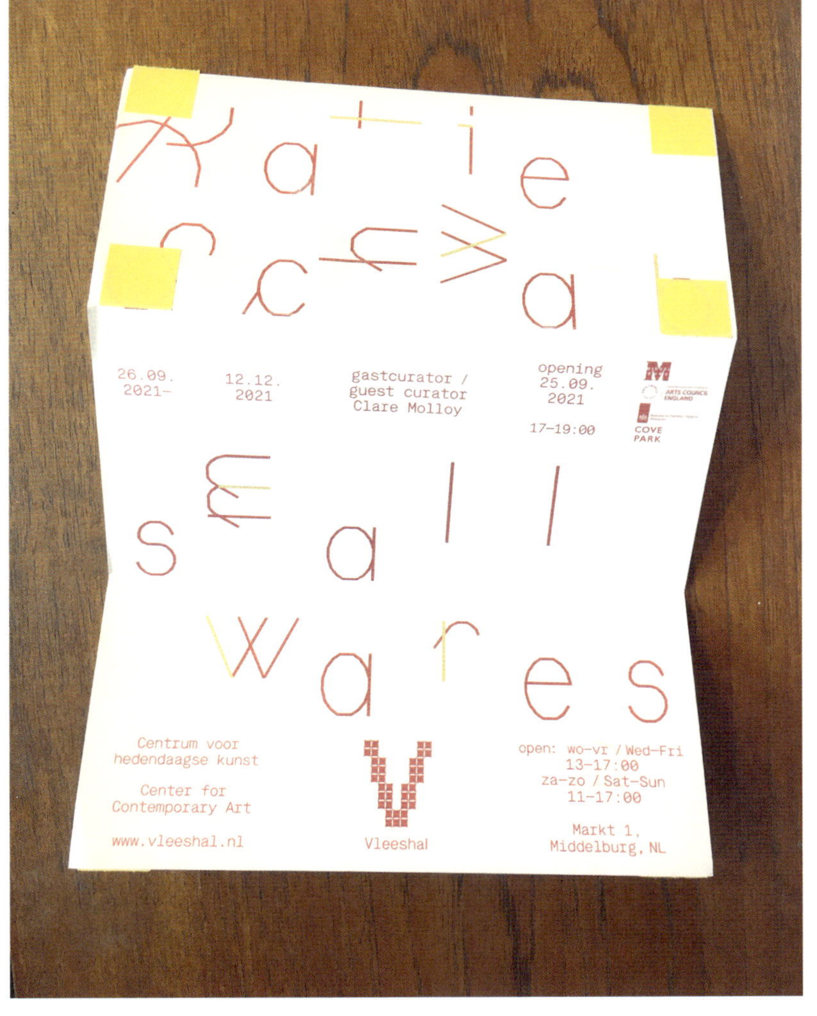
Katie
chwal
small
wares
26.09.
2021–
12.12.
2021
gastcurator /
guest curator
Clare Molloy
opening
25.09.
2021
17–19:00
ARTS COUNCIL
ENGLAND
COVE
PARK
Centrum voor
hedendaagse kunst
Center for
Contemporary Art
www.vleeshal.nl
Vleeshal
open: wo-vr / Wed-Fri
13–17:00
za-zo / Sat-Sun
11–17:00
Markt 1,
Middelburg, NL

The Source
and Course of
Brabantine Gothic

Michiel Huijben

It's a crisp but sunny morning in the early spring of 1455. In a stone quarry northeast of Brussels, dust particles dance in the morning light, shimmering in mid-air. The sharp, high-pitched sound of chipping stone bounces off the rocky walls and returns from every corner. A hand picks up a brick from one of the large, neat piles dotted around the premises. This is our brick. Brushing over its linen-coloured surface it feels coarse like sandpaper, marked all over with flecks and dents and scuffs. The bright sun makes it appear almost bone white.

This pale, chalky sandstone is only found here, in the south of the Duchy of Brabant, where it's mined from the 44-million-year-old Lede rock formation underfoot. It's soft and malleable, easy to cut. A mineral transformed into bricks, a material turned into objects: the perfect size and shape to be handled by a mason.

Actually, the hand holding our brick does belong to a mason: a master mason named Andries Keldermans. He has been sent here by the Middelburg City Council to buy more stone for their new city hall, the construction of which began four years ago.

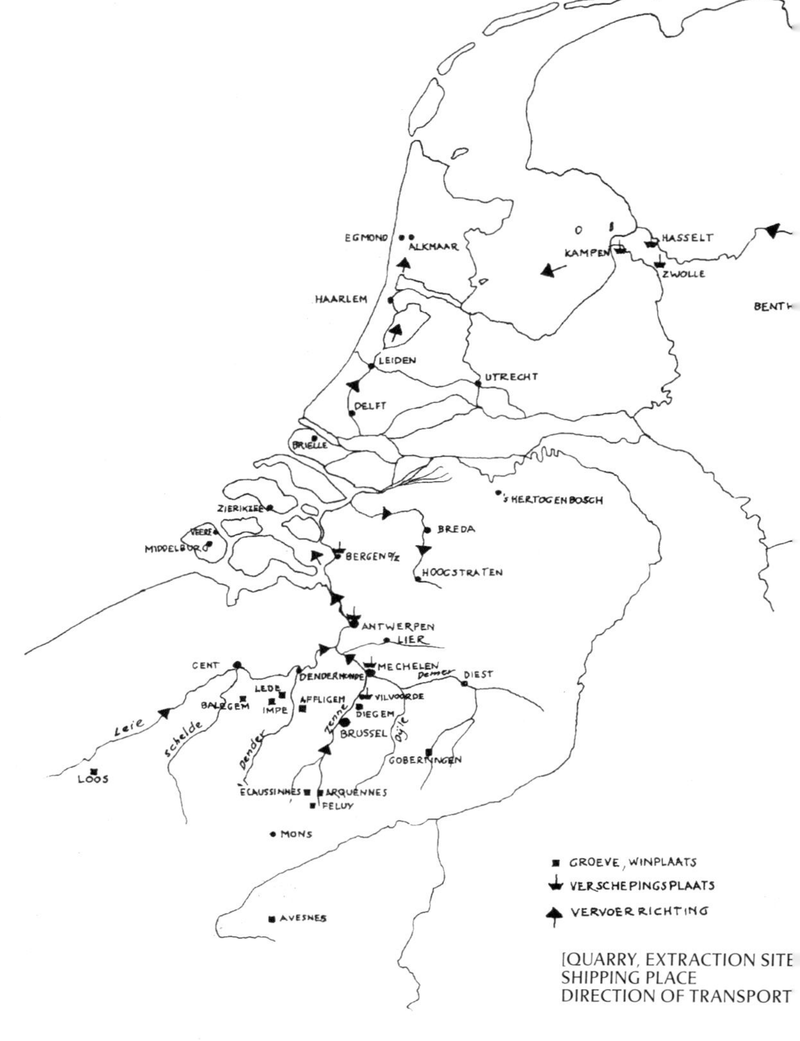

[QUARRY, EXTRACTION SITE
SHIPPING PLACE
DIRECTION OF TRANSPORT

River Scheldt
Transportation of natural stone and stone carvings at the
time of the Keldermans family

Coming from a lineage of architects, sculptors and masons, Andries knows this stone well. In fact, his family's business model depends on it: the Keldermans family is well known in Brabant for building cathedrals, churches and city halls from this very material. Their work is tied closely to the region and they supply all of their building plans, raw materials and even sculpted ornaments from their own quarries and workshops around the cities of Brussels and Mechelen. It's this level of efficiency that earned generations of the Keldermans family a considerable amount of fame and money.

Indeed, their success is owed more to their entrepreneurial skill than to architectural originality. After all, their signature style, Brabantine Gothic, is clearly just a variation on the classic French Gothic. But, in contrast to buildings like the Notre-Dame de Paris or the Reims Cathedral, those graceful structures that reach confidently skyward, the Keldermans' adaptations are squat and often seem wider than they are tall. As if to make up for a lack of classical grace, they're richly decorated with sculptures carved from Lede stone by one of the Keldermans brothers, who all trained as masons.

Andries scrapes the brick with his thumbnail and blows the dust off its surface. He looks at the fresh marking and nods. Putting the brick back on the pile, he places a large order with the quarry master.

***

With the wind in its sails, a boat sets off for the city of Middelburg, a journey that will take less than a day. At twenty metres long, this boat, a *pleit*, carries piles and piles of Lede bricks under its hatches – and nestled among them lies ours. As it travels down the Scheldt our brick passes the fortified walls of Antwerp, sounds of the bustling city escaping from beyond them. When the boat turns into the Scheldt Estuary, the scenery changes. A landscape of meadows pans by slowly, every now and then obstructed by a wall of reeds. Soon, the boat will head westward to the port of Middelburg.

The way there is heavily trafficked with similar boats. In recent centuries, the river system connected to the Scheldt Delta has given merchants access to a host of local markets, transforming the river into a busy trade route. Carrying sacks of rye or wheat, bales of cloth, or large kegs filled to the brim with wine, merchant boats impatiently make their way downstream. At every market town along the way, they dock to sell their goods.

***

It's a market day in Middelburg and the town square is bustling with people wandering from stall to stall or standing around, chatting in small groups. The square is covered with the lingering,

109

pungent smells of wine, milk and leather, mixed with mud and shit. Farmers from out of town sell their eggs and grains to buy the beer and bread they will take back home. Vendors shout from behind their tables to bring attention to their wares. A cow walks around calmly, undisturbed by the chaos.

In the background, the shrill clank of a blacksmith's hammer sounds across the square with the persistence of a metronome. The construction of the city hall is well under way. Some market-goers look up as ornaments are fixed to its exterior. Gothic niches, worked into the walls, await their future occupants; statues of the region's dukes and duchesses. With every floor, the façade grows denser and denser with the arches, spires and leafy capitals typical of the Gothic style.

Because its exteriors are so perforated by windows and openings, and traced with columns and ornamentation, some say that Gothic architecture is made in spite of the brick. As Gothic buildings reach up towards the heavens, the eye is dazzled not by solid, modular mass, but by an intricate structure of ornaments. Inside, light floods in through stained-glass windows.

On the ground floor of Middelburg City Hall, however, the walls are thick, the windows high up and half shuttered. With construction fast advancing, the future meat market at the back of the building is crowded with workers. Masons climb up and down the heavy wooden scaffold that supports the vaulted ceiling. When a shout blares down from the scaffold, two men on the ground start pulling the extruding spokes on a large wheel to make it turn and a pulley hoists up another stack of bricks. Around them, sunlight creeps in through the windows and, in between the slim pillars of light touching down on the floor, a mason pants as he kneels by one of the thick walls. He picks up a brick from a pile to his side. Our brick has arrived in Middelburg.

At first, Lede bricks are only found close to the Keldermans' quarries, but when their work begins to follow the trade route of the River Scheldt, it gradually advances downstream. Wherever merchant boats pull into a harbour, they are almost always met with a Keldermans building – the river commanding the course of Brabantine Gothic.

The mason lays the brick into the wall and tops it with another one, and then one more, and then another. He pauses to wipe the dust from his eyes and resumes his rhythm; picking up and laying down each individual brick. As the mason keeps stacking, our brick recedes into the wall, disappearing into the whole with each additional block of Lede stone.

Katie Schwab: Learning by Working[1]

Rebecca Lewin

Katie Schwab makes work that is thoroughly collaborative,
from the research she undertakes to the processes she employs.
Voices, skills and knowledge from other artists and makers,
from interview subjects – even from curators and friends such
as myself – are allowed to inform and even direct aspects of the
artworks she makes and the spaces they inhabit. Visiting one
of her exhibitions might require the drawing aside of a curtain
in order to sit on a chair or rug to watch a film – a series of
movements that choreograph visitors' bodies while simultaneously
bringing them into direct contact with her works. This necessary
interaction also results in a co-produced experience, in which
the elements Schwab has brought together encourage repose
and focused observation, not just of her own interventions
but also of the architecture that holds them, an outcome that
is reflective of her larger project: to investigate materials and
processes in order to reveal the politics and infrastructure that
has brought them together.

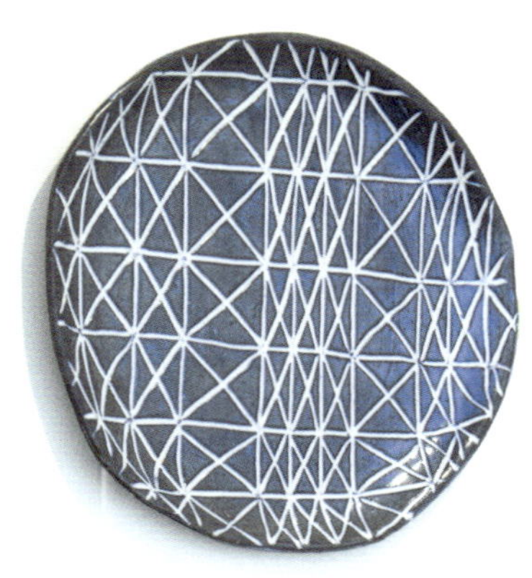
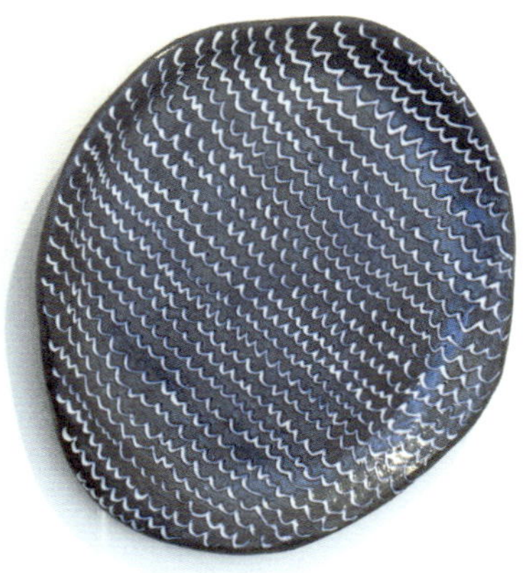

Alexei (2013), *Nisha* (2013)
Glazed stoneware, dimensions variable
Installation view, *The Palace of Green Porcelain*, Breese Little, London, 2013

Hardwood mainly from Africa, some from South America, but all the veneer in the Chamber is from Burma.

Still from *Civic Centre/City Centre* (2019)

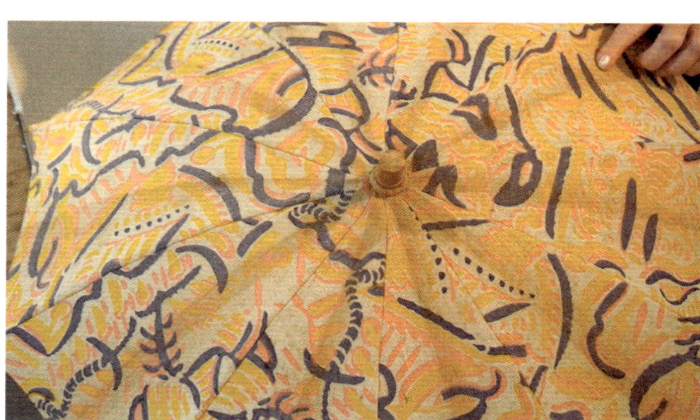

Still from *This Interesting and Wonderful Factory* (2019)

In addition to intentionally blurring the edges of her own authorship, Schwab is acutely aware of her position within the art world's capitalist project of global culture, wherein materials and objects of high value are shipped context-free around the world, and has developed a protocol of resistance to it. An invitation to make new work prompts her to begin research into the history of industrial or craft production in the region where a gallery or museum is located. She then conducts a series of site visits: to the gallery itself, to local civic museums, to craft shops, even to charity shops. She wants to understand how and where her own interests in the aesthetics of post-war design and especially the invisible labour of female makers might intersect with the inherited experiences of an area's inhabitants and with the materiality of their daily lives.

The open-ended outcomes of her research always respond to the variety of source material that she encounters. When I invited her to collaborate with sound artist Dan Scott on the exhibition that later became *The Palace of Green Porcelain* at Breese Little, London in 2013, their conversations around the impressibility of clay as a sonic recording device led to the production of a series of ceramic objects that were named after friends with whom she had discussed the project, or simply spent time with. I was struck by the continuity of Schwab's thinking, linking the properties of clay and her own body as a vessel that transferred the impressions she had gathered from the people she was spending time with back onto plates, pots and abstract forms. Her project for The Gallery at Plymouth College of Art in 2019, titled *A Working Building*, brought together the responses of local students to the architecture and design of buildings in Plymouth that are in part responsible for organising their lives, with her own responses to the design details of those buildings. This film, titled *Civic Centre/City Centre* (2019) was placed alongside another film, *This Interesting and Wonderful Factory*, also made in 2019, which responded to the material output of another location, the Cryséde textile factory in Newlyn and later St Ives, in the neighbouring county of Cornwall that was active in the 1920s and 1930s. Both films quietly observe the extractive and exploitative legacies of the British Empire that are embedded in everything from hardwoods like Myanmarese Teak and African Muhuhu included in architectural details in Plymouth, to the names of fabric designs produced at Cryséde.

In Middelburg, for the development of her exhibition *small wares* at Vleeshal in 2021, Schwab came upon a collection of eighteenth-century *stoplappen*, or darning samplers, in the local Zeeuws Museum, the colours of which became a reference point for her palette. A nineteenth-century loom located at the TextielLab in Tilburg offered a starting point for her decision to weave a ribbon, and her investigation into madder, a plant dye that had been grown across the Zeeland region for centuries further informed her colour choices. Extensive exploration of the Vleeshal building and conversations with its current team, particularly Kees Wijkers, whose physical and institutional memory of the marks left on the space by the installation of previous exhibitions determined her selection of hanging points from which her own work could be installed. Her decision to respond to the site and make use of its history rather than impose

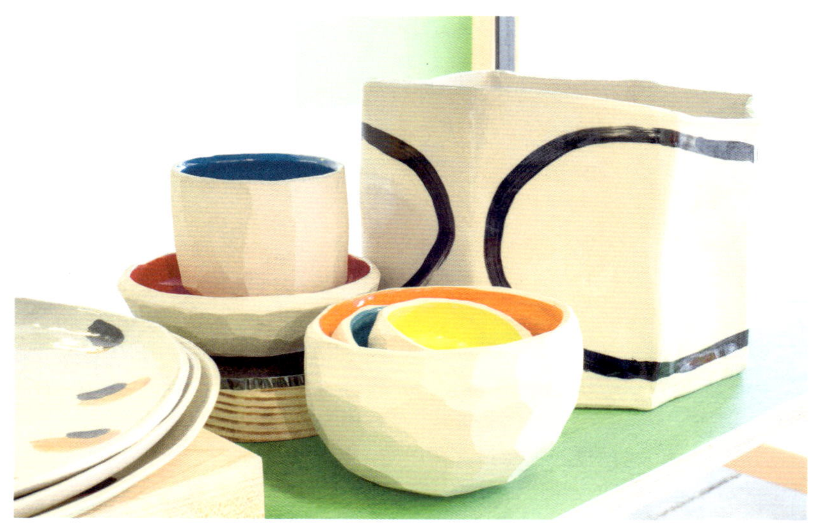

Installation view, *Making the Bed, Laying the Table*, Florence Dwyer,
Katie Schwab, Simon Worthington, Glasgow Sculpture Studios, Glasgow, 2016

or import demands allowed her to minimise her own impact on Vleeshal, while simultaneously drawing attention to the site's history and the care and exertions of its staff.

Schwab has always woven together existing materialities with her own creative interventions, an approach that also speaks to her concern with histories of labour. She describes much of her work as stemming from a long-standing interest in "craft histories that have been overlooked, maybe [consigned to] the realm of 'women's work.'"[2] She is able to trace one of the origins of this interest to a set of wools and books on stitching, embroidery and tapestry inherited from her maternal grandmother, and to compare her grandmother's hobby with her own position as an artist. Craft, as it has long been perceived in the West, could be described as the offspring of the uneasy relationship between paid and unpaid labour. As writer and activist Silvia Federici remarked in 1975, "to re-appropriate that money which is the fruit of our labour – of our mothers' and grandmothers' labour – means at the same time to undermine capital's power to command forced labour from us."[3]

Schwab's response has been to not only shed light on the kinds of techniques practised on a domestic scale, but also to question her own role as an individuated author. Sometimes she works alone, sometimes with others or as part of a collective, always learning from and crediting communities and experts, thereby making space for other hands, and other voices, to be made visible.

An exhibition from 2016 at Glasgow Sculpture Studios, *Making the Bed, Laying the Table* was largely populated by furniture that had been co-designed and made with artists Florence Dwyer and Simon Worthington. The three were housemates at the time, thinking about what furniture could populate a future form of communal living, while simultaneously using the economic and spatial possibilities provided by the exhibition to design for the present. *Together in a Room*, an exhibition at Collective, Edinburgh, also in 2016, saw Schwab experiment with some of the stitches learned from her grandmother's books or adapted from the work of Bauhaus weavers Anni Albers and Gunta Stölzl to produce a large embroidery, *Sampler* (2016) stitched on hessian using her Grandma's wool, a work that already signalled her interest in darning samplers. For Collective she also interviewed teachers, specialists and friends who had worked – or in my case, lived – with design processes in the 2016 film *Dedicated to my great teachers (Becky Lewin, St Catherine's College, Oxford; Madeleine Ladell, Phoenix Pottery, London; Mia Schwab, London)*. For Vleeshal, the work *small wares & hard wares* (2021) credited "passementerie expert Veva van der Wolf" and design elements, colours and patterns arose out of conversations with Van der Wolf, rather than being purely pre-determined by Schwab.[4]

The careful crediting of the collaborative labour involved in the production of an artwork is reflected in the way that Schwab draws on and embeds material processes. She has so far embraced ceramics, furniture design, enamel tiles, wallpaper, rug making, weaving and filmmaking. The enamel tiles included in the exhibition *A Working Building*, for instance, drew on the patterns

117

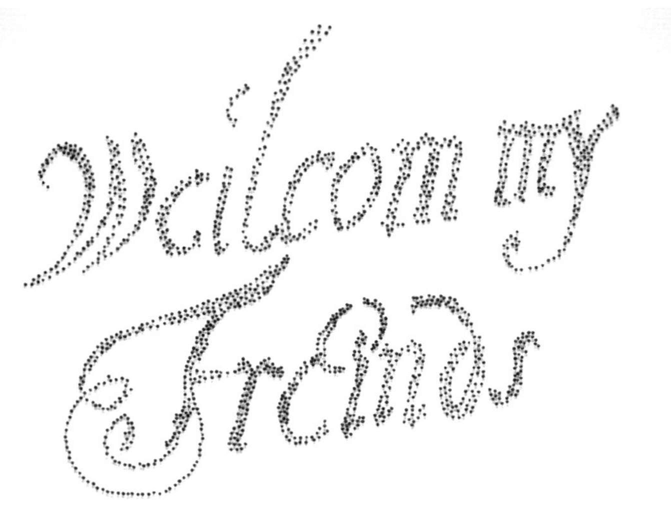

Weilcom my Freinds (2020)
Hand-forged steel nails, dimensions variable
Made in collaboration with Stephen Thompson
Installation view, *Another Crossing – Artists Revisit The Mayflower Voyage*, Fuller Craft Museum, Brockton, MA, 2021

of flooring in Plymouth City Council's building, and the colours of the bias binding of *strength study* (2021) were taken from the colours of stained glass in some of the Vleeshal's window panes. For one of the pieces she made for the group exhibition *Another Crossing* at Fuller Craft Museum in Massachusetts, which addresses the cultural influences, colonial legacies and exchanges brought about by the 1620 Mayflower voyage, Schwab commissioned a number of hand-forged nails from Plymouth maker Stephen Thompson. These were hammered into the gallery wall to read *Weilcom my Freinds*, the design of which she had found on a piece of English Delftware from 1661. By drawing on a largely lost skill to copy the design of an English plate that had itself borrowed techniques from the Netherlands, Schwab calls attention to the evolving network of knowledge that all craft – and by extension, visual culture – draws on to survive.

Schwab's foregrounding of collaboration throughout her practice is a radical approach that consciously moves away from the invisible labour of late capitalism. From an interrogation of the framework and infrastructure of locations, to the tracing of materials to their point of origin, and making visible the time and physical exertion of multiple bodies that are involved in all stages of production, she reminds us that the creation of objects and surfaces is simply the visible part of a collection of knowledge and materials, the origins of which reach far beyond the experience of the individual artist, the walls of the gallery or the temporality of the exhibition.

Notes

1. Anni Albers, "Design Anonymous and Timeless," *Magazine of Art* 40, no. 2 (1947): 51–53.

2. Katie Schwab, in conversation with the author, 19 November 2021.

3. Silvia Federici, *Wages Against Housework*, (Bristol: Falling Wall Press, 1975), 5.

4. *small wares*, (Middelburg: Vleeshal, 2021). Exhibition booklet.

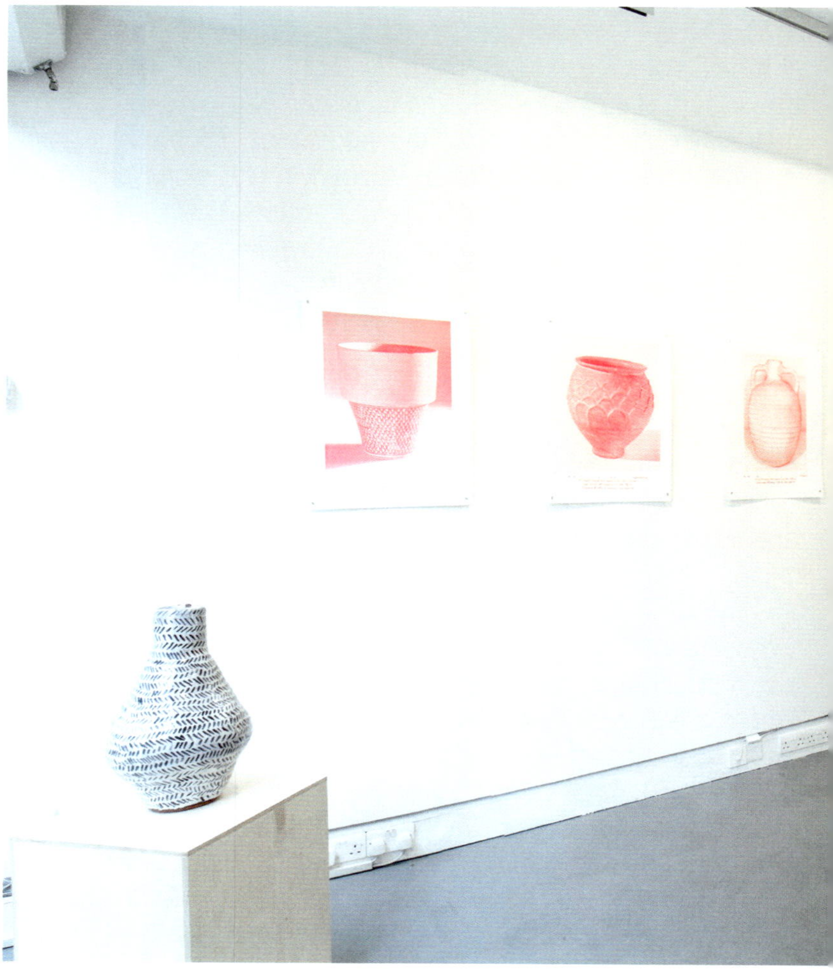

Installation view, *The Palace of Green Porcelain*, Breese Little, London, 2013

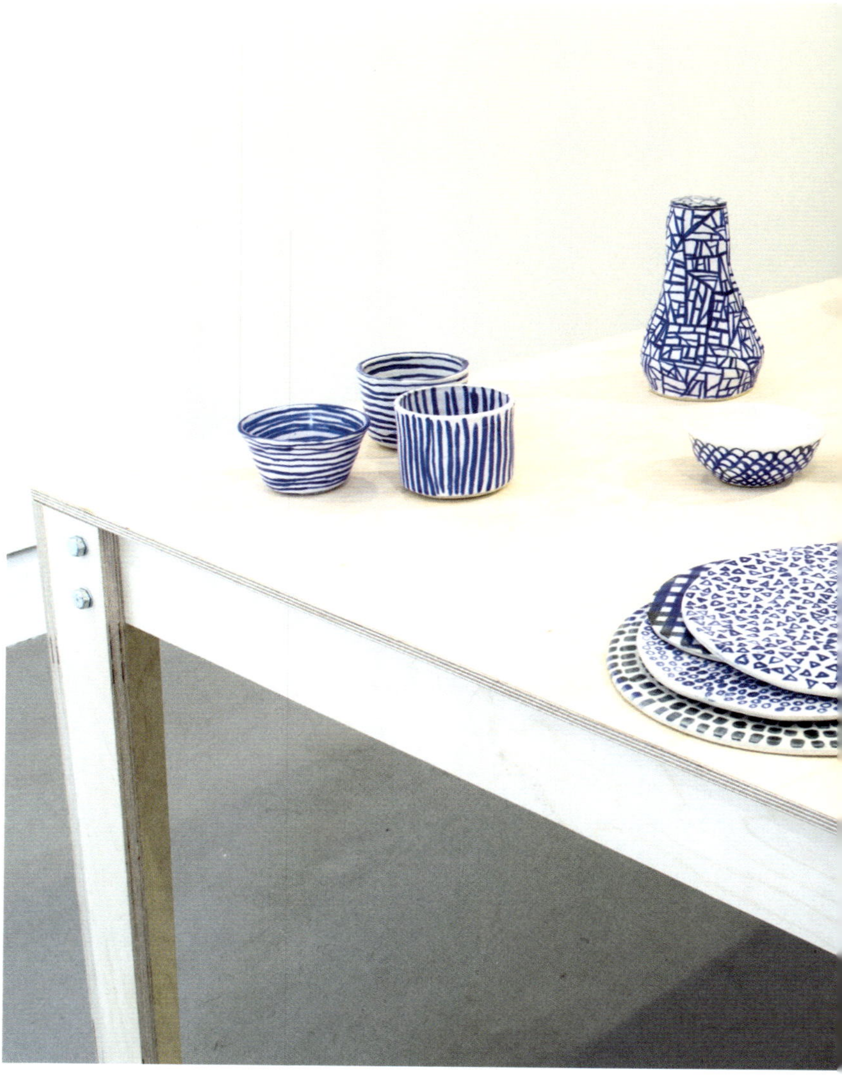

Elly, Ellie, Ella, Chloe, Monica, Ruth, Dave, Dan, Jonathan, Katy, Kitty, Kate, Rosanna, Melissa, Becky, Irene, Lizzie, Darcy, Amy, Antonia (2013)
Glazed stoneware, table by Jonathan Tibbs, dimensions variable
Installation view, *The Palace of Green Porcelain*, Breese Little, London, 2013

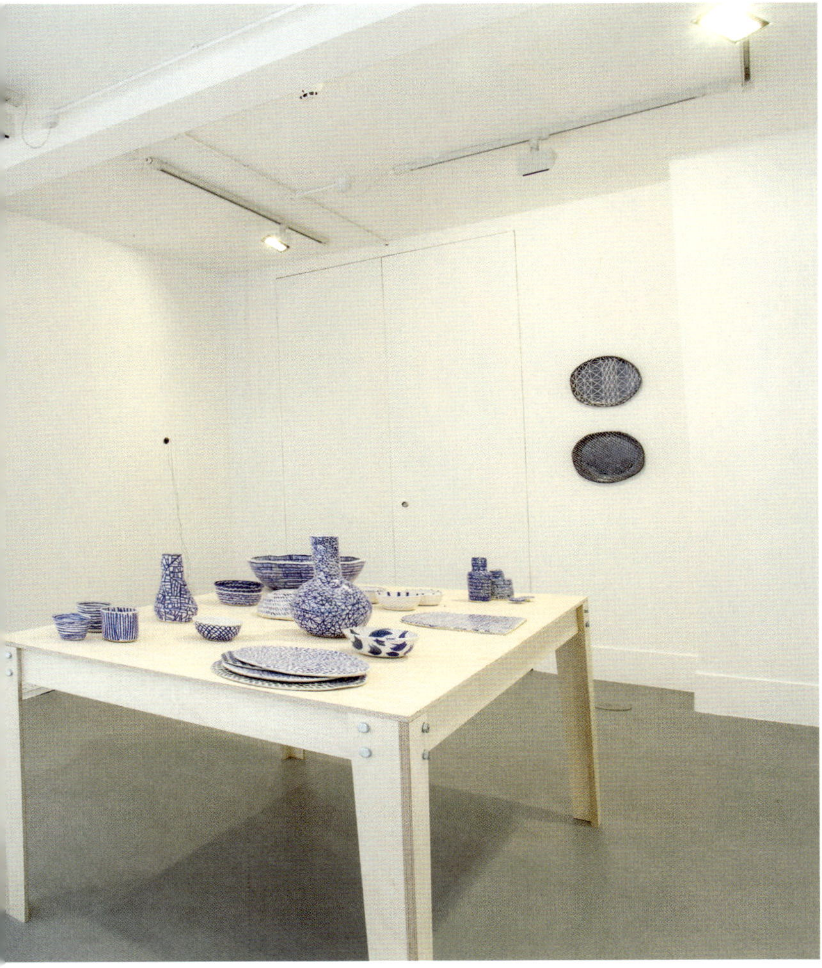

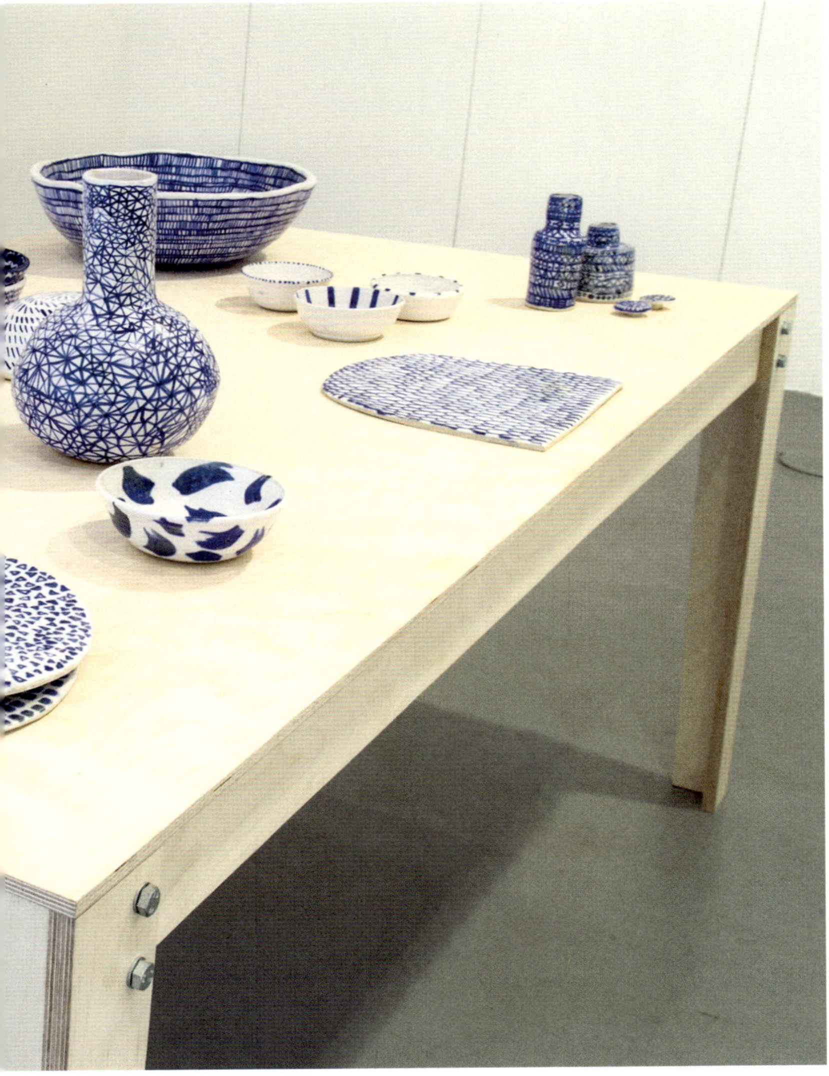

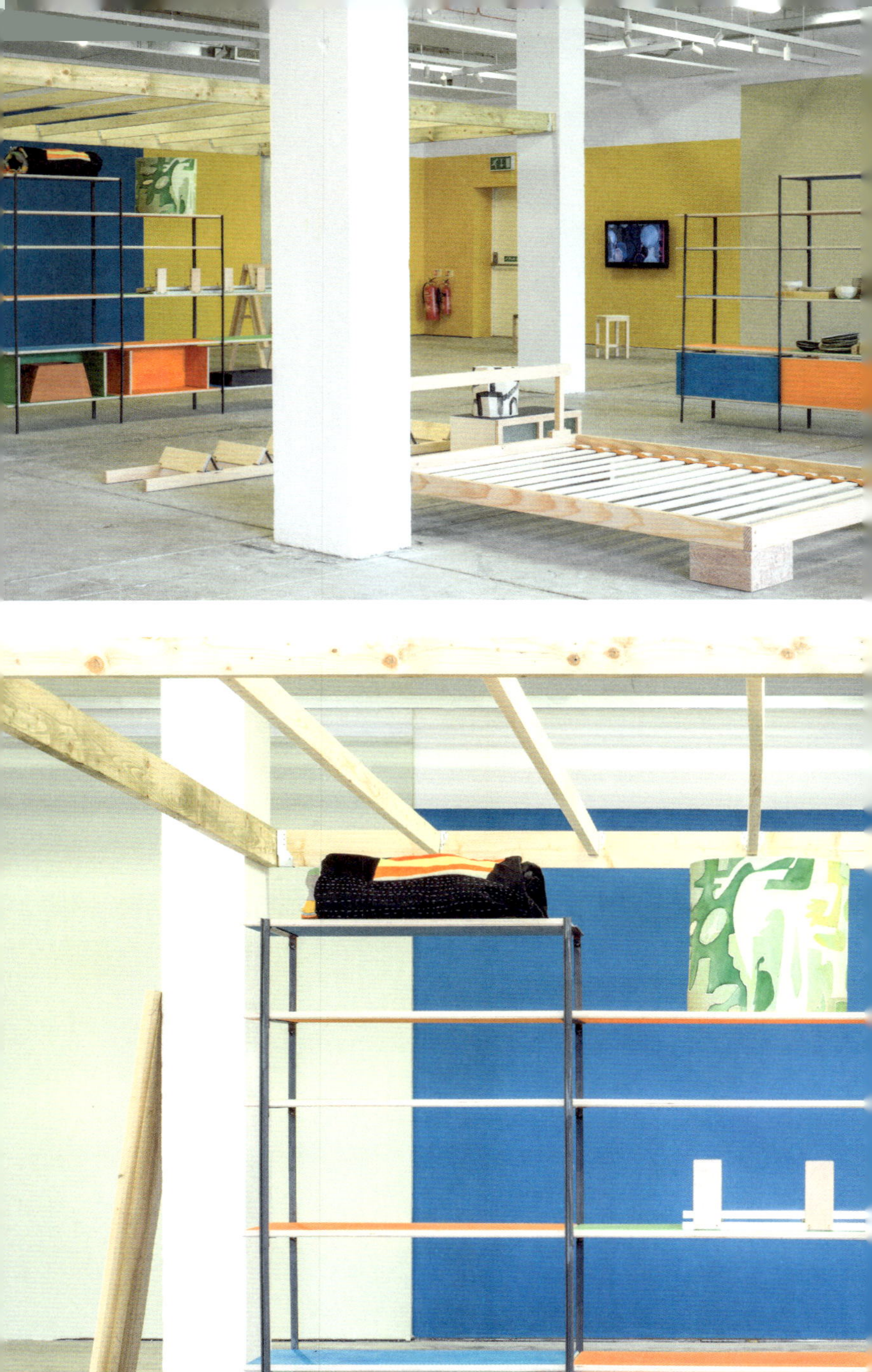

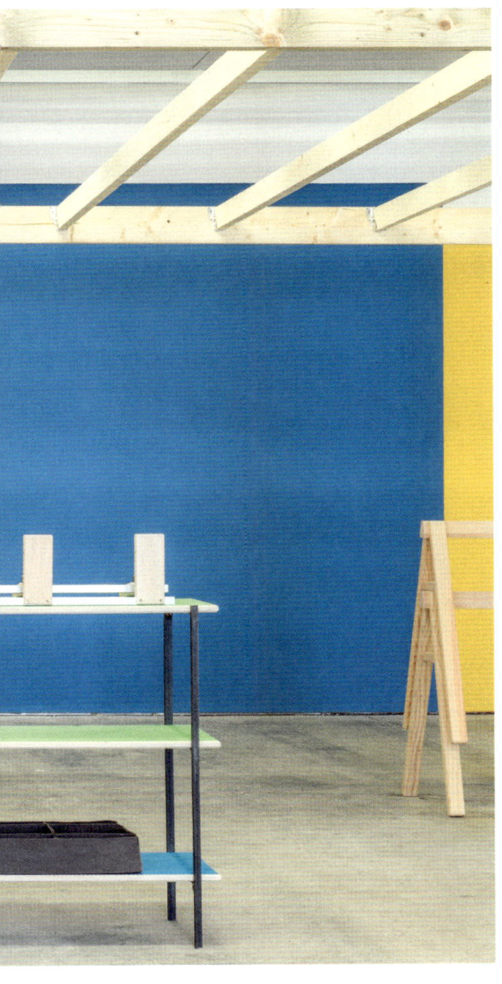

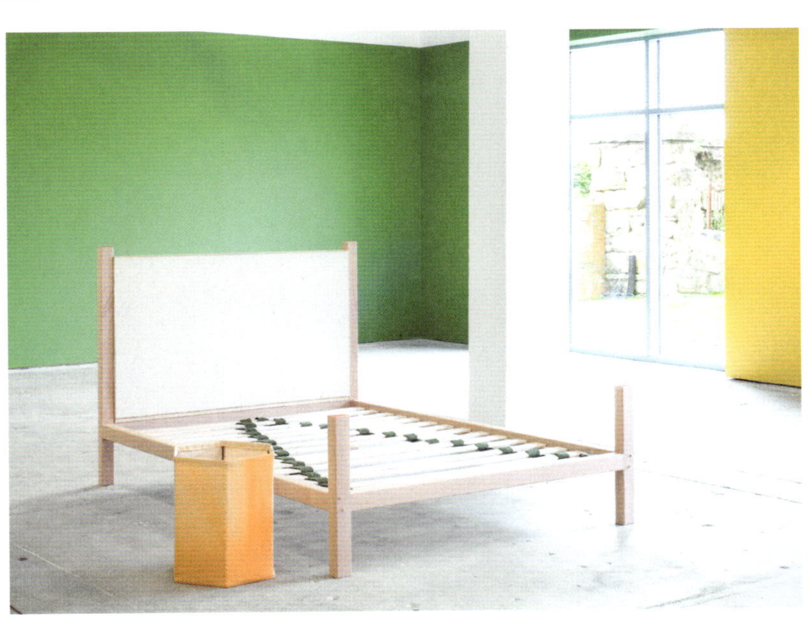

Installation views, *Making the Bed, Laying the Table*, Florence Dwyer, Katie Schwab, Simon Worthington, Glasgow Sculpture Studios, Glasgow, 2016

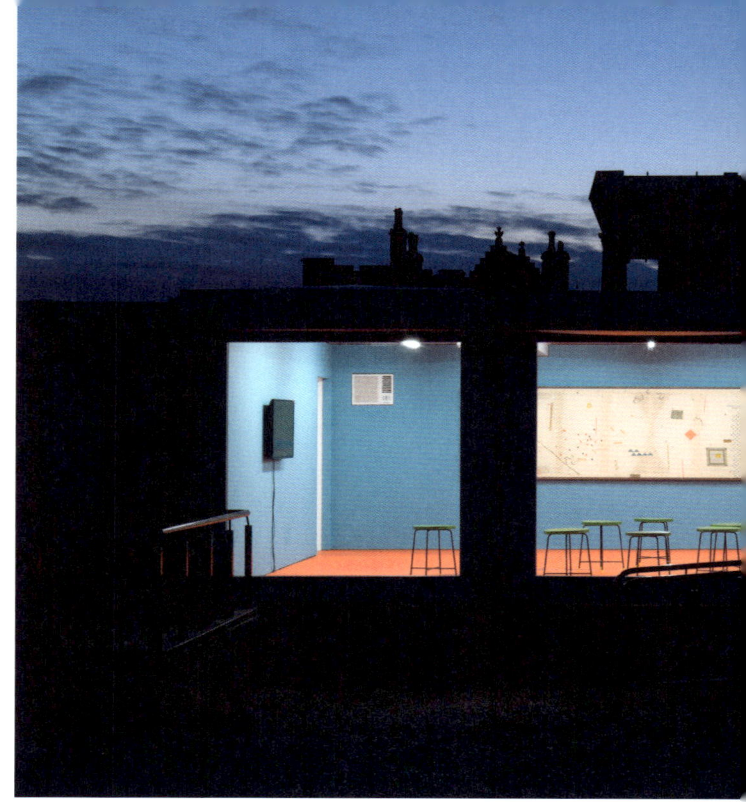

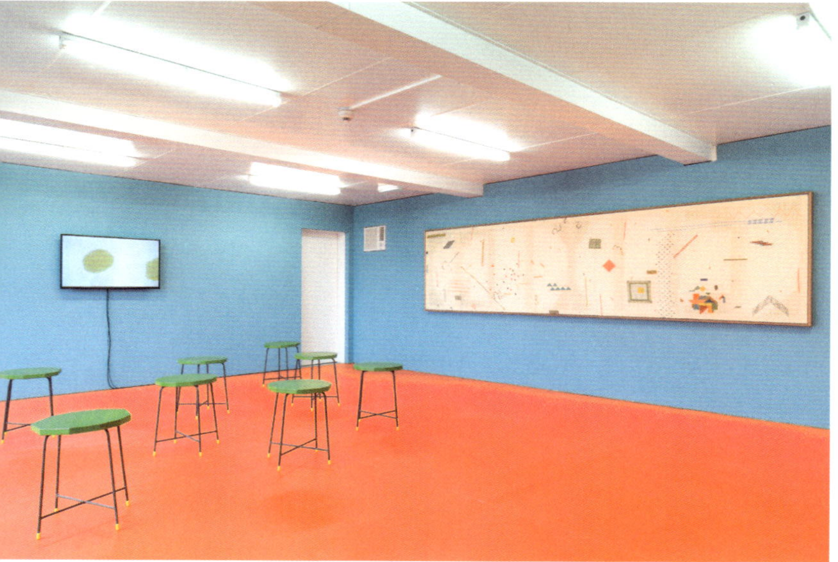

Installation view, *Together in a Room*, Collective,
Edinburgh, 2016
(clockwise from right)
Sampler (2016)
Hessian, Grandma's wool, pine, sapele, 400 × 150 cm,
framed

Ten stools made with Simon (2016)
Douglas fir, steel, wood stain, PVC, dimensions variable

*Dedicated to my great teachers (Becky Lewin, St Catherine's
College, Oxford; Madeleine Ladell, Phoenix Pottery London;
Mia Schwab, London)* (2016)
HD video and hand-painted 16 mm film transferred to HD,
10 mins. 14 secs.

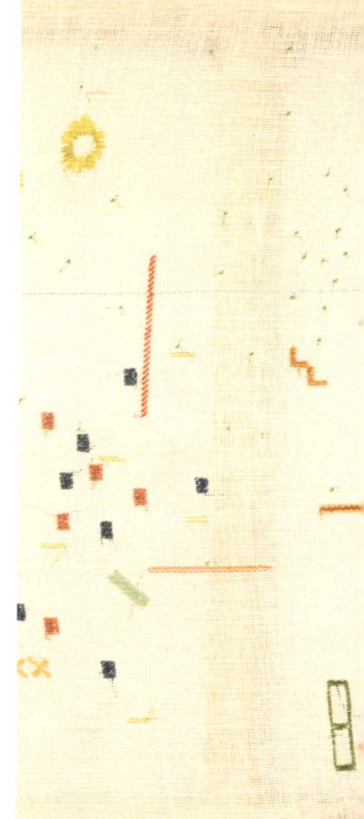

Sampler (2016)
Sampler (2016), detail
Installation view, *Together in a Room*, Collective,
Edinburgh, 2016

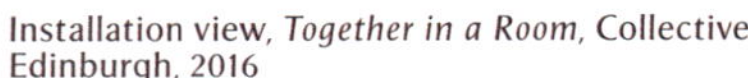

Installation view, *Together in a Room*, Collective, Edinburgh, 2016

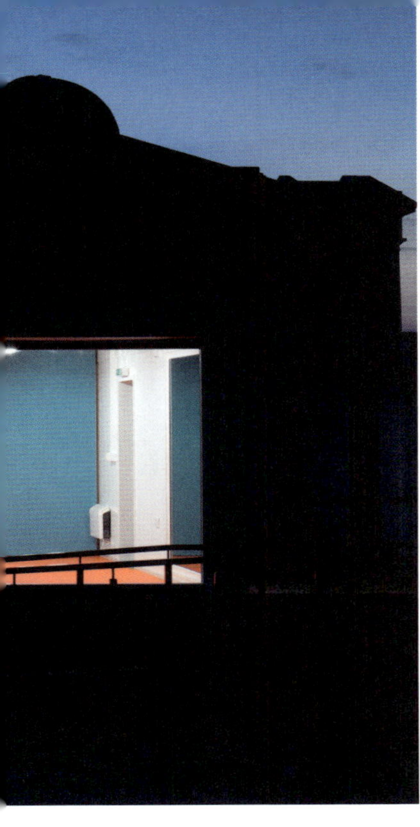

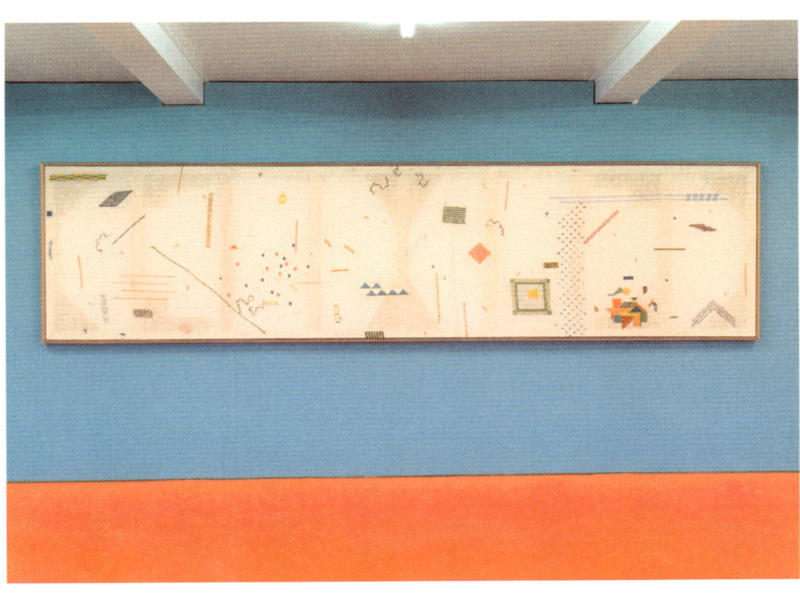

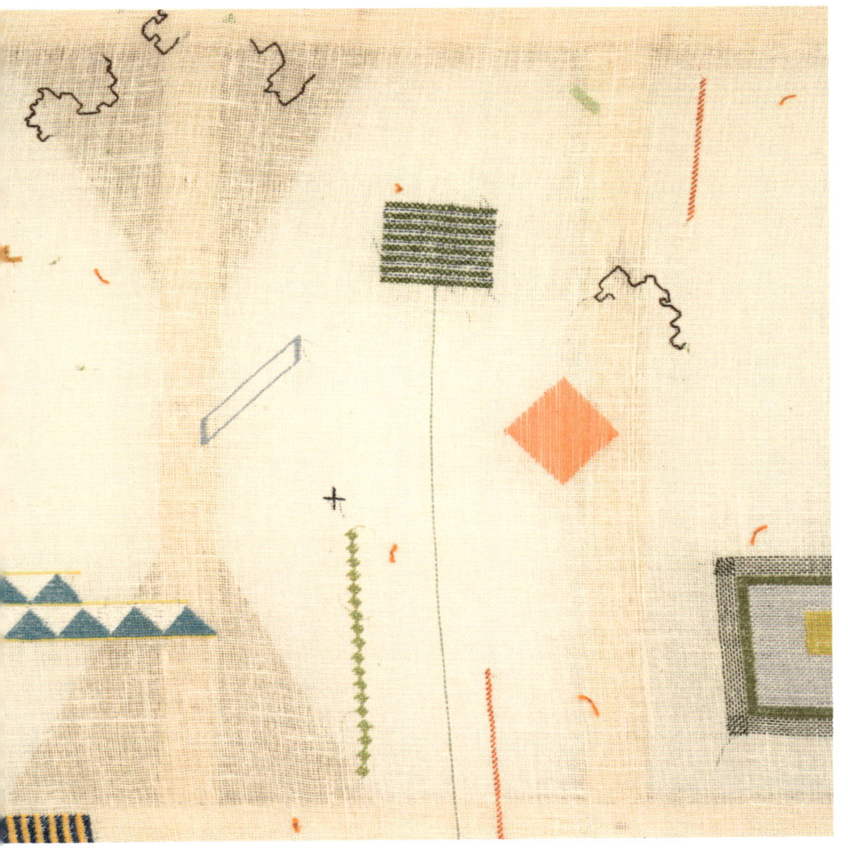

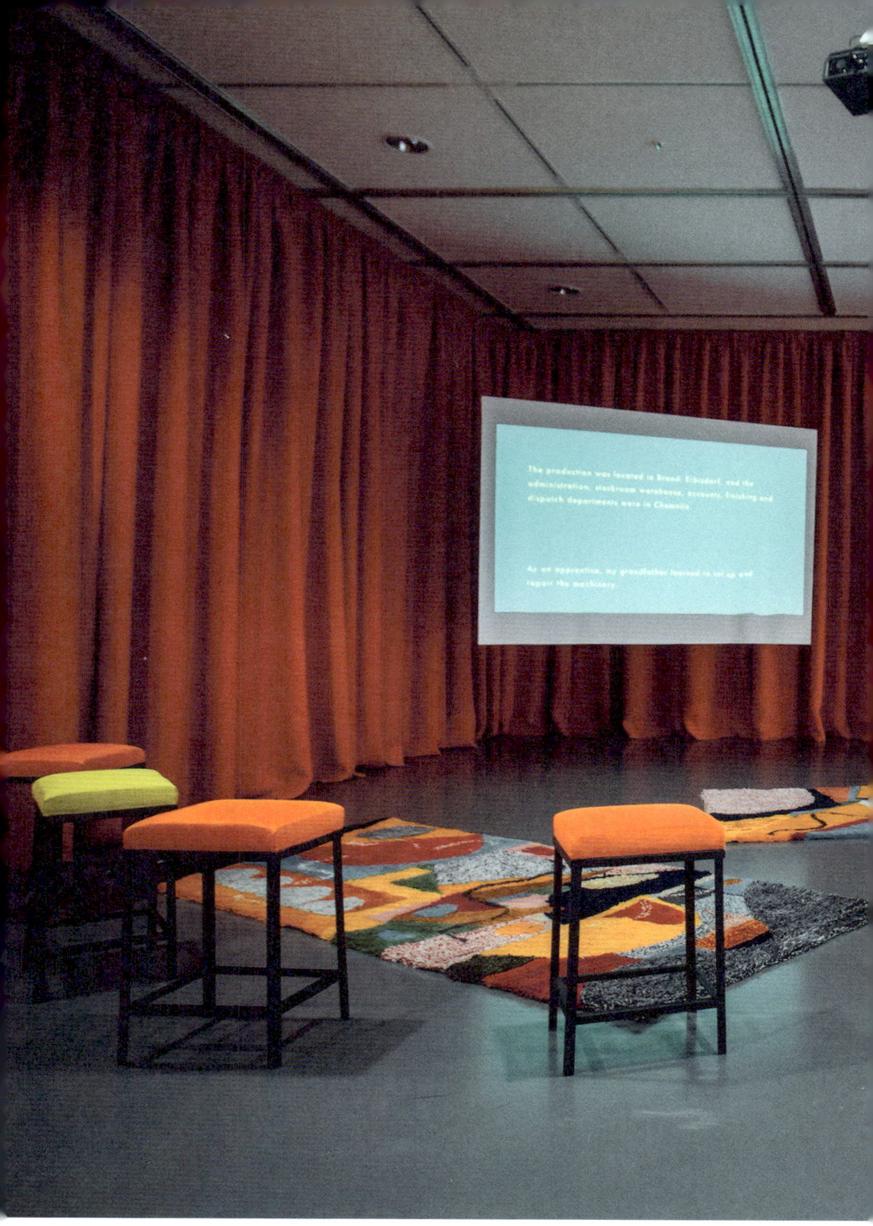

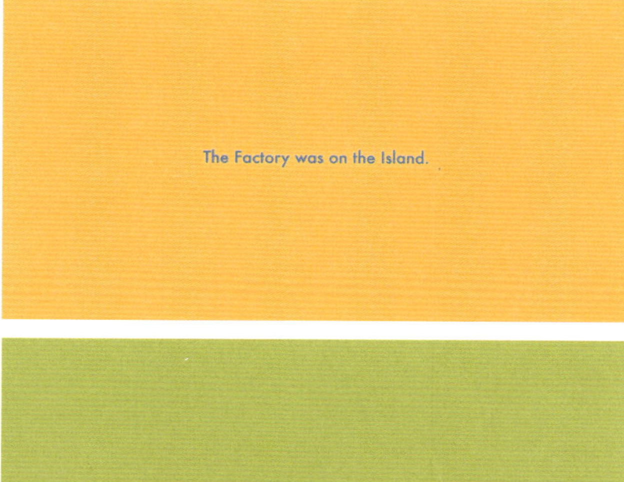

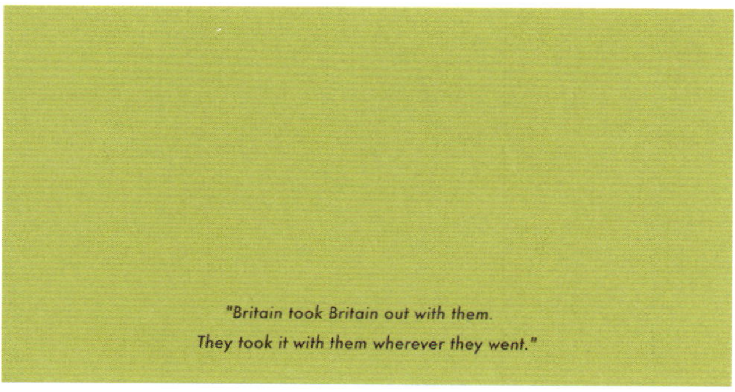

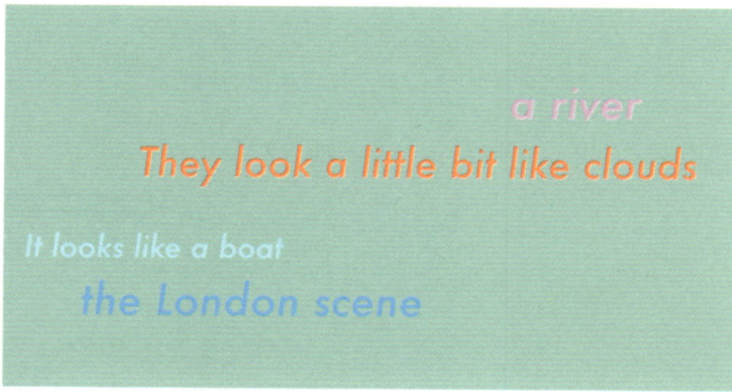

Stills from *This Interesting and Wonderful Factory* (2019)

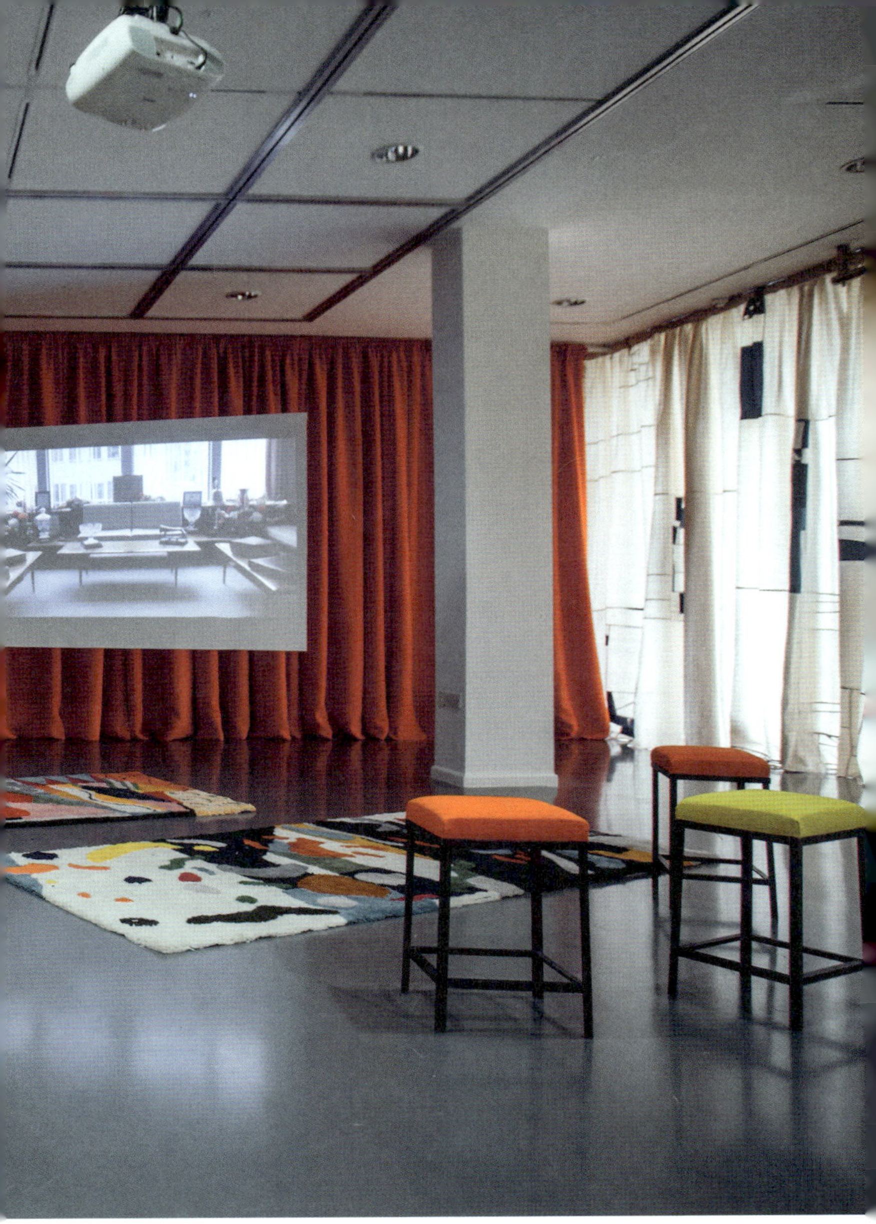

Installation view, *A Working Building*, The Gallery at Plymouth College of Art, 2019
(clockwise from top left)

This Interesting and Wonderful Factory (2019)
Digital and 16 mm video, digital photographs, scanned 35 mm hand-developed photograph, text
Digital footage: Alban Roinard, 16 mm footage: Katie Schwab, 11 mins. 29 secs.

Civic Centre/City Centre (2019)
Digital video, digital photographs and stop-frame animation
Digital footage: Robert Marshall and Katie Schwab, 17 mins. 45 secs.

Indigo Curtain (2019)
Indigo-dyed cotton dust sheets, cotton dust sheets, thread, Indigo fabric dyed with Sarah Johnson, St Ives, 2017, and leftover fabric from *A Portable Mural*, Serpentine Galleries, London, 2017, and *Jerwood Solo Presentations*, Jerwood Space, London, 2016, dimensions variable

Stripes (reconstituted) (2016/2019)
Steel, plywood, reconstituted foam, hessian, dimensions variable

Reconfigured stools from Jerwood Solo Presentations, (2016) Jerwood Space, London, 2016, dimensions variable

Plymouth Rugs (2019)
Yarn, mesh, 122 × 270 cm each

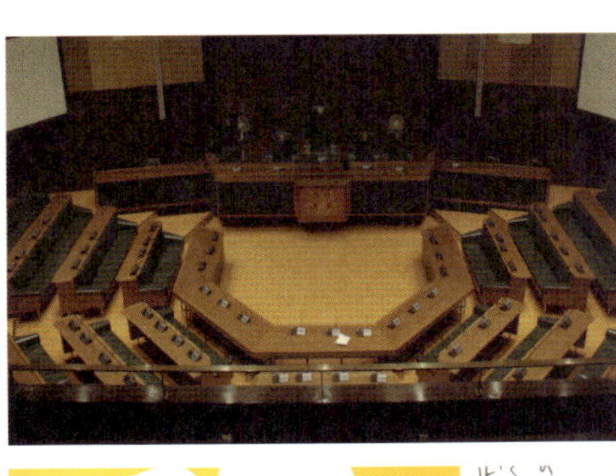

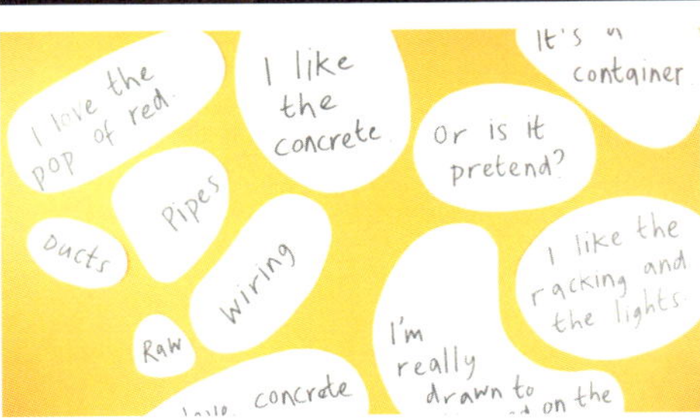

Stills from *Civic Centre/City Centre* (2019)

Published by Vleeshal and Dent-De-Leone
in conjunction with Katie Schwab's solo exhibition *small wares*
at Vleeshal, 26 September–12 December 2021
Curated by Clare Molloy

Authors: Ann Coxon, Roos Gortzak, Michiel Huijben,
Rebecca Lewin, Clare Molloy, m. patchwork monoceros,
Katie Schwab and Rosalie Sloof
Copyeditors: Jonathan Beaton and Clare Molloy
Editor: Clare Molloy
Graphic Designer: Åbäke
Managing Editors: Alix de Massiac and Julia Steenhuisen
Proofreader: Jonathan Beaton

Clare Molloy and Katie Schwab would like to express their sincerest thanks to Roos Gortzak, Hanna Verhulst, Luuk Vulkers and Kees Wijker at Vleeshal Center for Contemporary Art for their generosity, endless support and great sense of humour.

Immense gratitude to all those who guided the process of the exhibition and the making of *Katie Schwab: Sample Book*, including Åbäke, Meg Andrews, Gieneke Arnolli at Fries Museum, Jonathan Beaton, Johanna van Benthem, Anniek Brattinga and Marianne Noordzij at Werkplaats Typografie, Filip Caranica, James Champion, Peder Clark, Cove Park, Ann Coxon at Tate Modern, Jantiene van Elk, Wilma Kieboom and Elles van Vegchel at TextielMuseum, George Erml, Sam Fish at Swarf, Andy Ford, Stephan Helms at Alte Nationalgalerie, Gemma Holt and Maki Suzuki at Dent-De-Leone, Thomas Horak, Michiel Huijben, Marieke de Jongh at Musea Zutphen, Magali Junet at Fondation Toms Pauli, Emily Kemp, Karina Leijnse and Peter Blom at Zeeuws Museum, Rebecca Lewin at the Design Museum, Catherine Long, Merel Maissan, Kathleen Mangan and Hannah Robinson at Lenore G. Tawney Foundation, Jozef Marlow and Peter Rennie at Bridgeman Images, Alix de Massiac, Gunnar Meier, the Molloys, Tom Nolan, m. patchwork monoceros, Wayne Perry, Geeske Pluijmers, Nanda Runge, Franz Müller-Schmidt, Alexei Schwab, Irene Schwab, Max Slaven, Rosalie Sloof at Nederlands Openluchtmuseum, Julia Steenhuisen, Michiel Vermet, Veva van der Wolf at TextielLab, all those who visited *small wares*, and the women and girls behind the Dutch darning samplers. Finally, a hug for Emil Schwab, who arrived as the pages of this book were taking shape.

Published by Vleeshal and Dent-De-Leone
Edition of 800
Printed at SYL
Set in Vleeshal Sans, Janson text LT, Pascal ND regular and *Pascal ND italic*
ISBN 978-1-907908-71-2
© 2023 the artist and the authors, Vleeshal, Middelburg and Dent-De-Leone, London

This publication is supported by:

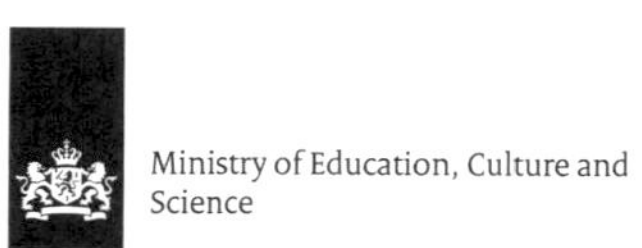

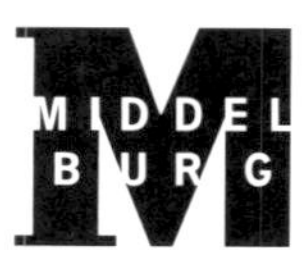

Image credits
James Champion, @jameschampionphotog, pp. 19, 24–25; Collection Historisch Museum De Bevelanden, Goes. Courtesy of Meg Andrews, megandrews.com, p. 13; Collection Nederlands Openluchtmuseum, Arnhem, inv. no. H10–61. Photo: Merel Maissan, pp. 62–65; Collection Rijksdienst voor het Cultureel Erfgoed, Amersfoort, doc. no. #019748, #019749, #019751, #019758, pp. 15, 28; Collection Staatliche Museen zu Berlin, Nationalgalerie, Berlin. Photo: Jörg P. Anders, p. 44; Collection Zeeuws Museum, Middelburg. Photo: Katie Schwab, p. 16; George Erml. Courtesy of Lenore G. Tawney Foundation, New York, p. 75; image sourced from Oliver Fairclough and Emmeline Leary, *Textiles by William Morris and Morris & Co. 1861-1940* (Birmingham: Birmingham Museums and Art Gallery, 1981), p. 21; Andy Ford, pp. 126–127; Thomas Horak, pp. 114, 120–121; illustration sourced from H. Janse and J.H. van Mosselveld, *Keldermans, een architectonisch netwerk in de Nederlanden* (The Hague: Staatsuitgeverij, 1987), p. 108; Emily Kemp, pp. 114, 127; illustration sourced from Ann Ladbury, *Sewing*, (Faraday Cl: Littlehampton Book Services, 1978), p. 33; Merel Maissan, pp. 62–63; Gunnar Meier, pp. 17, 36–43; Clare Molloy, pp. 26–27, 29–30, 35; Franz Müller-Schmidt, pp. 70–71, 84–95, 100–101, and front, back and inside cover; Tom Nolan, pp. 124–125; Marianne Noordzij, p. 34; Alice Pauli archives, Lausanne. © Fondation Toms Pauli, Lausanne, p. 74; Wayne Perry, p. 118; Private collection. © Christie's Images/Bridgeman Images, p. 21; Alexei Schwab and Katie Schwab, pp. 114, 126; Katie Schwab, pp. 9, 20, 22–25, 28, 32–33, 44, 104–105; Max Slaven, pp. 116, 122–123; Rosalie Sloof, pp. 60–61; Stadhuiscollectie Gemeente Middelburg, Middelburg. Photo: Ivo Wennekes, c/o Pictoright Amsterdam, 2023, p. 28; Sam Fish, pp. 45–46; Michiel Vermet, pp. 46–47, 82–83, 96–99, 102–103; Kees Wijker, p. 33.